COLLECTIVE BARGAINING AND COLLECTIVE ACTION

This book offers a unique contribution that examines major recent changes in conflict, negotiation and regulation within the labour relations systems and related governance institutions of advanced societies. The broad scope of analysis includes social welfare institutions, new forms of protest including judicialisation, transnational structures and collective bargaining itself. As the distinguished group of participating authors shows, the accumulation of numerous crucial changes in the interactions of unions, employers, political parties, courts, protestors, regulators and other key actors makes it imperative to reframe the study of collective bargaining and related forms of governance. The shifting dynamics include the growing relevance of multi-level interactions involving transnational entities, states and regions; the increasing tendency of workers and unions to turn to the courts as part of their overall strategy; new forms of solidarity among workers; and the emergence of new populist and nationalist actors. At the same time, sectors of the workforce that feel under-represented by existing institutions have contributed to new types of protest and 'agency'. Building on classical debates, the book offers new theoretical and practical approaches that insert the study of collective bargaining into the analysis of governance, solidarity, conflict and regulation, as they are broadly construed.

Oñati International Series in Law and Society

A SERIES PUBLISHED FOR THE OÑATI INSTITUTE
FOR THE SOCIOLOGY OF LAW

Recent titles in this series

Regulatory Transformations
Rethinking Economy-Society Interactions
Edited by Bettina Lange, Fiona Haines and Dania Thomas

Life Imprisonment and Human Rights
Edited by Dirk van Zyl Smit and Catherine Appleton

Trust in International Police and Justice Cooperation
Edited by Saskia Hufnagel and Carole McCartney

Human Rights Encounter Legal Pluralism
Edited by Eva Brems, Giselle Corradi and Mark Goodale

Transitional Justice and the Public Sphere: Engagement, Legitimacy and Contestation
Edited by Chrisje Brants and Susanne Karstedt

Law and the Precarious Home: Socio Legal Perspectives on the Home in Insecure Times
Edited by Helen Carr, Brendan Edgeworth and Caroline Hunter

Criminologies of the Military: Militarism, National Security and Justice
Edited by Andrew Goldsmith and Ben Wadham

Law and the Precarious Home: Socio Legal Perspectives on the Home in Insecure Times
Edited by Helen Carr, Brendan Edgeworth and Caroline Hunter

**For the complete list of titles in this series, see
'Oñati International Series in Law and Society' link at
www.bloomsburyprofessional.com/uk/series/
onati-international-series-in-law-and-society**

Collective Bargaining and Collective Action

Labour Agency and Governance in the 21st Century?

Edited by
Julia López López

Oñati International Series in Law and Society

A SERIES PUBLISHED FOR THE OÑATI INSTITUTE FOR THE SOCIOLOGY OF LAW

•HART•

OXFORD • LONDON • NEW YORK • NEW DELHI • SYDNEY

HART PUBLISHING

Bloomsbury Publishing Plc

Kemp House, Chawley Park, Cumnor Hill, Oxford, OX2 9PH, UK

HART PUBLISHING, the Hart/Stag logo, BLOOMSBURY and the Diana logo are trademarks of Bloomsbury Publishing Plc

First published in Great Britain 2019

A catalogue record for this book is available from the British Library.

Library of Congress Cataloging-in-Publication data

Names: López López, Julia, editor.

Title: Collective bargaining and collective action : labour agency and governance in the 21st century? / edited by Julia López López.

Description: Oxford [UK] ; Portland, Oregon : Hart Publishing, 2019. | Series: Oñati international series in law and society | Includes bibliographical references and index.

Identifiers: LCCN 2018049671 (print) | LCCN 2018050023 (ebook) | ISBN 9781509923175 (Epub) | ISBN 9781509923168 (hardback)

Subjects: LCSH: Collective bargaining—Law and legislation. | Collective bargaining—International business enterprises. | Labor unions—Law and legislation. | Collective labor agreements. | Labor laws and legislation.

Classification: LCC K1730 (ebook) | LCC K1730 .C65 2019 (print) | DDC 344.01/89—dc23

LC record available at https://lccn.loc.gov/2018049671

ISBN: HB: 978-1-50992-316-8
ePDF: 978-1-50992-318-2
ePub: 978-1-50992-317-5

Typeset by Compuscript Ltd, Shannon

Acknowledgement

The Editor would like to express gratitude to the Spanish Ministry of Economy and Competitiveness (Reference DER 2015-69652-P) and the Oñati International Institute for the Sociology of Law for research support making possible the scholarly interchanges leading to this volume.

Contents

Editor and Contributors

Julia López López is Professor of Labour Law and Social Security Law at the Universitat Pompeu Fabra Law School in Barcelona, where she leads the Research Group on Labour Law (GreDTiss). Her current research is focused on precarious work and labour rights, flexisecurity, discrimination by age and gender, the judicialisation of the labour system, collective bargaining, governance and labour market reforms. Her publications include: 'Age as Factor of Discrimination and Collective Dismissals' in M Rönnmar and JJ Votinius (eds), *Festskrift till Ann-Numhauser Henning*, (Lund, University of Lund, 2017); 'Responding to Anti-union Legal Reforms: Labor Movement Strategies in Contemporary Spain' (2017) 38 *Comparative Labour Law and Policy Journal*; 'The Increasing Trend to Formalize the Segmentation of Workers' Rights: Tensions Among Regulatory Levels' in J López López (ed), (2015) 36(2) *Segmentation and Labor Rights, Monographic issue of the Comparative Labor Law and Policy Journal*; 'Solidarity and the Re-socialization of Risk: Analysing ETUC Strategies to Face the Crisis' in N Contouris and M Freedland (eds), *Resocialising Europe in a Time of Crisis* (Cambridge: Cambridge University Press, 2014); and 'Social Rights in Changing Labor Markets: Caring for Caregivers in the European Union' in K Stone and H Arthurs (eds), *Rethinking Workplace Regulation: Beyond the Standard Contract of Employment* (New York: Russel Sage Foundation, 2013).

Alan Bogg joined the Bristol Law School in 2017 as Professor of Labour Law. Previously he was Professor of Labour Law in the University of Oxford and a fellow of Hertford College, Oxford. He is interested in exploring these areas from philosophical, doctrinal and comparative perspectives. His current research projects are examining freedom of association; common law fundamental rights; the role of criminalisation in work relations; and the future of the social democratic constitution.

Assaf Bondy is Research Fellow in the ERC project 'Human Trafficking from a Labor Perspective'. He has been coordinator of the Young Researchers Community in the Israeli Industrial-Relations Research Association. His current research is focused on the erosion of industry-level collective bargaining, and the segmentation of the Israeli industrial relations system.

Dulce María Cairós Barreto is Senior Lecturer in Labour and Social Security Law at the University of La Laguna. Her teaching covers labour and social security law, European labour law and international labour law. Her main research interests are the contract of employment, collective labour relations, European and international labour law, and occupational risk prevention.

Sergio Canalda is Lecturer at the Pompeu Fabra University, Barcelona and a member of the UPF Research Group in Labour Law and Social Security. His research interests involve transnational collective bargaining and union activism, though recently he has focused his work on working poor and employment policies.

Consuelo Chacartegui is Associate Professor at the Pompeu Fabra University, Barcelona, Vice Dean of Labour Relations at the Faculty of Law and member of the UPF Research Group in Labour Law and Social Security. Her research interests are focused on labour law and social protection, European social law and gender discrimination. Her current research includes the areas of human rights at work and sustainability.

Alexandre de le Court is Lecturer in Labour Law and Social Security at Pompeu Fabra University, Barcelona and a member of the UPF Research Group in Labour Law and Social Security. His research interests include the comparative study of labour law and social security, European social law, precarious work and labour rights in a multilevel context.

Mark Freedland is Emeritus Research Fellow in Law at St John's College, Oxford and Honorary Professor at the Faculty of Law of University College London. His university teaching has been in the fields of labour law, international and European employment law, and comparative public law. He has acted as the Director of Graduate Studies for the Law Faculty, as Vice-Chair of the Law Board, and as Director of the Institute of European and Comparative Law. In previous years he has held visiting professorships at the Universities of Paris I and Paris II. He has written extensively on the law concerning contracts of employment and personal work relations. His main research interest are in the areas of labour law and public law.

Guy Mundlak is Professor at Tel Aviv University, with a joint appointment between the Buchmann Faculty of Law and the Faculty of Social Science, Department of Labor Studies. He is currently Visiting Professor at Cornell Law School. His research deals with the impact of law on the labour market and the welfare state. He is interested in the relationship between labour law and industrial relations, the internalisation of employment standards, and on the rights to social security and work, the effects of globalisation on labour markets, and the efficacy of international instruments.

Tonia Novitz has been Professor of Labour Law at the University of Bristol since 2008. Her research interests focus predominantly on labour law, international and EU trade and the protection of human rights. She is also a member of the executive committee of the Institute of Employment Rights and an honorary member of Old Square Chambers. She writes in the areas of labour law, international and EU law, jurisprudence and legal mechanisms for the protection of human rights.

Margarita I Ramos Quintana is Professor of Labour Law and Social Security at the University of La Laguna. She has been a member of the Economic and Social Council of Spain and is Coordinator of the research group Labour Law and Social Security-ULL. Her main lines of research are labour migration, gender equality, European social law, collective bargaining, the right to strike, employment contracts, productive organisation, occupational safety, and health and social security.

Mia Rönnmar is Dean and Professor in private law, working as a researcher and teacher in labour law at the Faculty of Law at Lund University. Her research areas are Swedish, comparative and EU labour law and industrial relations. She has been a visiting researcher at inter alia the London School of Economics, the European University Institute and Sydney Law School. She is President-Elect of the International Labour and Employment Relations Association (ILERA).

Katherine V.W. Stone is a leading expert in labour and employment law in the United States. She was awarded a Guggenheim Fellowship Award in 2008 and a Russell Sage Fellowship for 2008–09 for her work on the changing nature of employment and the regulatory implications. Professor Stone has been a member of the faculty of the UCLA School of Law since 2004. She received her BA magna cum laude from Harvard University and her JD cum laude from Harvard Law School.

Introduction

JULIA LÓPEZ LÓPEZ

MODES OF COLLECTIVE ACTION IN DEFENCE OF SOLIDARITY

THIS IS A book about collective bargaining and its insertion in changing dynamics of collective action. Our perspective on bargaining places this fundamental component of the system that regulates labour relations in the context of the forces, processes and principles that influence its transformations. The volume's approach makes it possible to identify and make sense out of major contemporary transformations in bargaining, their determinants and their consequences. By placing collective bargaining in a broader 'family' of closely related phenomena – most prominently including collective action – the contributions collected here make it possible to understand alterations in current institutional practice more fully than is possible with conventional framings of bargaining that focus exclusively on formal institutional features. Much of our analysis examines legal instruments and institutions, but by placing those themes in a broad framework we contribute to an understanding of legal regulation and social realties that looks beyond narrow disciplinary boundaries in order to promote an understanding of changes in the world itself. In this volume's view, legal analysis and the study of other types of social interaction are most effective when scholars take full cognisance of interactions and connections as we constantly seek to do in this volume.

Collective action includes various forms of joint conduct developed by actors seeking to promote the shared interests of groups of persons engaged in collective conflict. Collective action transcends individual interests and centres on collective ones. For this reason, the idea of solidarity thoroughly impregnates collective action and therefore offers a useful analytic frame for its study. The complexity of the concept was posed by Mancur Olson in his classic study *The Logic of Collective Action* (1965). Olson is concerned to identify foundations in individual rationality – and in material incentives underpinning such calculations – for efforts that benefit large groups of persons. For Rolfe,[1]

[1] See M Rolfe 'Collective Action' in P Bearman and P Hedström (eds), *The Oxford Handbook of Analytical Sociology*, Oxford Handbooks Online, June 2017.

collective action processes include the coordination of collective and individual interests, and rely on both cooperative and conflictual elements. In his perspective, mechanisms of both consensus and conflict underpin the complex dynamics of action shaped by the political and social frames of actors. It seems clear that collective bargaining is built on both consensus-oriented and conflict-oriented forms of collective action.

Solidarity plays a crucial role in collective action in two ways. First, it is a principle that helps to explain why individuals support group goals and actions. In this sense solidarity can be focused on the joint actions of workers, unions, employers and so on. However, solidarity can also be concerned with the society as a whole and with its most vulnerable members. Durkheim's classic understanding of solidarity, and his distinction between organic and mechanical forms of it,[2] has to do with society-wide social cohesion in this sense. We are concerned here with both group-oriented and society-wide solidarity.

Much of our work concerns the translation of collective action into legally recognised collective rights, including freedom of association and the rights to collective bargaining and to strike. In this way we see collective bargaining as a centrally important component of a larger range of actions and institutions, all of them shaped by the evolution of labour law. Thus we locate institutionalised forms of conflict regulation within the broader study of modes of collective action or, in the influential formulation of sociologist Charles Tilly,[3] 'repertoires of contention'. The repertoires of protest and action and of collective bargaining models are to a large degree the result of the evolution of labour law in response to the solidarity principle and efforts to improve the regulation of labour. Of course, other interests and conceptions, such as neoliberal ones, have also played a role in the changing nature of labour law. As Bogg and Freedland argue in their chapter in this volume, collective action and the robust use of the freedom of association are crucial to offer responses to the rise of populism, authoritarian tendencies, and the reduction of social rights.

One of the main parameters of collective activity is the multilevel scenario that regulates the conduct of actors and the institutional regulation of their interactions. Legal norms, protest and collective bargaining itself are all articulated in different legally defined territories and levels of governance. The interrelationship between those levels is subject to change over time. Multilevel dynamics are crucial for our themes of study.

A main reference in the construction of the meaning of collective activity is the Charter of Fundamental Rights of the European Union. The Charter has many points of relevance for collective action, including the freedom of association, the right to collective bargaining and to protest, and the right to strike. Crucially, the Charter constitutionalises these collective rights as part of its

[2] E Durkeim, *The Division of Labor in Society* (The Free Press, 1984) 31–38.
[3] C Tilly, *Regimes and Repertoires* (Chicago University Press, 2006) chapter 3.

definition of solidarity. As Catherine Barnard,[4] in an analysis of the reinforcement of labour standards, has argued, Article 28 of the Charter of Fundamental Rights has as a prior reference Article 6 of the European Social Charter, which integrates within the right to bargain collectively various other important principles and activities, including voluntary negotiation, mechanisms of conciliation and arbitration and collective action including strikes. The integration of all these rights, including strikes, under the principle of solidarity serves to remind us that collective action involves processes of both consensus and disagreement.

This integration of collective action within the Charter's reading of the principle of solidarity offers protection to collective bargaining, protest, strikes, workplace information and consultation as a deliberative process, as well as other matters. The Charter further recognises, in the same definition, decent work as fair labour conditions guaranteed under the right of dignity; protection against termination of contracts as a matter of stability; and social security and social assistance as collective rights constituting the main stone in the definition of solidarity as supporting the agency of collective actors. An interdependent principle of solidarity is raised in the Charter, recognising both individual rights and collective ones as connected to this principle. The inclusion of protection against dismissal and collective rights together under the umbrella of solidarity provides support for the argument that there is an important interaction between individual, plural and collective social rights. This, in turn, offers an avenue to constructing challenges to neoliberal legal policies on labour conditions and unions. The value of this principle, not only at the EU level, but also at the national level, can potentially increase the role of courts in the application of both individual and collective rights and principles.[5]

The increased level of individualisation of labour relations is an important theme in the debate on collective action. The political underpinnings of labour law have been conditioned during the last decade by the globalisation of the economy and markets, the increasing pace of technological innovation, and, at the same time, by the rise of nationalism and the emergence of disruptions produced by financial crisis and the massive movements of people due to poverty or war. The changing context has produced a non-ceasing sequence of new challenges for the functioning of existing institutions and forms of practice. New actors, institutions and sources of regulation have emerged from this reality. The regulation of labour in this period of time has been shaped most powerfully by the politics of austerity programmes; the economic goals of governments have informed the politics of labour regulation around the world. The individualisation of labour employment regulation, the segmentation of rights, increased

[4] C Barnard, 'Using Procurement Law to Enforce Labour Standards' in G Davidov and B Langille (eds), *The Idea of Labour Law* (Oxford University Press, 2011).

[5] N Busby, 'The EU Charter of Fundamental Rights' in A Bogg, C Costello and ACL Davies (eds), *Research Handbook on EU Labour Law* (Edward Elgar, 2016).

vulnerability for individual workers, anti-union policies and the repression of protest[6] have all emerged as major labour law tendencies in this period of time. Both individual-level labour guarantees and collective rights have been reframed by certain institutional actors. In this sense, the previously predominant social models have been affected by the financial crisis and other macro-level factors. The new environment has also been marked by new forms of spillover between the national and supranational levels.[7] These shifts in regulatory logics, and the conditions that promoted their emergence, have of course been met by transformations in the actions and strategies of workers as well as unions. These changes pose the need for scholars, as well, to reframe their studies and analyses, a broad and complex challenge that we collectively take up in this volume.

Difficulties have emerged in the pursuit or defence of solidarity because the individualisation of labour regulation has been a central feature of the dominant institutional approach in the new context. A clear example of this tendency is the Commission Green Paper 'Modernising Labour Law' (2006),[8] which 'modernised' its subject matter without any reference to *collective rights*. This shift has, in turn, generated important socio-economic consequences such as more inequality and growing vulnerability for underprivileged people. These dynamics have been expressed in various ways, including the upsurge of precarious contracts that undercut the viability of 'decent work'.[9] The goal of labour law has historically been to reduce inequality, not only in labour markets, but also in society at large. However, this goal can only be successfully defended through combinatory strategies involving workers' representation not only within enterprises or the labour relations system, but also via the use of 'political voice' and other forms of collective expression to defend labour.[10]

The elements of complexity in the changing panorama of labour legislation and conflict are quite considerable. Employment regulation increasingly involves interactions between soft and hard law, while the transformed regulatory scenario of workers' rights has developed growing tensions among the different layers of the legal order, leading to important debates about the

[6] See T Novitz, 'The Restricted Right to Strike: Far-reaching ILO Jurisprudence on the Public Sector and Essential Services' (2017) 3 *Comparative Labor Law and Policy Journal* 353. See T Novitz, *International and European Protection of the Right to Strike* (Oxford University Press, 2003).

[7] See JE Delvik and A Martin, 'From Crisis to Crisis: European Social Models and Labor Market Outcomes in the Era of Monetary Integration' in JE Dolvkand and A Martin (eds), *European Social Models from Crisis to Crisis. Employment and Inequality in the Era of Monetary Integration* (Oxford University Press, 2015) 385.

[8] Commission Green Paper of 22 November 2006 entitled 'Modernising Labour Law to Meet the Challenges of the 21st Century' COM (2006) 78 final.

[9] See G Davidov, *A Purposive Approach to Labour Law*, Oxford Monographs on Labour Law (Oxford University Press, 2016) 36–37.

[10] K Ewing, 'The Importance of Trade Union Political Voice. Labour Law Meets Constitutional Law' in A Bogg and T Novitz, *Voices at Work. Continuity and Change in the Common Law World* (Oxford University Press, 2014) 277.

autonomy of labour law.[11] Judges have emerged as newly predominant actors of governance. In this panorama, labour has tried to reorganise and unions have promoted new global structures to increase their agency in the multilevel dynamics of the current era; the initiatives of labour organisations are often expressed through globalising initiatives and discourse,[12] as well as a newly cosmopolitan activism.[13]

In this context, the goal of this volume is to reframe our understanding of collective bargaining to fully incorporate within it several phenomena that are rooted in the pursuit of solidarity. These solidarity-related phenomena include collective action, labour's agency, especially through conflict itself, and the placement of bargaining within broader governance structures. This broad reframing of collective bargaining and labour regulation draws within the broadly construed study of bargaining the processes through which workers come to be entitled to rights and freedoms as well as initiatives in which labour participates in deliberative interactions and in decisions on the implementation of rights. The institutional outlets and forms of expression for such strategies can be thought of as ways to channel solidarity. This volume's reframing fully embraces the need to study, and technically master, the institutional and legal forms taken by labour regulation but it places these phenomena within a multi-actor interactive framework.

Collective bargaining, in our reading, is not an institutionally isolated process limited to the insertion of efficiency into labour markets' regulation. Instead, as both the political theory and sociological approaches to labour relations argue, collective bargaining is embedded in a constellation of collective rights and political processes; its evolution is interrelated with such dynamics and, by extension, forms part of broader patterns of governance. For this reason, a number of key concepts have cross-over relevance for studying multiple collective phenomena including collective bargaining, other labour strategies or labour regulation mechanisms, and the broader contextual forces that shape these phenomena. These concepts include, for example, consensus, discontent, solidarity, disruption and many others that are present in all forms of collective activism. However, many of the relevant concepts involve institutional structures rather than dynamics of protest within the parameters set by such structures. The multilevel nature of the institutions and actors that express and channel conflict – with spillover results – is reflected in regulation of various types, the courts, unions and forms of collective bargaining. We are interested precisely in the interrelations between institutional forms and types of conduct on the one hand and expressions of conflict on the other hand, given our view

[11] See A Bogg, C Costello, ACL Davies and J Prassel (eds), *The Autonomy of Labour Law* (Hart Publishing, 2015).

[12] See RM Fishman, *Democracy's Voices* (Cornell University Press, 2004).

[13] See S Tarrow, *The New Transnational Activism* (Cambridge University Press, 2005).

that these dynamics are interrelated. Indeed, the process of negotiation is called *bargaining* because 'each side is able to apply pressure on the other' – in the case of workers most importantly through strikes.[14]

The starting point for us is to define modes or repertoires of collective action, including collective bargaining, strikes and other forms of activism and protest such as the judicialisation of conflict. All these forms of mobilisation reflect both conflict and some form of institutionalisation of it; they channel dispute management through mechanisms that involve institutional forms of one sort or another – such as collective bargaining or – in the case of judicialisation – the externalisation of the ultimate resolution to a judge. All these forms also involve a process of deliberation, negotiation and ultimately resolution, embedded in labour law regulation. Although these various modes of collective action all involve micro-level dynamics, they are all shaped by macro-level processes that are historical in nature.

The changing historical context has also exerted an important impact on the model of the strike. The growth of de-contractual employment relations because of the increasing incentives to self-employment – very clearly manifested in the European Union in (and following) 'Modernising Labour Law' – has imposed on social actors the need to invent new forms of protest. This dynamic has been reinforced by the evaporation of pre-existing workplace geographies, not only due to the globalisation of production, but also generated by the impact of new technologies. The resulting innovative forms of action have faced the challenge of trying to capture the diverse forms of the employment relation generated in a segmented labour market. The increase of judicialisation of labour disputes responds quite directly to this challenge – and to the new constraints that underpin it.

The judicialisation of labour relations can be specified quantitatively by delineating over time change in the number of cases. This indicator, which can be understood to reflect a form of protest, has increased during the last decade not only at the national level, but also at the supranational one. To fully appreciate the basis for reading judicialisation as reflective of collective activism it is necessary to take into account increasing instances of the repression of strikes and protest not only in non-democratic regimes, but also in democratic ones. Government strategies to cut back social rights – including, in some cases, collective rights relevant for the conduct of strikes and other forms of protest – have often ended up promoting the tendency of actors to channel their actions in new ways, such as judicialisation.

The definition of labour-related collective action as a matter of rights protected in the law has been reinforced by the European Court of Human

[14] H Clegg, *Trade Unionism Under Collective Bargaining. A Theory Based on Comparisons of Six Countries*, Warwick Studies in Industrial Relations (Basil Blackwell, 1976) 5.

Rights' finding in the cases of *Demir and Baykara v Turkey* (2008)[15] and *Enerji-Yapi-Yol Sen v Turkey* (2000).[16] The decision on these cases declares that

> Article 11 of the European Convention on Human Rights includes a right to collectively bargain and precludes a blanket ban on the right to strike. This crucial judicial decision treats both strike activity and collective bargaining as interrelated components of one overarching process that in effect involves the dialectic between consensus and disruption, thereby protecting against the repression of protest.[17]

Collective action, as the different chapters in this volume demonstrate, presents multiple patterns of interaction with regulatory systems. This multiplicity is reflected both in the strategies of the actors and in their impact on individual rights. As Assaf Bondy and Guy Mundlak argue in their chapter, solidarity is a fundamental underpinning of the coordination needed for collective bargaining. In her chapter, Julia López López argues that solidarity informs unions' activism in the judicial arena in the defence of collective rights. Her chapter discusses criticisms of European Court of Justice (ECJ) jurisprudence on the right to strike, arguing for the relevance of this form of protest to the exercise of workers' agency. As Margarita I Ramos Quintana and Dulce María Cairós Barreto show in their chapter, the new tendency towards de-contractualisation of labour law has reshaped how workers pressure for improved labour conditions through protest or strikes. New types of solidarity in collective action are analysed in Katherine Stone's examination of the gig economy and new employment forms. Her chapter shows how new forms of collective action serve to countervail the evaporation of labour rights in emergent types of production systems.

COLLECTIVE ACTION AS AGENCY IN A MULTILEVEL CONTEXT

One of our central concerns in reframing the idea of collective bargaining in this volume is to underline the process of agency that all the forms of conflict which we examine entail for unions and workers. It is crucial to embed our analysis in a historically oriented perspective in which various evolving phenomena – economic crisis, the elimination of social rights and above all the effort of some institutional actors to reduce unions' agency – challenge existing mechanisms for the defence of workers' rights. The global labour market, the initiatives of global actors, the growing gig economy and the political increase of nationalism all stand as major contextual factors conditioning changes in collective action of all sorts.

[15] *Demir and Bakara v Turkey* App no 34503/97 (ECtHR, 12 November 2018).

[16] *Enerji Yapi-Yol Sen v Turkey* App no 68959/01 (ECtHR 21 April 2009).

[17] See KD Ewing, 'The Dramatic Implications of Demir and Baykara' (2010) 39(1) *Industrial Law Journal* 2–51.

The main legal, and rights-based, reference for our subject matter is freedom of association, not only at the national level, but also at the supranational one. Despite the attacks that this right has suffered during the last decade, the right to organise is a fundamental entitlement for workers from the national level to the International Labour Organization (ILO) Convention, the EU's Charter of Fundamental Rights and the European Social Charter. This is a very important point to underline because this collective right serves as a foundation to reconfigure collective strategies in the current economic and political scenario. Indeed, the various forms of conflict and conflict regulation that interest us are reflective not only of economic dynamics and concerns, but also of political ones. This is crucial because political processes involve not only the pursuit of self-interest, but also collective action in the defence of broader principles, especially solidarity. These political processes and the structures in which they are embedded place our subject matter within the broader study of governance.

Models of collective bargaining have experienced an evolution similar in many respects to those of other instruments of regulation. The multiple actors involved in conflict over labour matters – typically interacting through political dynamics and other institutional processes, including those centred in the courts – have created a universe of regulation instruments of varying efficacy. The centralising and decentralising components of the collective bargaining system have been evolving in most national cases towards hybrid systems not only in the combination of firm and sector levels, but also in the level of stability of the relevant instrument – be it a conventional collective contract or some other type of agreement or settlement.

From the perspective of the actors, collective bargaining involves multilevel features both in its process and contents, thereby creating important spillover results linked to the interactions between levels of action and regulation. Agreements reached at one level tend to generate multiple consequences at other levels. The agency of unions and workers' representatives opens a new geography of strategies at the national level. Unions' global federations and supranational or transnational workers' councils are some of the relevant examples. As the chapters in this volume by Sergio Canalda and Tonia Novitz underscore, various transnational negotiations, arrangements and agreements – with transnational actors as the main protagonists, but also involving national level actors – point to the growing relevance of collective action beyond the traditional national level. The combination of levels in collective action has proved highly relevant for the elaboration of the national good practices which some unions have achieved in responding to the new challenges of the gig economy and other processes of change related to economic globalisation. The combination of the local and national levels in labour action facilitates the defence of workers' rights.

The chapters in this volume share the perspective that collective action is integral to both the regulatory process and the conduct of several institutions, such as collective bargaining and the judicial system itself. Our work, as presented in this volume, assumes that protest in its various forms promotes and indeed reflects workers' agency – both individually and collectively – and that it is intimately related to both the freedom of association and the principle of solidarity. In our view protest does not stand in contradiction to regulatory institutions but instead is intrinsically related to their proper functioning. Indeed, the exercise of solidarity stands at the roots of much that we examine and argue in this volume; its study is interrelated with the other themes emphasised in the book. Solidarity should be read also as emblematic of agency for collective actors in a multilevel scenario. The chapter by Tonia Novitz provides an excellent example of how unions have been able to create an institutional network for exercising agency at the global level in their interactions with multinational firms – a capacity that has generated important consequences in labour rights. Solidarity in multilevel interactions is also manifested in the actions of works councils, supranational structures of workers' representation with increasing importance in information, consultation and the concluding of agreements, as Sergio Canalda shows in his chapter. Consuelo Chacartegui's chapter underlines the important role played by collective bargaining in coping with the failure of the European Union to fulfil obligations to refugees. In all of these instances institutional practice is reflective of solidarity. But solidarity also implies inclusion, and governance can be understood as a platform for pursuit of that objective.

COLLECTIVE ACTION AND INCLUSIONARY GOVERNANCE

The topic of governance in labour relations, understood from a perspective that stresses the principle of solidarity, necessarily leads us to debates on collective action, broadly construed. After all, the concept of governance places institutional practice and decision making within a broader range of interrelated social processes. Bargaining, for us, fits within that broader range of governance-related phenomena. Tensions between political and economic objectives of collective action and between levels of regulation hold great relevance in how governance processes shape labour regulation, as several chapters in the volume underscore.

A fundamental issue concerns the origin of pressures that have led national regulatory systems to weaken labour rights. The chapter by Mia Rönmar raises the question of how pressures exerted by the European Union have impacted the Swedish model of collective bargaining. She shows how this supranational source of influence has tended to undermine the agency of collective actors and the viability of solidarity-oriented outcomes in this case. Social protection for the unemployed as a type of solidarity that is pursued through collective bargaining is discussed by Alexandre de le Court in his chapter analysing the cases of the Netherlands, Sweden, France and Italy.

This volume's approach assumes that labour regulation should be studied and understood from a perspective that incorporates the significance of governance structures and arrangements. Forms of governance hold multiple consequences for workers' rights. Governance structures are often rooted in international agreements and principles. Governance as a set of rules to orient policies is a main reference for the United Nations, the Universal Declaration of Human Rights, the ILO Conventions, the Decent Work Agenda and the UN Global Compact. These instruments and their preoccupation with governance are crucial for constructing a fair globalisation. Collective action implies the notion of governance through its de facto promotion of deliberation and consultation. Regulation mechanisms that include these components can be understood as forms of governance. The governance side of collective action involves setting the rules that guarantee labour rights and which obviously presuppose freedom of association as a foundation for exercising social agency.[18]

One of the principal debates over governance involves the relation among levels of deliberation, action and regulation. The impact that EU strategies have had at the national level has often been to promote cutbacks in social guarantees although at the same time EU legal structures – such as the ECJ – have often had the reverse effect. In both cases, the role of multilevel dynamics is of central importance. One of the purposes of complex governance structures is to monitor the enforcement of law and regulations; the institutions that play an important role monitoring decent work as part of the broader effort to guarantee fundamental rights[19] include not only structures of workers' representation, but also judges and the overall legal system. Our subject matter constitutes a complex interrelated whole. This perspective is relevant not only for the study of Europe, but indeed for the analysis of the larger worldwide arena. This is underscored by the ILO action of the Committee of Freedom of Association, case number 3018, 11 of June 2016, regarding a complaint against the Government of Pakistan presented by the International Union of Food (IUF) where the Committee urged the government 'to take measures to encourage and promote free and voluntary negotiations between the union and the employer'. Collective bargaining is embedded in a complex transnational system of governance, anchored in a conception of collective rights.

In sum, the structure of the volume is organised around the themes specified above. The chapters by Bogg and Freedland, López López, Ramos Quintana and Cairós Barreto, Bondy and Mundlak, and Stone all conceptualise forms of conflict and labour regulation as modes of collective action. Their studies place the reframing of collective bargaining and related dynamics within the scholarly context of analyses of multiple forms of collective action. The chapters by Novitz, Chacartegui and Canalda emphasise the complexities and the challenge of sustaining labour's agency in an interactive context characterised

[18] See A Bogg and KD Ewing, 'Freedom of Association' in M Finkin and G Mundlak (eds), *Comparative Labor Law* (Edward Elgar, 2015) 329.

[19] See A Stone, 'The European Court of Justice and the Judicialization of EU Governance' (2010) *Faculty Scholarships Series*, Paper 70.

by profoundly multilevel dynamics. Their analyses deepen and elaborate our understanding of the connections between the national and transnational or supranational levels. The chapters by Rönmar and de le Court centre on the possibilities for an inclusive governance in an increasingly globalised order of interactions. Their scholarship provides institutional and case-sensitive substance to our analytical understanding of this terrain.

Taken as a whole, the chapters in these three thematic clusters all contribute to our collective reframing of collective bargaining and other forms of labour conflict and regulation as collective action informed by the principle of solidarity.[20]

[20] S Stjernø, 'The Idea of Solidarity in Europe' (2011) 3 *European Journal of Social Law*.

Part I

Modes of Collective Action and Solidarity

1

Labour Law in the Age of Populism: Towards Sustainable Democratic Engagement

ALAN BOGG AND MARK FREEDLAND*

As Lord Wedderburn emphasised throughout his long and distinguished career, labour law is indisputably political.[1] We believe that this discourse of 'political labour law' has been valuable in exposing the variety of ways in which personal work relations are sites of conflict over interests and values. Further, that the adjustment of those conflicts should be regarded as political adjustments, located principally within the public rather than the private sphere.

This chapter reflects upon another dimension to 'political labour law' which we now regard as of the utmost importance. Our fundamental claim is that sustainable democratic institutions in the polity are dependent upon sustainable democratic institutions in the sphere of work and work relations. In this way, we think that it is time to disrupt the assumption that 'industrial' or 'social' citizenship is developmentally or normatively posterior to 'political' citizenship. It is better to regard these elements as co-equal dimensions of 'democratic citizenship at work'. To put it bluntly, liberal democratic institutions are now teetering dangerously on a populist precipice; and a significant contributing factor to this political instability has been the spread of rank economic and social precariousness in personal work relations. In this way, the collapse of 'social' citizenship threatens the basic stability and integrity of 'political' and 'civil' citizenship.[2]

* Professor Bogg would like to record his gratitude to the Leverhulme Trust for its generous support of his work. He would also like to record his gratitude to Franz Ebert and Tonia Novitz for their kind invitation to deliver the keynote lecture at the Max Planck Institute in Heidelberg, where some of these ideas were presented and discussed.

[1] KW Wedderburn, *The Worker and the Law*, 1st edn (Harmondsworth: Penguin, 1965) 339.

[2] This influential typology is of course attributable to TH Marshall, *Citizenship and Social Class* (London: Pluto Press, 1992).

We explore these issues through the lens of populism. We regard the development of populism as a real and dangerous political phenomenon that has significant traction at the current time. Building on recent work in political philosophy and political science, we specify what populism entails as political ideology and as statecraft. The chapter then examines the anti-totalitarian labour law developed by Otto Kahn-Freund. We suggest that there is no straightforward path from the anti-totalitarian restriction of popular participation to the current wave of populism. We then explore the symbiotic connections between, on the one hand, populist politics and, on the other hand, the degradation of personal work relations. We do so by examining some recent examples of populism in labour law within the nation-state, and beyond the nation-state. The chapter concludes by suggesting some possibilities for an anti-populist labour law, building upon Kahn-Freund's notion of the 'pluralistic constitution'. This provides a potential basis for sustainable work relations and sustainable democratic citizenship.

I. THE POLITICS OF POPULISM

If the late decades of the twentieth century were the 'age of neoliberalism', we now appear to have entered the 'Age of Populism'.[3] In countries as diverse as the United States, Russia, Hungary, Venezuela, Poland, Turkey and Italy, governments described as 'populist' now wield political power. More generally, there has been a disintegration of traditional political parties and the rapid emergence of new political parties and movements opposed to 'elites' and the political establishment.[4] These spanned the political spectrum from Left to Right: SYRIZA in Greece, Podemos in Spain, the Five Star Movement in Italy, PEGIDA, or AfD, in Germany, UKIP in the United Kingdom. Recently, the French President Macron has even been heralded as a benign populist antidote to more dangerous forms of populism at large in Europe.[5] It is timely, therefore, to reflect upon the importance of this shift in the political context, and its potential implications for labour law. In particular, we believe that some precision is necessary if populism is to be useful as an analytical framework. Otherwise, there is a risk that 'populist' simply becomes another label to signal general normative disapproval of labour law policy that we happen not to like. The allegation of populism then becomes a cheap rhetorical device. That would be regrettable, not least because we think populism represents a real political phenomenon with its

[3] This memorable description is offered by Ivan Krastev, 'The Populist Moment', available at www.eurozine.com/articles/2007-09-18-krastev-en.html, 2018, cited in Jan-Werner Müller, *What is Populism?* (Harmondsworth: Penguin, 2016) 2.

[4] Yascha Mounk, *The People vs. Democracy: Why Our Freedom Is in Danger and How to Save It* (Cambridge: Harvard University Press, 2018) 32.

[5] Philip Collins, 'Macron, the populist antidote to populism', available at www.thetimes.co.uk/article/macron-the-populist-antidote-to-populism-nwvnkc2hh.

own distinctive contours. Moreover, we believe that the 'Age of Populism' has the most profound implications in thinking about the future politics and regulation of work.

Two recent works have engaged with this populist turn in modern political practice, and both provide important insights into the meaning of populism, its causes, and how best to respond to populist mobilisation. In *What is Populism?* Jan-Werner Müller provides a precise and lucid examination of populism in contemporary political thought and practice.[6] Specifically, Müller challenges the view that populism is best understood in terms of an orientation that is critical of established elites. As Müller explains, it is possible to be critical of elites without thereby being populist. Indeed, holding elites to account in the democratic process is a virtue of liberal democratic citizenship. While populists are critical of elites, *the distinctive mark of populism is its 'antipluralism'*.[7] In this way, populists do not repudiate political representation of 'the people'. Rather, populists assert a claim to be the exclusive moral representatives of 'the people' as a homogeneous entity. This is 'a particular moralistic imagination of politics, a way of perceiving the political world that sets a morally pure and fully unified … people against elites who are deemed corrupt or in some other way morally inferior'.[8] This feature of populism is of the first importance. As labour lawyers, our disposition is often to be critical of established power structures and the role of political and business elites in supporting those structures. All too often, the powerful have invoked 'populism' as a de-legitimating rhetoric to protect the status quo from critique. Müller's work identifies the fallacy of this move and the basis for its rejection.

While populist discourse is superficially democratic – indeed, Müller describes populism as the 'permanent shadow of representative politics'[9] – its modalities of governance are antithetical to liberal democratic institutions. The idea of 'The people' is understood as a mystical 'substance' or 'spirit', rather than a genuinely plural or aggregative concept that takes seriously the equality and separateness of persons.[10] Accordingly, those who dissent from the populist's divination of 'the people' are subject to a kind of civic banishment: they are traitors to the 'real' people. According to Müller, this repression of pluralism is reflected in the anti-democratic techniques of populist governance: colonising state institutions such as the civil service and judiciary; mass clientelism providing discriminatory benefits to supporters of the regime; and systematic suppression of autonomous sites of resistance in civil society.[11] In extreme cases, populist governments may even institute populist constitutions that entrench the political suppression of pluralism.

[6] Müller (n 3).
[7] ibid 3.
[8] ibid 20.
[9] ibid 101.
[10] ibid 27–29.
[11] Müller (n 3) esp chapter 2.

In *The People vs. Democracy: Why Our Freedom Is in Danger and How to Save It*, Yascha Mounk mounts an urgent and powerful critique of populist threats to liberal democracy across the world.[12] Mounk identifies two distinctive trajectories within a general pattern of the degradation and decomposition of liberal democracy. The first is 'democracy without rights' or 'illiberal democracy', which describes a situation where the expanding reach of populist mobilisation interferes with the rights of minorities and undermines the bulwarks of political pluralism. This would be reflected in, among other things, the democratic legitimation of discrimination against those individuals adjudged to be outside the moral community of citizens (often on ethnic or religious grounds); the capture of media outlets and attacks on the free press; and the suppression of 'foundations, trade unions, think tanks, religious associations, and other nongovernmental organizations'.[13] It may be that the Polish case is an exemplar of 'illiberal democracy'.

The second is 'rights without democracy' or 'undemocratic liberalism', which describes a situation where democratic participation and collective democratic agency are curtailed in favour of technocratic expertise. This would be reflected in, for example, strong constitutional review through an independent judiciary, independent central banks insulated from political accountability, the growth in bureaucratic law-making through secondary legislation, and international treaties and organisations that limit national sovereignty.[14] It may be that the EU is an exemplar of 'undemocratic liberalism'. While 'undemocratic liberalism' ensures that fundamental rights are insulated from the sway of democratic majorities, it is highly vulnerable to populist attacks. The minimisation of popular democratic influence is alienating for citizens, particularly precarious citizens who experience the economic turbulence and social dislocation of a globalising economy. It also lends itself to populist portrayals of technocratic institutions as a corrupt conspiracy of self-serving elites. Mounk provides a wide-ranging evaluation of the causes of these trajectories, as a prelude to examining effective policy interventions to reconsolidate liberal democracy. He discusses the role of social media, the impact of economic stagnation and growing inequality, and the rise of nationalism as a basis of moral community. Each of these elements has been corrosive of liberal democratic citizenship.

While there are certainly differences between Müller and Mounk,[15] both scholars identify populism as a most profound threat to sustainable democratic

[12] Mounk (n 4).

[13] ibid 45.

[14] ibid chapter 2.

[15] Müller deprecates the terminology of 'illiberal democracy' as a description of populist political orders because he takes the view that populism is by its nature antithetical to democracy (see Müller (n 3) 50). By contrast, Mounk argues that the terminology is useful in identifying the raw democratic pulse that often animates populist mobilisation (see Mounk (n 4) 51–52). Both scholars agree that populist political movements, in virtue of the totalising logic of populism, tend to undermine democratic institutions in the long run.

governance. Their work also enables us to understand the overlapping connections with nationalism and authoritarianism in the practices of populist governance. According to Müller, the logic of populism is not necessarily aligned with nationalism.[16] Certainly, populism depends upon some basis for demarcating the morally pure 'people' from the morally debased 'others' who stand outside of the political community. While those markers may be based upon nationality and ethnic identity, it is also possible for the ethical community to be defined in other ways such as religion or class-based identities. Still, it is important to acknowledge that even if the overlap between nationalism and populism is contingent, it is highly salient at the current time. For example, Taggart has drawn attention to the alignment of some populist movements with 'ethical nationalism' and isolationism in foreign policy.[17] In a similar vein, Mounk has identified 'exclusionary nationalism' as a virulent strand in modern populist movements,[18] and he reflects upon strategies to 'domesticate' nationalist sentiments into more inclusive forms of civic engagement.

The alignment between populism and authoritarianism is also strong. Populist governance is directed at the suppression of pluralism, and the repressive techniques of governance reflect its antipluralism. It is for this reason that Müller is circumspect about the term 'illiberal democracy' insofar as it confers democratic credentials on populist regimes. This is because populist constitutionalism attacks 'freedom of speech and assembly, media pluralism, and the protection of minorities'.[19] When populism, nationalism and authoritarianism converge, the resulting political constellation is utterly poisonous to sustainable democracy.

Should we not acknowledge the normative difference between 'Left' and 'Right' populism? That is to say, 'Right' populism is especially toxic because it is prone to xenophobic nationalism and authoritarian repression. By contrast, 'Left' populism may represent a noble cause in mobilising working people to challenge the forces and structures of neoliberal oppression. In this way, 'Left' populism operates as a corrective to the gross deficiencies of representative democracies under modern capitalism. The negative connotations of the populist label provide a convenient rhetorical move for criticised elites to delegitimise the mobilisation of disempowered groups seeking recognition in the democratic process. Progressive labour lawyers should be wary of playing into the hands of political and business elites who might invoke populist anxieties to justify the restriction of collective mobilisation.

We acknowledge the superficial appeal of a positive populism of the Left. As Müller explains, populism has often been aligned with 'producerism'.[20]

[16] Müller (n 3) 25.
[17] Paul Taggart, *Populism* (Buckingham: Open University Press, 2000) 96.
[18] Mounk (n 3) 199–201.
[19] Müller (n 3) 55.
[20] ibid 23.

This ideology pits 'the pure, innocent, always hardworking people against a corrupt elite',[21] and in so doing it elevates work as a source of civic honour and the basis of membership in 'the people'. The political marginalisation of work and the worker has become so entrenched in liberal capitalism that this political shift to 'producerism' is no doubt an alluring one. The rebalancing of political concern with production alongside consumption may be positive. Furthermore, the historical roots of populism in the Russian ideology of *narodnichestvo* may also account for the normative ambiguities of Left populism at the current time. This ideology represented a faith in the agrarian peasantry as an elevated form of community that provided an egalitarian alternative to the debased character of the tsarist regime.[22] This historic ideal of 'going to the people' may now resonate with the modern emancipatory concerns of labour law, at least 'in the sense of favoring the least advantaged or bringing the excluded into politics'.[23]

Nevertheless, we think that it is important to repudiate populism in all its political guises. The mobilisation of working people can be democratic without being populist. In this respect, we agree with Müller that 'the demand for a specific "left-wing populism" to oppose austerity policies (or, for that matter, to counter the rise of right-wing populism) in many parts of Europe is either redundant or dangerous'.[24] Its redundancy lies in the fact that it is entirely possible for working people to mobilise, to criticise elites, to hold the powerful to democratic account, and to seek justice, in a non-populist way. This mobilisation need not occur using the totalising garb of populist rhetoric. Inclusive pluralism requires democratic mobilisation to be couched in terms of 'we are also the people'.[25] This would reject the totalising and exclusionary logic of populism. 'Left' populism is dangerous precisely because it leads to the eventual destruction of constitutional checks and balances. It thus poses a simultaneous threat to democratic institutions and to basic political freedoms. That is no less of a concern in Venezuela than it is in Poland or the United States.

We are also deeply suspicious of 'producerism' as an ideology of identity. In populist governance, this may degrade into further exclusionary distinctions based upon migration statuses, gender, disability/inability to work, unemployment and so forth. 'Producerism' then operates in an exclusionary fashion that valorises the 'British worker' or the 'male worker'. In so doing, it denigrates those who do not count in the political community of the 'real' workers. How might we reconceive of work as a politically significant activity in a non-populist pluralistic democracy? We think that the most promising possibility lies in a notion of 'democratic citizenship at work', and we will return to this idea in the

[21] ibid.
[22] Taggart (n 17) 46–58.
[23] Müller (n 3) 19.
[24] ibid 98.
[25] ibid, citing Catherine Fieschi, 'A Plague on Both Your Populisms!' Open Democracy, 19 April 2012, www.opendemocracy.net/catherine-fieschi/plague-on-both-your-populisms.

final section of the chapter. In the meantime, we would emphasise that we envisage this as a universalist category not circumscribed by national citizenship. It also transcends the distinctions between employees, workers, some at least of the self-employed, the unemployed and people engaged in unpaid reproductive labour.

In developing this normative ideal of non-populist worker mobilisation, the work of Müller and Mounk suggests that there are three aspects to be considered. The first aspect reflects a more general concern with institutional design and achieving a sustainable balance between democratic accountability and technical expertise in governance. Specific issues here would include the role of courts in securing fundamental rights, and the ways in which the specification of fundamental rights might be democratised. There are likely to be different legitimacy challenges depending upon whether we are considering transnational courts, such as the European Court of Human Rights (ECtHR) or Court of Justice of the European Union (CJEU), or national courts, such as the United Kingdom Supreme Court (UKSC). This would also extend to a consideration of other forms of institutional design, especially at the transnational level, such as International Labour Organization (ILO)-style tripartism and dialogue-based mechanisms for developing and applying norms. Most generally, it would require an exploration of the ways in which organisations such as the EU are excessively technocratic, and the ways in which EU institutions might be democratised.

The second aspect concerns the substantive contours of an anti-populist labour law for sustainable democratic governance. To this end, Mounk sets out a range of considerations under the general rubric of 'fixing the economy'.[26] This includes measures to improve productivity through education and training, increasing the bargaining power of workers, facilitating the portability of social and welfare rights to support employment mobility, and reflecting on the possibilities for 'meaningful work' in an increasingly automated gig economy. The overarching concern with all these discrete initiatives would be to empower workers' collective agency over the material and social forces that would otherwise seem overwhelming to them. The experience of powerlessness is demeaning and corrosive of a sense of effective civic agency. These reflections also acknowledge the different ways in which precarious work engenders precarious democratic citizenship.

The third aspect concerns the centrality of migration regulation to sustainable democratic governance. According to Mounk, this requires a dual recognition: that 'all legal residents of a country be treated the same irrespective of their color or creed' but that 'secure borders can help to win popular support for more generous immigration policies'.[27] For Müller, what he describes as 'the boundary problem' (who is included in 'the people'?) in liberal democracies

[26] Mounk (n 4) chapter 8.
[27] Mounk (n 4) 214.

must be addressed through ongoing democratic debate.[28] The democratic specification of 'criteria for belonging'[29] will be bound up with considerations of labour market access for migrant workers and the terms upon which such access is granted. The neuralgic point here is how sustainable democracies approach the question of fundamental entitlements for those among us who are not, in Mounk's terms, 'legal residents of a country'.

II. ANTI-TOTALITARIANISM, POPULISM AND THE POLITICS OF LABOUR LAW

Why have European democracies been so vulnerable to populist mobilisation? The answers to this question are no doubt exceedingly complex. Müller offers some important contributions to these debates. We believe that the crux of that contribution lies in his identification of the post-war institutional response to totalitarianism in the twentieth century:

> Now, in Western Europe, one of the peculiarities of the aftermath of the high point of totalitarian politics in the 1930s and 1940s was the following: both post-war political thought and post-war political institutions were deeply imprinted with anti-totalitarianism ... They relied on an image of the past as a chaotic era characterized by limitless political dynamism, unbound 'masses', and attempts to forge a completely unconstrained political subject.[30]

This was reflected in a distrust of popular sovereignty and a constitutional concern to limit politics through checks and balances, strong constitutional review through courts, and transnational mechanisms to entrench liberal democracy such as the Council of Europe and the EU.[31] According to Müller, the technocratic response to the financial crisis emboldened populist groups to attack that post-war democratic settlement because the critique gains 'some legitimacy on the grounds that the postwar European order really is based on the idea of keeping "the people" at a distance'.[32] This critical stance is also pursued by Mounk, who identifies the EU as an example of 'undemocratic liberalism'.[33]

We think that Müller's reflections on the institutional traction of minimalist theories of democracy in the post-war period are highly plausible. For example, Joseph Schumpeter's influential critique of participatory democracy

> echoed closely the opinions of many Western commentators and politicians at the time who felt 'excessive' participation might produce the mobilization of the demos

[28] Müller (n 3) 81.
[29] ibid 103.
[30] ibid 93–94.
[31] ibid 94–96.
[32] ibid 96.
[33] Mounk (n 4) 12.

> with highly dangerous consequences: among the experiences uppermost in their minds were no doubt the Bolshevik revolution and the mass rallies which signalled the advent of Nazi Germany.[34]

Schumpeter's theory of democracy was to emphasise its credentials as a method for choosing between governing elites at periodic elections between competing political parties. It was based upon a pessimistic view of the political competence and capacities of ordinary citizens. It depended upon a functioning system of competition between political parties, and it required a working consensus on the constitutional ground rules that shaped the formulation of competing political programmes.[35] The work of pluralist democratic theorists such as Robert Dahl supplemented this competitive theory of democracy by examining the role of pressure groups in the democratic process. The competitive clash between pressure groups in interest group bargaining ensured that a wide range of individuals could exert some influence over public decision making.[36]

While these theories shaped the architecture of the European post-war settlement, they also shaped the theorisation of labour law in the post-war period in the UK. Indeed, British labour law in the post-war period may be understood as an exemplar of anti-totalitarian labour law, given the biography of Professor Sir Otto Kahn-Freund as a German Jew and refugee. Kahn-Freund famously described the 'rapidly developing pluralistic character of the British Constitution' in his seminal essay 'Labour Law'.[37] The constitutional manifestation of this pluralistic approach was that 'the line between "State" and "society" has been blurred very deliberately, or to put it differently, the "pressure" of pressure groups has been so organised as to work inside the legislative, administrative, judicial and policy making processes'.[38] This pluralism was reflected in, among other things, the inclusion of 'representative organisations' in the machinery of investigation,[39] adjudication,[40] and regulatory processes setting binding standards. As such, this pluralistic constitution envisaged the devolution of regulatory tasks to autonomous trade unions in civil society. In industrial relations, trade unions operated as a form of competitive democratic opposition to employers, a conceptualisation that had obvious affinities with Schumpeter's work.[41]

[34] David Held, *Models of Democracy* 3rd edn (Cambridge: Polity, 2006) 142, discussing Joseph Schumpeter, *Capitalism, Socialism and Democracy* (London: Allen and Unwin, 1976).

[35] Held (n 34) 150–51.

[36] RA Dahl, *A Preface to Democratic Theory* (Chicago: University of Chicago Press, 1956).

[37] O Kahn-Freund, 'Labour Law', in O Kahn-Freund, *Selected Writings* (London: Stevens & Sons, 1978) 1, 8.

[38] ibid 10.

[39] See, eg, the procedures for triggering the operation of the Cotton Manufacturing Industry (Temporary Provisions) Act 1934. For discussion, see Douglas Brodie, *A History of British Labour Law 1867–1945* (Oxford: Hart Publishing, 2003) 200–01.

[40] See, eg, Industrial Court Act 1919, s 1.

[41] See HA Clegg, *A New Approach to Industrial Democracy* (Oxford: Blackwell, 1960).

This anti-totalitarianism shaped the core motifs of pluralist labour law: the democratic need for trade unions to perform an oppositional role in industry and in national politics; liberal scepticism about the 'common good' as a constraint on free bargaining; the central role of collective bargaining as a form of interest group bargaining; the dangers of 'integration' of free associations into the apparatus of the employing organisation or the state; and the institutionalisation of legitimate conflicts of interest to be mediated through free collective bargaining.

In recent years, some labour lawyers have retrieved and reworked older paradigms of labour law scholarship.[42] Is this historical turn useful in the light of the populist threat? Müller's assessment of the post-war European legacy is circumspect. He avoids simplistic and crude causal accounts that postulate a direct link between post-war minimalist democracy and the recrudescence of populism at the current time. Nevertheless, there is evidently a need for caution in using Kahn-Freund's work to inspire a new political and legal cartography. Like many great thinkers of his time, Kahn-Freund's political commitments were shaped by the terrible shadow of totalitarianism. Müller's work demonstrates that anti-totalitarian political structures and anti-populist political structures may have very different institutional shapes leading to very different political outcomes. The flight from totalitarianism may translate into the denigration of citizens' capacities for democratic participation, leading to the insulation of public decision making from popular democratic influence. Should we surprised when citizens kick back at technocrats and experts during times of economic crisis and uncertainty?

Despite this, we think that there is some value in reflecting upon the 'pluralistic constitution'. At the outset, it is important to acknowledge that it embodied many enduring political virtues, the loss of which has inflicted grave costs on our democratic settlement. Kahn-Freund never shared in the post-war denigration of citizens' civic capacities. For example, he was greatly impressed by the 'direct democracy' of workplace bargaining through 'shop stewards',[43] and more generally the mediating role of trade union representation in a liberal democracy. He was also deeply moved by the freedom and 'autonomy' of British trade unions, and in this respect the contrast with the integration of the German trade union movement into the state apparatus was very striking to him. 'Freedom of association' was vital in a healthy liberal democracy. Moreover, Kahn-Freund's theory was explicitly pluralist and hence repudiatory of the antipluralism of populist political thought.

[42] For a notable example, see Ruth Dukes, *The Labour Constitution* (Oxford: Oxford University Press, 2014), which develops the classic work of Hugo Sinzheimer.

[43] O Kahn-Freund, 'Labour Law and Industrial Relations in Great Britain and West Germany' in Lord Wedderburn, R Lewis and J Clark (eds), *Labour Law and Industrial Relations: Building on Kahn-Freund* (Oxford: Oxford University Press, 1983) 1.

Nevertheless, using populism as a refractive lens exposes four difficulties with the pluralistic constitution that have sometimes been obscured. The first difficulty lies in a hesitation about the role of law to entrench and expand democratic institutions in workplace governance. Most notably, Kahn-Freund was committed to industrial democracy through voluntary methods of collective bargaining. He remained sceptical about institutional experimentation through company law reform or institutionalised works councils. This scepticism was strongly rooted in his commitment to pluralism, and the fear that structural integration of trade unions would compromise their independence and oppositional role. More generally, Kahn-Freund was sceptical about the positive value of 'direct' auxiliary support for collective bargaining, such as legal good faith duties. In retrospect, a more strongly constitutionalised set of structures for democratic participation may have been more enduring in the neoliberal decades that were to follow from 1979 onwards.

The second difficulty lies in the uncertain position of constitutional courts in the pluralistic constitution. Certainly, this ambivalence was never dogmatic. In his inaugural Goodhart lecture in the University of Cambridge, Kahn-Freund remarked that

> it is very easy for judges to read their own notions of policy into the bill of rights. To enact a bill of rights may involve a shifting of the function of law reform from Parliament, the Government and the Law Commission to the Bench and to the Bar. Some may consider this as a risk, others as an opportunity.[44]

There is thus a great sensitivity to the democratic consequences of constitutionalisation, whereby political questions in the hands of elected politicians are transmuted into legal questions in the hands of unelected judges. From the perspective of avoiding populism, this concern to stymie the colonisation of politics by law and unelected judges might be regarded as attractive. Nevertheless, the virtues and vices of constitutionalisation are rather finely balanced. We speculate that some form of constitutional entrenchment of fundamental social rights might have restrained the most egregious manifestations of neoliberal politics that have dominated the UK over the last 40 years. This could have mitigated some of the worst manifestations of social and economic precariousness that have facilitated the growth of populist movements in the UK.

The third difficulty is the conservative bias of the pluralistic constitution. This critique was developed by Richard Hyman, who emphasised that the scope of *reasonable* pluralism in the pluralistic constitution was in fact highly constrained.[45] The pluralist emphasis on consensus and constitutional

[44] O Kahn-Freund, 'The Impact of Constitutions on Labour Law' (1976) 35 *Cambridge Law Journal* 240, 270.

[45] Richard Hyman, 'Pluralism, Procedural Consensus and Collective Bargaining' (1978) 16 *British Journal of Industrial Relations* 16.

stability meant that legitimate interests were restricted to narrow forms of material concession that could be adjusted through bargaining. The constraining effect of shared constitutional rules meant that 'radical social and economic transformation ... would strain intolerably the institutions of pluralistic industrial relations'.[46] This meant that pluralist institutions tended to support and maintain existing distributions of property and economic power. Once again, insulating basic social and economic structures and the resulting inequalities from strong democratic control left the pluralistic constitution particularly exposed to neoliberal reforms.

Finally, the notion of pluralism in the pluralistic constitution was too narrow to offer a credible political response to the significant societal changes occurring in European societies. The pluralism in Kahn-Freund's work was formulated in narrowly material terms. It did not address the facts of pluralism in liberal societies where there were significant moral and political disagreements between citizens with different religious commitments and moral values. Kahn-Freund was apt to emphasise the 'homogeneous' character of British society.[47] Whatever the historical accuracy of this description, it was certainly not true in the latter decades of the twentieth century. This failure to develop an account of 'reasonable disagreement', and to acknowledge its constitutional significance, identifies an important gap in the pluralistic constitution. Nor are there any easy answers to it. The existence of reasonable disagreement about justice has led liberal theorists to develop ideas of 'public reason' as a basis for respectful dialogue across difference in the public sphere.[48] Still, this leaves many very difficult questions unresolved: does 'public reason' lead us to a betrayal of 'true reason'? When does disagreement cease to be 'reasonable'? Does reasonable pluralism extend to the interests of employing entities? And which institutions should have priority in the face of reasonable disagreement where those disagreements relate to fundamental rights such as the right to strike?[49]

In these short reflections, we hope at least to have identified some ways in which Kahn-Freund's intellectual struggles resonate with our own struggles today. While his resolution of them may have been imperfect, it is important to recognise that the current state of our democratic predicament cannot easily be traced back to the pluralistic constitution. Rather, we think that the current economic context to populism is of great and decisive importance. The seeming unsustainability of our democratic institutions has resulted from successive

[46] ibid 33.

[47] Kahn-Freund (n 37) 37.

[48] The literature is forbiddingly large. For a nice introduction, see Jonathan Quong, 'Public Reason', available at https://plato.stanford.edu/entries/public-reason/.

[49] For an attempt to begin thinking about the importance of disagreement in theory-building in labour law, see Alan Bogg, 'Labour Law and the Trade Unions: Autonomy and Betrayal' in Alan Bogg, Cathryn Costello, ACL Davies and Jeremias Prassl (eds), *The Autonomy of Labour Law* (Oxford: Hart Publishing, 2015) 73, 100–05.

decades of deregulation, the collapse in private sector trade unionism and collective bargaining, the explosion in precarious work and sham self-employment, and the declining democratic role of working class organisations in the political process. In other words, populism represents the civic consequences of neoliberal politics and economics. The pluralistic constitution was insufficiently embedded to impede this development. It may have been more deeply embedded had there been greater openness to the constitutional entrenchment of fundamental social rights, at least in the UK context. Perhaps this explains why the 'Age of Populism' has followed on from the 'Age of Neoliberalism'.

We think that it would be valuable to relate this back to the work of political theorists such as Müller and Mounk. In the UK, for example, the last bastion for the protection of fundamental rights of 'irregular' migrant workers have often been the courts.[50] This has also been true of the fundamental right of access to a court. The UKSC recently struck down the tribunal fees regime, which had led to the effective exclusion of precarious workers from the legal process through the imposition of prohibitive fees.[51] Where worker-citizens and their representative associations are socially and economically weakened, democratic procedures can become paralysed through the intransigence of the powerful. We think that ILO tripartism around the 'right to strike', and the fundamental repudiation of the right to strike by the ILO Employers' Group, provides an excellent recent example of this phenomenon. This suggests that we need to explore the *complementarities* between political and legal institutions in the domain of fundamental rights, rather than to view the problem in terms of a simple institutional trade-off between 'democracy' and 'liberalism' (and the excessive dominance of the latter).

III. LABOUR LAW POPULISM WITHIN THE NATION-STATE

The convulsions around Brexit have shed light on the rise of populist politics in UK labour law. In 2016, two pieces of legislation were enacted which, on their face, were unconnected. The Trade Union Act 2016 introduced a restrictive body of norms directed at trade union political and industrial activity, including further curtailment of the right to strike. The Immigration Act 2016 introduced a new set of penal offences that criminalised the daily activities of 'irregular' migrants, especially their working activities. The populist frame exposes the normative continuities between these two statutes as constructing an antipluralist vision of the 'British worker'.

The Trade Union Act 2016 covers a wide range of trade union matters although its most notable provisions were (i) restrictions on the right to strike,

[50] *Hounga v Allen* [2014] UKSC 47.
[51] *R (on the application of UNISON) v Lord Chancellor* [2017] UKSC 51.

especially in relation to new ballot thresholds and notice requirements; (ii) tightening the law on picketing and protest; and (iii) restricting the political voice of trade unions by switching to an 'opt-in' scheme for trade union political funds for new members. The provisions that have attracted the most attention are the revised thresholds for pre-strike ballots. Section 2 stipulates a requirement that 50 per cent of those entitled to vote did so, in order for the ballot to constitute a valid authorisation of the industrial action. Section 3 stipulates a further requirement where 'the majority of those who were entitled to vote in the ballot are at the relevant time normally engaged in the provision of important public services', that 'at least 40% of those who were entitled to vote in the ballot' supported industrial action. The meaning of 'important public services' will be confined to services falling within the categories of health services; education of those aged under 17; fire services; transport services; decommissioning of nuclear installations and management of radioactive waste and spent fuel; and border security.

In a valuable work on strike law reforms during the 1980s in the UK, Simon Auerbach drew attention to the balance between 'internal' and 'external' justifications for the imposition of balloting requirements on trade unions.[52] 'External' justifications were especially concerned with the minimisation of the effects of strike action on external constituencies, such as employers, service users and customers, or the wider 'public'. Strict balloting requirements would tend to disinhibit precipitate strike action, so that the weapon was only deployed by trade unions as a last resort. 'Internal' justifications were especially concerned with the relations between the trade union leadership and its members. This often rested on a perception that a militant leadership might be subjected to internal democratic constraint by a more moderate 'rank and file' membership.

It is the 'external' justification that has been most dominant in the new provisions on 'important public services'. This represents a view of strike law that places a premium on maintaining social order, avoiding the disruptive impact of strike action on public services, and suppressing pluralist conflicts of interest between 'public sector' workers and users of public services. On this view, the 'real worker' is the hard-working non-unionised worker in the private sector, whose interests and values are threatened by the selfish actions of the unionised and cosseted public sector worker.

This antipluralist reading is supported by the proposals to restrict public protest through the criminal law. In July 2015 the Department for Business, Innovation and Skills (BIS) commenced a consultation on the reform of picketing and protest law in parallel with the introduction of the Trade

[52] Simon Auerbach, *Legislating for Conflict* (Oxford: Clarendon Press 1990) 118.

Union Bill.[53] Ostensibly, this consultation was directed at considering new legal measures to prevent the 'intimidation of non-striking workers' during industrial disputes. The specific proposals for consideration in the BIS Consultation disclosed an important shift in governmental strategy. Thus, the Consultation stated that 'Employers report that enforcing civil offences through the courts can be time-consuming and potentially expensive and slow'.[54] The Consultation contemplated the increased use of criminal sanctions in the restriction of 'leverage' protest. It identified as a 'key challenge' the need to 'promote effective policing and prosecution of intimidation and other offences arising in the context of industrial disputes'[55] and suggested that the government would work with the police and the Crown Prosecution Service to ensure that the existing catalogue of criminal offences (including anti-social behaviour provisions) was used more extensively and effectively against protesters using 'leverage' tactics.[56] Alongside the push for greater utilisation of existing criminal offences by the police and prosecuting authorities, the Consultation also raised the prospect of *further* criminalisation in the form of a new offence of 'intimidation on the picket line'.

In the end, these measures proposing extended criminalisation were not enacted. The responses to the Consultation were overwhelmingly hostile. Moreover, the government had been weakened politically by the impending vote on Brexit. Nevertheless, these proposals for criminalisation may be resurrected at a later date and they give an important insight into the government's antipluralist view of public protest.

The Trade Union Act 2016 also contained important new provisions restricting the political role of trade unions. Section 11 provides that it is unlawful for a union member to be required to make a contribution to the political fund if the member has not given the trade union an 'opt-in notice' (or if the member has given notice of withdrawal from an 'opt-in' notice). The trade union is also subject to an obligation to notify its members of their right to withdraw from the political fund. The 'opt-in' regime is subject to a transitional arrangement and it applies only to members who join at the end of a period not less than 12 months following the entry into force of the relevant provisions. This was coupled with cumbersome reporting obligations. While the final provisions in the Act are intrusive, these measures are significantly diluted from the original

[53] Department for Business, Innovation and Skills, 'Trade Union Bill: Consultation on Tackling Intimidation of Non-Striking Workers' (BIS/15/415, July 2015). Available at www.gov.uk/government/uploads/system/uploads/attachment_data/file/445439/BIS-15-415-tackling-intimidation-of-non-striking-workers.pdf (BIS/15/415).

[54] ibid para 8.

[55] ibid para 37.

[56] ibid paras 37–38.

proposals in the Bill, which had envisaged a universal 'opt-in' scheme for all members, requiring renewal on a five-year cycle.

The House of Lords Select Committee on Trade Union Political Funds and Political Party Funding considered that this switch to an opt-in system 'could have a sizeable negative effect on the number of union members participating in political funds',[57] translating into a significant drop in the funding for the Centre-Left opposition party, the Labour Party.[58] In the view of the Select Committee, 'If any government were to use its majority unilaterally to inflict significant damage on the finances of opposition parties, it would risk starting a tit-for-tat conflict which could harm parliamentary democracy'.[59] The suspicion that this was part of a longer game to undermine political opposition was given further support by the announcement in the Spending Review and Autumn Statement 2015, published on 25 November 2015, which proposed the reduction of Short Money allocations to opposition parties by 19 per cent and then freezing them for the remainder of the Parliament.[60] It is difficult to resist the conclusion that this represents an incremental strategy to undermine the ability of other political parties and civil society groups to mount a credible and effective opposition to the Conservative government. Müller argues that the suppression of a critical civil society is one of the core features of populist governance. In our view, this provides a very powerful perspective on the political significance of the Trade Union Act 2016 in its broader context.

One of the central political controversies in the Brexit referendum was control over immigration. Specifically, many supporters of Brexit were hostile to the loss of sovereign national control over borders as a corollary of free movement of workers. In the field of labour law, it manifested itself in the populist slogan, 'British Jobs for British Workers'. It was here that concerns about the oversupply of cheap labour, particularly from Eastern European Member States, were most acute. Sometimes this centred upon diffuse concerns with the impact of migration flows upon the cohesiveness and character of local communities. It mainly crystallised around specific concerns about the effects of an oversupply of cheap labour on the living and working conditions and employment opportunities of indigenous workers.

It is against this political backdrop that the interactions between migration law and labour law have occurred. These intersections have increasingly been mediated by the role of the criminal law. The criminal law has performed two main functions in this context. We might identify these as the 'worker-repressive' and 'worker-protective' functions of the criminal law. First, from a

[57] Trade Union Political Funds and Political Party Funding Committee, *Report of Session 2015–16* (HL 2015–16, 106) para 74.

[58] ibid para 100.

[59] ibid para 115.

[60] Richard Kelly, 'Short Money' (Briefing Paper 01663, House of Commons Library 22 March 2016). Available at http://researchbriefings.parliament.uk/ResearchBriefing/Summary/SN01663#fullreport.

'worker-repressive' perspective, there has been a growing use of criminal law to regulate the employment of 'irregular' migrants. This has led to the creation of new criminal offences that target employers employing 'irregular' migrants *and* migrant workers who are working illegally. Second, from a 'worker-protective' perspective, the criminal law is increasingly being used to target highly exploitative and abusive employment practices that tend to be associated with migrant labour. Most obviously, this has been reflected in criminalisation of trafficking and 'modern slavery' practices.[61] New forms of criminalisation are also addressing more specific labour abuses, such as the failure to pay the minimum wage. These functions were brought together in the Immigration Act 2016, which constitutes an important piece of labour legislation, albeit one in which the Home Office had a decisive hand.

To begin with the 'worker-repressive' functions of the criminal law, the Immigration Act 2016 creates new offences for workers working illegally and for the employers employing them. Thus, section 34 creates a new offence of 'illegally working'. This offence is committed where the worker (P) works where he is disqualified from doing so on the basis of his immigration status, and 'at that time P knows or has reasonable cause to believe that P is disqualified from working by reason of P's immigration status'. It covers an extremely broad range of contractual arrangements for the provision of work, even extending to self-employment. Conviction for the offence may be punished by a maximum of 51 weeks' imprisonment and/or a fine. In addition, the legislation makes provision for a confiscation order under section 70 of the Proceeds of Crime Act 2002, which would cover the remuneration earned as a result of working illegally. Section 35 expands the existing criminal liability for employers engaged in the employment of 'irregular' migrants. Specifically, it provides that an employer is liable for an offence where he employs a migrant who is disqualified from working where he 'has reasonable cause to believe that the employee is disqualified from employment by reason of the employee's immigration status'. This is accompanied by powers for immigration officers to order the closure of workplaces where the employer has previously been convicted or held civilly liable for employing migrant workers illegally.[62] These criminal law measures build upon the extensive set of civil penalties regulating the behaviour of employers that already existed in the UK.[63]

The 'worker-protective' criminalisation in the Immigration Act 2016 is concerned to tackle the worst forms of exploitation through the techniques of the criminal law. This involves using criminal sanctions as an auxiliary enforcement mechanism for certain established employment rights, such as the right

[61] See, e.g., Modern Slavery Act 2015.

[62] Section 38 and Schedule 6.

[63] For discussion, see Bernard Ryan, 'Employer Checks of Immigration Status and Employment Law' in Cathryn Costello and Mark Freedland (eds), *Migrants at Work* (Oxford: Oxford University Press, 2014) 239.

to a minimum wage. Its effect is to create new mechanisms of public enforcement through the criminal law, alongside civil litigation. In support of this public enforcement through criminal prosecution, the legislation creates a new position of 'Director of Labour Market Enforcement' to coordinate the enforcement activities of public agencies concerned with licensing of certain employing entities and the enforcement of labour rights. In some respects, this might be regarded as a positive development. It signals an acknowledgement of the practical reality that the most vulnerable migrant workers will often lack the wherewithal to enforce their employment rights through the civil process. However, as ACL Davies' powerful analysis of the Immigration Act framework demonstrates, the reality is rather more ambivalent.[64] Specifically, the legislative framework is designed 'to build, rather than break down, connections between labour law enforcement and immigration enforcement' by facilitating cooperation between the 'Director of Labour Market Enforcement' and the public authorities concerned with immigration enforcement.[65]

Overall, the new regime of the Immigration Act 2016 marks a step change in the authoritarian character of state intervention in labour law. This is reflected in a greater willingness to use the stigmatic and punitive techniques of the criminal law to enforce immigration control in the sphere of work. Criminalisation is of great symbolic and practical importance since the processes of criminal investigation, prosecution and punishment are a public matter and so within the jurisdiction of public rather than private law. The web of civil and criminal liabilities effectively co-opts private employers into the public task of immigration law enforcement.[66] This blurring of the public and the private both intensifies the private coercive power of employers while simultaneously expanding the public coercive power of the state. It has contributed to a public discourse of national community that we regard as deeply troubling. The 'British worker' represents the dark side of a 'producerist' ideology which, in populist hands, translates into a form of exclusionary nationalism. We have described the phenomenon of 'worker-protective criminalisation' and we regard this as a very real legislative tendency. As a form of worker protection, is it not benign? We do not believe that it is. Indeed, it is profoundly disquieting when we ask which worker is the object of protection. For it is unquestionably the non-migrant worker. The suppression of extreme forms of labour market exploitation of migrants is justified in terms of protecting the working conditions of the native British worker.

[64] ACL Davies, 'The Immigration Act 2016' (2016) 45 *Industrial Law Journal* 431.

[65] ibid 441.

[66] The food chain 'Byron Burger' cooperated with the immigration authorities, which led to the arrest and deportation of 25 workers. It has been subject to protests by campaigning groups in the light of its cooperation in the arrests of its workers. See 'Protesters target Byron burger branch over immigration raid', 1 August 2016, www.theguardian.com/uk-news/2016/aug/01/byron-burger-chain-asks-protesters-to-respect-customers-safety. See further K Bales, 'Immigration Raids, Employer Collusion and the Immigration Act 2016' (2017) 46 ILJ 279.

Reflecting back on some of the general themes developed in the earlier sections of the chapter, we think that two features of this legislative activity warrant particular emphasis. The first is the relatively limited constraints imposed on this national legislative activity by European human rights law, both under EU law and the norms of the Council of Europe. The concepts of 'legislative competence', 'subsidiarity' and 'margin of appreciation' have always left Member States with significant room for legislative manoeuvre, and this is especially true in the domain of collective labour law. We do not proffer this as a political critique of supranational courts such as the ECtHR. Rather, it is an important reminder of the need to be precise when characterising transnational legal orders as 'undemocratic' because they interfere unduly with national sovereignty. Otherwise, critiques of populism risk playing right into the hands of the populists by giving legitimacy to inaccurate caricatures of supranational law making and adjudication. Under current legal conditions there is a great deal of scope for Member States to develop human rights norms in ways that are sensitive to local values and social practices and give national democracy its appropriate due.

The second is the risk of overuse of populism as a descriptive and critical nomenclature. We recognise this risk as a very real one. In our view, 'neoliberalism' in labour law discourse suffered that very fate and it lost some of its critical edge as a result. Can we really describe the current situation in the UK as a form of 'populist' authoritarianism, akin to the constitutional situation in Hungary? The critic might allege that this is hyperbolic, and hyperbole threatens the credibility of our analysis. Nevertheless, we think that ours is a defensible characterisation of the current UK situation given Müller's and Mounk's analytical presentation of populism. Three aspects of their presentation should be emphasised. First, populist governance tends to occur 'step by step' rather than through some dramatic constitutional moment. Specific measures examined singly might be defensible in their own terms. It is nevertheless important to examine constitutional developments cumulatively as they develop over time, rather than deriving a characterisation from a snapshot of the detail.[67] Second, populism should be understood as a matter of degree rather than as a binary category.[68] Finally, even if the current Conservative government is not itself 'populist', and Theresa May is not a 'populist' leader, it is important to recognise that it may be appropriating populist policy positions from populist parties such as UKIP for its own electoral advantage. As Müller observes, 'no right-wing populist has come to power in Western Europe or North America without the collaboration of established conservative elites'.[69] Where this collaboration is identified, politicians who have exploited this collaboration for electoral advantage must be held to democratic account.

[67] Müller (n 3) 50.
[68] ibid 40.
[69] ibid 109.

IV. OPPOSING LABOUR LAW POPULISM BEYOND THE NATION-STATE

In the foregoing sections, drawing on the work of Jan-Werner Müller, Yascha Mounk, and reverting to Otto Kahn-Freund's account of 'the pluralistic constitution', we have examined the growing threat of populism to institutions and practices of democratic engagement, concentrating our inquiry primarily upon the European region and upon the domain of labour law. In this section, we suggest that this threat seems to amount to the evolution of a populist genre of labour law which is especially opposed to supranational labour law – so much so as eventually to undermine labour law and its practices of democratic engagement, even at the national level. We argue that it is of great importance to oppose this wave of labour law populism, and we try to identify the best ways of conducting that struggle.

The first step in that argument is to identify and face up to the extent of labour law's vulnerability to populism and to acknowledge the special vulnerability of supranational labour law, taking as our case in point the supranational labour law of the European region as embodied in the norms and institutions of the European Union, the Council of Europe, and, in the larger background, those of the ILO. In times of social, political and economic upheaval, such as the present ones in the UK and in various other European countries, it is predictable that the norms and institutions of labour law will come under great pressure and that they will be subjected to a severe populist critique. This is not unexpected; but it is nevertheless fair to say that the severity of the populist onslaught upon those norms and institutions has taken the world of labour law scholarship by surprise and has found it somewhat unprepared. Perhaps the key element of this surprise consists in the brutal reminder that, when political discontent reaches a certain degree of severity, populist leaders of opinion both on the extreme Right and on the extreme Left of the political spectrum may quite suddenly converge upon a nihilistic rejection of existing norms and institutions, including those which, however imperfectly and unsatisfactorily, provide the basis for pluralist consensus and democratic engagement in the society in question.

In a large and general sense, historical instances of this phenomenon are abundant; and at the time of writing, Italian politics seem to be providing a text-book example of it, consisting in the formation of a coalition government composed of parties of the extreme Left and the extreme Right which seems to display precisely those characteristics. Our concern at this point is not, however, to test out the validity and extent of this proposition as a general historical paradigm, but rather to home in on particular cases where it is instantiated in the domain of labour law and, in particular, with regard to the supranational labour law of the European region. We concentrate upon two such instances of national crises, which became theatres of populism and in which areas of dissatisfaction with EU labour law (using that term in the widest sense) have been at or near the centre of the national political stage. The first such case is that of Greece's Austerity Crisis, which crystallised early in 2010, and the second such case is that of the UK's Brexit Crisis (we think it can now be regarded and styled as such) which has unfolded from early 2016 onwards.

In the evolution of the Greek Austerity Crisis, a prominent contributor to political and popular discontent with the EU in general, and its labour law regime in particular, was the insistence on the part of the so-called Troika of intervening supranational authorities – the European Commission, the International Monetary Fund and the European Central Bank – on a scaling down of the collective and individual protections for workers in the events of redundancy or corporate re-organisation whereby those protections were reduced from high-standard to very low-standard on the spectrum of European labour law. In the development of the UK Brexit Crisis, on the other hand, a key area of the terrain of populist contestation surrounding the Referendum of 2016 was the EU regime for labour migration, embodied in its foundational provisions for the freedom of movement of workers and their families between EU Member States and in its regulation of the 'posting' of workers by corporate employers between Member States. In both cases, EU labour law in the broad sense of that term could be presented as a source of the difficulties and discontent which the ordinary people of those countries were experiencing in times of austerity and economic and social upheaval.

The discourses of discontent with the labour market and labour migration regimes of the EU which thus developed in Greece and in the UK come straight out of the playbook of populism which the works of Müller and Mounk have placed on display to us and could be regarded as key locations for the political fire alarms which those authors are sounding, quite rightly in our view. The point here is that, when the going gets rough in times of austerity, it is those supranational regimes of the EU which are especially vulnerable to populist attack because they can be portrayed – not entirely without a germ of reason, of course – as the impositions of remote supranational technocrats and judges upon the essentially more democratic national systems of government and governance, depicted as more truly responsive to the respective national needs and aspirations of each Member State. It is a point which both these authors specially make, and which indeed Mounk, as we observed earlier, takes to the lengths of identifying the EU as an exemplar of 'undemocratic liberalism'. Indeed, the EU's interaction with Greece might be characterised as an exemplar of 'undemocratic *il*liberalism'. Through a series of economic measures, developed by supranational institutions lacking political accountability, embedded social rights in the Greek Constitution were de-constitutionalised.[70] These events occurred in a zone of 'liminal legality' that was also effectively insulated from constitutional supervision by the CJEU.[71]

[70] Ioannis Katsaroumpas, 'De-constitutionalising Collective Labour Rights: The Case of Greece' *Industrial Law Journal*, dwx019, https://doi.org/10.1093/indlaw/dwx019.

[71] Claire Kilpatrick, 'The EU and its Sovereign Debt Programmes: The Challenges of Liminal Legality' (2017) 70 *Current Legal Problems* 337.

This observation brings us to a key point of intersection between populist political discourse and scholarly legal policy discourse in which the theorists of labour law should, we suggest, regard themselves as deeply involved and implicated. We can arrive at this point by invoking a passage in Yanis Varoufakis' polemic of 2016, in which, under the title of 'And the weak suffer what they must',[72] he pinpoints what he regards as crucial flaws in the design of the European Union, which he thinks of as responsible for a fragmentation of Europe and a resurgence of racist extremism across the continent. Here, the Greek Austerity Crisis and the Brexit Crisis touch each other in a specially interesting way. In the Foreword to the paperback edition of his book, written in 2017, he describes how he came to Britain early in 2016, shortly following upon the original publication of his book, to campaign against Brexit because he believed that the problems with the European Union 'should be confronted from *within*, rather than through a series of exits'.[73] He records that

> [a]udiences were puzzled: 'How can you, given the way the EU treated you and your country, tell us that we should *remain*?'. The confusion was not eased by Michael Gove and other Brexiteers who heaped praise on my book, mischievously presenting it as the best argument for Britain to *leave* the EU.

Yanis Varoufakis was writing as the former Finance Minister in the SYRIZA Government of Greece, who had been at the heart of the negotiations between the Greek government and the EU concerning the Austerity Crisis. As a prominent politician with his own brand of more than slightly populist discourse, he might be regarded as having been just marginally disingenuous when he wrote that passage. But he seems to us to write as a political and economic theorist with a sense of historical responsibility for what he has to say, and as such he confronts us with a similar, if less publicly prominent, burden of responsibility for our own contributions to debates about the thorny topic of labour law in the 'Age of Populism'. We do or should experience an ambivalence comparable to that of Varoufakis: many of us who write about EU labour law have for a long time and often been profoundly critical of it. In particular, the *Viking* and *Laval* jurisprudence of the CJEU brought about a profound crisis of confidence in EU labour law on the part of labour law scholars which it has been very hard to repair. It came to epitomise the democratic dangers of a European juristocracy that was ever more remote from the national social democratic traditions of EU Member States. Still, there is an element of paradox here. Social democratic labour lawyers were not critical of judicial activism as such. They were critical of the specific crystallisation and treatment of fundamental rights

[72] Yanis Varoufakis, *And the Weak Suffer What They Must? – Europe, Austerity and the Threat to Global Stability* (London: Bodley Head, 2016; (paperback) London: Vintage, 2017).

[73] ibid 11.

in those decisions and the ways in which the judges undermined a European floor of social rights.

Nevertheless, we think there is still – indeed, more than ever – a moral duty to be constructive and creative in pursuit of democratic and pluralistic engagement at European level with the continuing agenda of labour law, very much including the increasingly pressing issues concerning the regulation of labour migration. We believe that EU labour law has to be at the heart of that continuing enterprise and we think that it would be unfortunate in the extreme if the wayward politics of Brexit placed the UK outside that zone of endeavour – as, it must be said, they currently threaten to do. We suggest that a promising methodology for this enterprise could consist of looking for ways of maximising the integration with each other of the different systems of supranational labour law which apply to or within the European region, that is to say the systems of the ILO, the Council of Europe and the European Union – seeking that integration, not just with regard to the formulation and interpretation of parallel norms such as those which articulate human and social rights in the sphere of the workplace, but more deeply and extensively with regard to the mechanisms of collective democratic deliberation such as the European Social Dialogue, which has languished somewhat in recent years.

In this respect, we think that the framing of the EU as 'undemocratic liberalism' is too stark. Certainly, there are ways in which European democracy can be revitalised, for example through the Social Dialogue. But it is inaccurate to suggest that the EU is 'undemocratic' simply because its democratic institutions are improvable. It is also important to avoid complacency about the EU's role in protecting fundamental social rights. In this respect, it has sometimes not been liberal enough, at least in the sense of providing a strong legislative and judicial underpinning to a floor of social rights in Europe, as a counter to the spread of precarity across Europe.

As crises of solidarity multiply and intensify in various European countries, so the prospects for such an enterprise appear more idealised even as the need for it intensifies. Some very valuable preparatory work is we think to be found in the symposium on 'Resocialising Europe'[74] to which we and various other authors of chapters in the present volume contributed, especially in the set of seven chapters of Part III of that work which concern themselves with 'Reinventing the collective dimensions of Social Europe'. Written in or around 2012, these chapters sought to address what seemed to be an already very real crisis in the European labour market and social sphere more generally. Now writing in 2018, we experience an even more keen sense of crisis in that domain, and we feel the need somewhat to re-examine the state of play accordingly.

[74] Nicola Countouris and Mark Freedland (eds), *Resocialising Europe in a Time of Crisis* (Cambridge: Cambridge University Press, 2013).

V. RECLAIMING THE PLURALISTIC CONSTITUTION: A MANIFESTO FOR SUSTAINABLE DEMOCRATIC ENGAGEMENT

What should labour law in the pluralistic constitution look like in the early decades of the twenty-first century? If we have learned anything from these recent reflections on populism, it is that this question must be approached with some humility. Constitution making should be a democratic and participatory process in which citizens and their intermediate associations have an audible voice. Such a constitution must be based upon an inclusive vision of democratic citizenship at work. The abstract values of dignity, autonomy and equal capabilities provide a normative structure to guide democratic deliberation about the parameters of the constitution. These values would also shape the more precise formulation of social rights in the constitutional order. A pluralistic democracy must take reasonable civic disagreement seriously and it must provide democratic opportunities for the adjustment of such disagreements in personal work relations. It must guard against antipluralist techniques of populist governance identified in Müller's work, such as the capture of independent state institutions; clientelism and 'discriminatory legalism'; and the repression of a critical civil society. In this respect, we are sympathetic to Müller's call for a reconstituted social contract as a basis for a pluralistic constitutional order.[75] This social contract would encompass the following:

Constitutional protection of the fundamental rights of migrants at work, and the imposition of a firewall between migration statuses and fundamental rights protections.

A universal floor of fundamental social rights must be guaranteed to all persons engaged in personal work, regardless of the technical character of their contractual arrangements. This would include the fundamental right to equality and non-discrimination. All citizens should enjoy the fundamental right of access to a public court to seek an effective remedy for rights violations.

There should be constitutionalisation of fundamental social rights such as those set out in the EU Charter's 'Solidarity Chapter', in both transnational and national constitutional orders. These rights should be implemented with due respect for national traditions, guided by the principle of subsidiarity. This should be developed as a European floor of social rights. These rights should be specified and implemented, wherever possible, through social dialogue between representative social partners. Beyond the floor, 'constructive human rights pluralism' should prevail,[76] allowing for dialogue and creative normative disagreement between different legal orders. This provides political space for

[75] Müller (n 3) 99.

[76] See C Costello, *The Human Rights of Migrants and Refugees in European Law* (Oxford: Oxford University Press, 2015).

contestation and democratic dialogue about the meaning and content of fundamental rights.

The pluralistic constitution would place particular emphasis on sectoral collective bargaining as a democratically encompassing mode of governance. Autonomous trade unions would themselves be democratic and pluralistic organisations, subject to duties of fair representation in sectoral bargaining. Sectoral collective bargaining would cover traditional issues such as pay and hours. Collective bargaining must also be directed at the implementation of new technologies in working practices at the sectoral level. This will be complemented by democratic institutions at the enterprise level, including representation in corporate structures.

The pluralistic constitution must be based upon a 'collaborative' conception of the separation of powers.[77] Political and legal institutions should be jointly responsible for the specification, implementation and enforcement of fundamental social rights. The balance between political and legal institutions should be subject to ongoing democratic dialogue.

The autonomy of trade unions, other civil society actors and political parties should be enshrined as a constitutional right. Such a right would be a collective rather than an individual right. Autonomy should be understood as the basis of an agonistic civil society which is a necessary counterpart of a pluralistic democracy. Autonomy is not absolute but must be balanced against other fundamental rights, especially the right to non-discrimination. This will promote more encompassing visions of democratic citizenship in the networks of civil society.

[77] A Kavanagh, 'The Role of Courts in the Joint Enterprise of Governing' in NW Barber, R Ekins and P Yowell (eds), *Lord Sumption and the Limits of the Law* (Oxford: Hart Publishing, 2016) 121, 132.

2

Modes of Collective Action: Judicialisation as a Form of Protest

JULIA LÓPEZ LÓPEZ

I. UNIONS AND PROTEST: JUDICIALISATION AS A MODE OF COLLECTIVE ACTION

THE INTERPLAY BETWEEN negotiation and activism contributes to regulating labour conditions in a great variety of ways conditioned by labour strategies, representation systems and other factors. Collective bargaining – the classic approach to the institutionalisation of conflict – involves a complex process of interaction among actors, encompassing deliberations and the search for effectiveness in the resolution of social conflicts.

The political theory approach to this terrain understands the legal guarantee of freedom of association to imply collective bargaining as well as multiple forms of activism – including strikes – intended to impact society through a diversity of strategies. In this theoretical logic, collective bargaining as a process includes elements not only of agreement, but also of discontent and discord. Alan Bogg, a prominent defender of the political theory approach, has constructed a definition of freedom of association as primary among the fundamental rights, writing that 'freedom of association matters more than other fundamental rights'[1] in the guarantees that underpin collective bargaining and a deliberative conception of the right to strike.[2]

Working within this same framework for the study of labour regulation and conflict, I argue that judicialisation is another form of protest that in effect 'externalises' the solution of conflict, placing it outside the labour relations

[1] A Bogg, 'Labour Law and the Trade Unions: Autonomy and Betrayal' in A Bogg, C Costello, ACL Davies and J Prassel (eds), *The Autonomy of Labour Law* (Hart Publishing, 2015) 105.

[2] A Bogg, 'The Political Theory of Collective Bargaining: Pluralism, Deliberation and the Duty of Bargain' in A Bogg (ed), *The Democratic Aspects of Trade Union Recognition* (Hart Publishing, 2009) 285. See also A Bogg, and C Estlund, 'Freedom of Association and the Right to Contest' in A Bogg and T Novitz (eds), *Voices at Work. Continuity and Change in the Common Law World* (Oxford University Press, 2014).

arena in its most narrow sense. The externalisation of labour conflict to the judiciary becomes increasingly common under certain circumstances. The goal of this chapter is first of all to underscore how various institutional processes and other forms of collective action should be seen as jointly reflective of underlying conflict in the labour sphere, and secondly to analyse the judicialisation of labour law – and its impact – as a form of protest, conflict and ultimately regulation. In this sense, this chapter analyses the judicialisation of labour law through the lens provided by debates over unions' agency, forms of activism and protest.[3]

The increasing role of courts in the resolution of labour disputes is one of the most important current trends in the ongoing transformation of sources of regulation in a multilevel context. Judicial decisions, adjudicating cases often brought by labour activists or organisations, have come to play an increasing role in setting the legal guidelines shaping work relations. Legal activism and law making have had an important impact on the interpretation of labour law not only at the national, but also on the supranational level. Given the multilevel and interactive nature of the judicial system, judicialisation should be understood as a dynamic process that is shaped by both initial trigger mechanisms and feedback effects.[4]

Modes of labour conflict should be interpreted as reflective of the encounter between the contending interests that inform the process of collective bargaining and alternatives to it. When the expression of conflict is 'externalised' so that it takes place *outside* the most narrowly construed terrain of labour relations, it may develop in several institutionally distinctive ways. One of those modes is through the judicialisation of conflict. Unions have participated as key actors in this process, making a multilevel use of courts to reinforce labour rights. Unions and organs of workers' representation have promoted judicial activism as a mode of conflict that permits them to channel their protest in often effective ways that ultimately generate new types of regulation.

Union strategies promoting judicialisation as a mode of protest have made creative use of the multilevel institutional context. Unions have taken their demands and aspirations not only to national courts, but also to supranational courts of human rights and the European Court of Justice (ECJ). This has promoted a series of legal interactions between these courts, thus generating new readings of labour rights that rest on the dynamic interconnections between judicial decisions reached at different levels of the system.

An important element of the trend towards increasing judicialisation, the *preliminary rulings* of the ECJ, have been conceptualised above all as an

[3] See J Lopez, 'Anti-austerity Activism Strategies: Combining Protest and Litigation in Spain' in A Blackett and A Trebilcock (eds), *Research Handbook on Transnational Labour Law* (Edward Elgar, 2015).

[4] A Stone Sweet, 'The European Court of Justice and the Judicialization of EU Governance' (2010) Faculty Scholarship Series, Paper 70, 4.

indicator of European political integration;[5] this important manifestation of increased judicialisation is often understood through the lens of a broad theoretical perspective focused on the process of Europeanisation. However, the preliminary rulings also carry an important set of specific implications in the field of labour regulation. In a multilevel context, the preliminary rulings of the ECJ represent an interesting example of the 'spillover' dynamic that places actors and institutions in interactive relations that often bring into play second-order effects that can be seen to constitute a 'spillover' extending beyond the initial institutional intent of the actors involved. This dynamic is quite visible in the case of ECJ preliminary rulings. In the current scenario, the evolution of labour law is driven to a significant degree by the decisions and actions of workers searching for different ways to counteract cutbacks in social rights and the increasingly unfavourable directions taken by social regulation. The increase in the judicialisation of labour conflict is a result of worker strategies developed in response to regressive labour market reforms not only at the national level, but also at other levels. I argue that if we examine this phenomenon from the standpoint of its causal origins, the preliminary rulings on labour matters are in large measure a manifestation of unions' agency.

Thus the concerns and strategies of workers and unions have been the crucial background condition for the growing turn to the courts. As argued above, this turn toward the courts in turn leads to an increase in multilevel dynamics in which the spillover effects of ECJ decisions are often quite considerable. An understanding of both the causes and consequences of increasing judicialisation inevitably leads one to focus on both actors and institutions. Court rulings play a crucial role in this dynamic.

There are important studies of labour regulation that connect unions, the broader collective power of workers (or other collective actors) and strikes, understanding their interconnections through a socio-political framework. Snyder, in his rigorous analysis of factors that explain variation in the strike rate, assigns more importance to organisational and political than to economic determinants of strike activity.[6] Fishman argues that even under Spain's repressive Franco regime (1939–75), the role played by politics was crucial, explaining the contradictory record of the regime on labour relations, jailing many labour activists and also institutionalising a representative labour structure. Among the consequences of this was that the strike rate in that period was relatively high despite the high level of repression.[7] Again showing the importance of political

[5] J Beckfield, 'European Integration and Income Inequality' (2006) 71 *American Sociological Review*.

[6] See D Snyder, 'Institutional Setting and Industrial Conflict: Comparative Analysis of France, Italy and United States' (1970) 3 *American Sociological Review*.

[7] See RM Fishman, *Working Class Organization and the Return to Democracy in Spain* (Cornell University Press, 1990) 120.

and institutional factors, Hugh Clegg emphasises the connection between efficient disputes procedures in democratic systems and lower rates of unconstitutional strikes.[8] All of these studies reach conclusions that emphasise the interconnections between institutional processes, forms of conflict and background conditions that influence such broader dynamics. I argue that similarly the judicialisation of labour matters needs to be understood as a phenomenon that is shaped by these overlapping processes.

The underlying conditions shaping collective action have been strongly transformed during the most recent decade by the global economic crisis and the continuing increase of technology as a factor of production. Employment relations have been deeply reconfigured, creating challenges for labour regulation and employees' rights. The multiplicity of sources of regulation, the increase of inequality and the growing segmentation of the working class are the parameters that one needs to understand in analysing the evolution of contemporary labour law. The complexity of the system has grown over time: channels of representation for employees are now multilevel in nature and unions share representation with non-union actors. Global unions, international trade agreements, elective structures of representation such as works committees, and national collective bargaining offer examples of this growth in complexity. Both collective action and its regulation are increasingly multilevel phenomena that link national and local dynamics to transnational ones.

A common theme in the comparative approach to the study of labour regulation is the existence of considerable differences among actors in their goals and strategies. The underlying conflict of interests is a fundamental reality that must be understood – as much of the classic literature emphasises. Labour law remains a set of institutions designed to channel and regulate social conflict through negotiation, the role of arbitrators or judicialisation. Conflict and its regulation imply both activism *and* negotiation. The connection between negotiation on the one hand and activism on the other hand is in this sense fundamental to labour law.

One component of the overall configuration of forms of conflict and of regulation that is often not recognised as such is the increasing role of the judiciary in defining labour regulation. This element of labour conflict and regulation has grown in prevalence during recent years. This development is driven in part by the reaction of labour against cutbacks in employees' rights, for in many crucial instances disputes reach the courts as a result of the decision of unions to pursue their objectives in this manner. Indeed, I argue that the growing judicialisation of labour conflict – and as a clear result, the increase in the number of court

[8] H Clegg, *Trade Unions Under Collective Bargaining. A Theory Based on Comparisons of Six Countries* (Basil Blackwell, 1975) 81–82.

cases on labour matters – is an indicator of the externalisation of social conflicts that have their origins in the same terrain as other types of labour conflict.

Given my concern to link judicialisation to other forms of conflict it is useful to turn now to data on strikes. The data offered by the European Trade Union Institute (ETUI),[9] as shown in Figure 2.1, shows there is a decrease in strikes in the EU but this decline has to be understood in combination with the identification and study of other ways to externalise conflicts, such as judicialisation. In other words, the decrease in strikes is reflective of substitution mechanisms through which conflict is expressed in other ways, including both judicial litigation and, crucially, public protests.

Figure 2.1 Days not worked per 1,000 employees

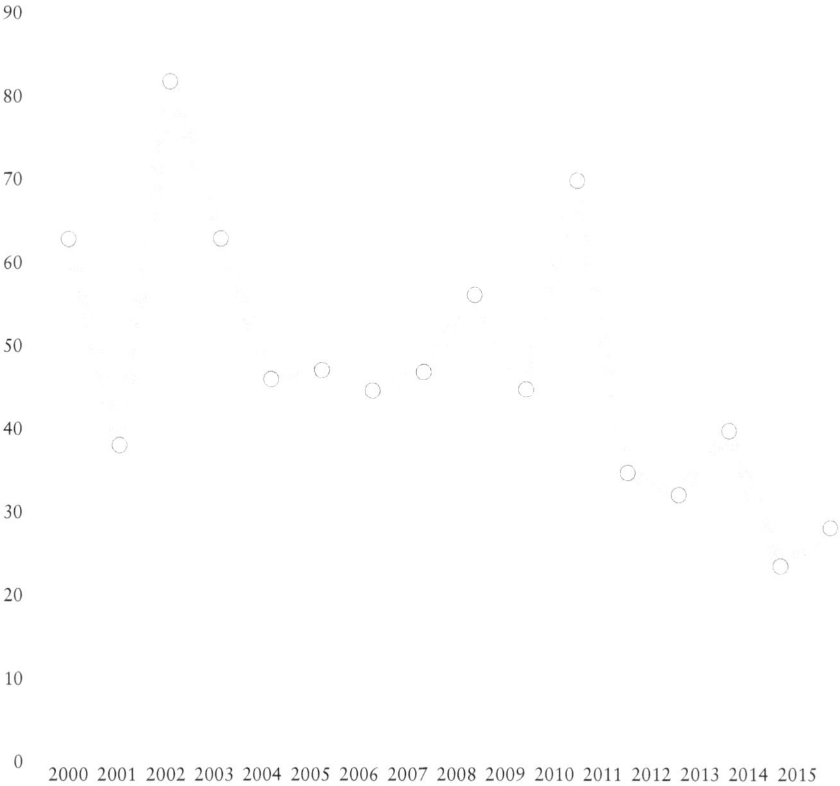

Source: Author's elaboration from ETUI Data.

[9] ETUI, 'Days not worked due to industrial action in Europe, 2000–2015'. Data on general strikes is kindly provided by Kerstin Hamann, Alison Johnston and John Kelly. See their publications: 'The Electoral Effects of General Strikes in Western Europe' (2016) 49(1) Comparative Politics 63–82; 'Striking Concessions from Governments: The Outcomes of General Strikes in Western Europe 1980–2009' (2013) 46(1) *Comparative Politics* 23–41; 'Unions Against Governments: General Strikes in Western Europe 1980–2006' (2013) 46(9) *Comparative Political Studies* 1030–57.

An interesting point to underline about public protest is that demonstrations – many of which concern labour and social matters – have incorporated a broader spectrum of themes than traditional Left-oriented demands and in the current scenario conservative groups also use strikes and demonstrations as a form of protest to express their discomfort with some policies.[10] Strikes, protest and the judicialisation of labour opposition to austerity policies have together composed the overall set of union actions to defend labour rights.

II. MULTILEVEL ACTIVISM AS UNIONS' AGENCY

The vital role of courts in labour law makes it important to specify the complex configuration of judicial actors not only at the multinational level, but also at the national one. The human rights courts, the ECJ, the constitutional courts and the other national courts within Member States in effect interact with one another in the substance of their rulings and thereby create spillover effects, extending the impact of their decisions on labour rights beyond the initial direct consequences. Despite the jurisprudence of the ECJ on collective rights, reducing social rights in favour of economic freedoms, the overall impact of the judicial process often tends to increase unions' agency; relevant components of the overall judicial process include the promotion of de facto deliberation among actors, new law making, and crucially the possibility for unions to bring cases to court, often in ways that construct new legal arguments for the defence of labour rights. Union strategies have made effective use of the judicial system's multilevel dynamics.

A. The Courts of Human Rights: Labour Rights as Human Rights

The courts of human rights are the core institutional location of efforts to defend labour rights as human rights. The globalisation of rights through reference to labour standards is the main challenge to be taken up in efforts to achieve a fair globalisation in the terms set by the United Nations. The freedoms of association and of participation have been declared as fundamental rights and as part of the Decent Work Agenda by the United Nations.

In this context, the Inter-American Court has provided an institutional framework for unions' agency. Recently, the Court[11] recognised the capacity of unions to defend and represent workers' interests, interpreting Article 8.1a of the Inter-American Convention. The Court recognised unions but not corporations

[10] M Torcal, T Rondond and MJ Hierro, 'Word of the Street: The Persistence of Leftist Dominated Protest in Europe' (2016) 2 *West European Politics* 326.

[11] Opinion consulting OC-22/16, February 26 of 2016.

as entitled to defend their interest in front of the inter-American system.[12] The Court ruled that unions are entitled to this right due to Article 44 of the San Salvador Protocol, which provides for the presentation of individual petitions in front of the Court in cases of rights violation by member states of the American Convention. In this institutional context unions act as the representatives defending workers interests; together the courts and unions have constructed the basis for the pursuit of solidarity through an approach that simultaneously defends individual and collective worker rights.

A second important judicial level is that of the European Court of Human Rights. This court has played an important role defending collective action in the global labour market. In the cases of *Demir and Baykara v Turkey*[13] and *Enerji v Turkey*,[14] the Court defined a concept of collective action, applying Article 11 of the Convention, recognising a broad spectrum of human rights incorporating the freedom of association, the right to collective bargaining and the right to strike. The Court considered international standards set by international instruments to be the core of these judicial rulings.

It is important to acknowledge that another important case, *RMT v UK*, has reduced the enthusiasm[15] created by the previously cited cases but the construction of the collective action rule by the European Court of Human Rights continues to provide a broad space of agency for unions to defend labour rights. The influence of this jurisprudence should be understood as having effects that are not only horizontal, creating a counterweight to the very regressive jurisprudence of the ECJ, but also vertical, with implications for the national courts in cases related to limits on the right to strike due to the proportionality principle.

A final reference at the global level is the Committee of Freedom of Association, an informal court that has applied international standards of labour law with important consequences for collective action. In 2017 the most frequent decisions of the Committee involved protections against anti-union discrimination, and matters of collective bargaining, trade union rights, civil liberties and the right to strike. Latin America is the region which has presented most complaints in the period 2000–17 with 762 cases. Europe presented 146 cases and North America 42 cases.[16] This Committee plays an important role, contributing to the legal foundations – and avenues – for unions' initiatives in defence of both individual and collective worker interests.

[12] See AB Cornell, 'Inter-American Court Recognizes Elevated Status of Trade Unions, Rejects Standing of Corporations' (2017) 3 *International Labor Rights Case Law*.

[13] *Demir and Bakara v Turkey* App no 34503/97 (ECtHR, 12 November 2018).

[14] *Enerji Yapi-Yol Sen v Turkey* App no 68959/01 (ECtHR, 21 April 2009).

[15] C Stylogianis, 'The Protection of the Right to Strike under the European Convention on Human Rights' (2017) 6 *UCL Journal of Law and Jurisprudence* 142.

[16] International Labour Office, Governing Body, 333rd Session, Geneva, Report Committee of Freedom of Association, 2017.

B. The Activism of Unions in the Judiciary: The European Court of Justice

A basic point of departure for much of the remaining analysis is the fact that EU law presents us with important cases of failures – with varying intensity – to fulfil obligations in the transposition and implementation of the EU's own norms. The ECJ has taken actions to obligate the Member States to achieve the goal of implementation. Figure 2.2 lays out the overall map of non-implementation. These data help to contextualise unions' judicial activism in the EU.

The ECJ offers data[17] on failures of Member States (from 1952 to 2016) to implement EU Regulations and Directives. The total count of such failures is quite high (3,859 cases), revealing substantial disaffection with EU rules. Furthermore, there are countries – such as Italy (642 cases), France (416 cases) and Greece (407 cases) – that manifest a higher level of 'failures' than other Member States such as Germany (289 cases) or Luxembourg (269 cases). Interestingly, the UK (140) is not among the countries with the highest counts of non-application, as captured by this indicator. There is a group of countries that stands out for its failures in applying EU obligations, a group essentially made up of south European countries with the exception of Portugal. Despite the referendum outcome in favour of Brexit, the UK presents better results than these countries in achieving EU goals.

Figure 2.2 provides data on one crucial aspect of ECJ preliminary rulings. The figure reports the identity of the institutions that initiate the preliminary ruling process in cases emerging from all of the affected Member States. This indicator offers valuable insights into the profile of mutual trust among multi-level institutions[18] and also serves to measure judicial activism. In 2017[19] the Member States which initiated the most requests for ECJ preliminary rulings were Germany with 149, Italy 57, the Netherlands 38, Austria 31 and France 25. In total there were 533 requests for preliminary rulings in 2017. I take these data not as an isolated matter but instead as a reflection of broader historical and contextual tendencies.

The last two decades have been marked not only by political events that have challenged the future of the EU, but also by crises that have had important implications for the EU. The economic crisis and measures responding to it have induced complex spillover effects not only at the supranational level, but also at the national level, increasing social conflict. I argue that this conflict, in turn, has created new relations among the courts engaged in ruling on labour law institutions. The call for preliminary rulings by the ECJ has been part of the

[17] See Court of Justice of the European Union, Annual Report 2016, Judicial Activity, 112.

[18] See E Brouwer, and D Gerard (eds), 'Mapping Mutual Trust: Understanding and Framing the Role of Mutual Trust in EU Law', 2016/13 EUI Working Papers, MWP.

[19] European Union Court of Justice, Annual Report 2017, Judicial Activity.

Figure 2.2 New references for a preliminary ruling (by Member State and by court or tribunal)

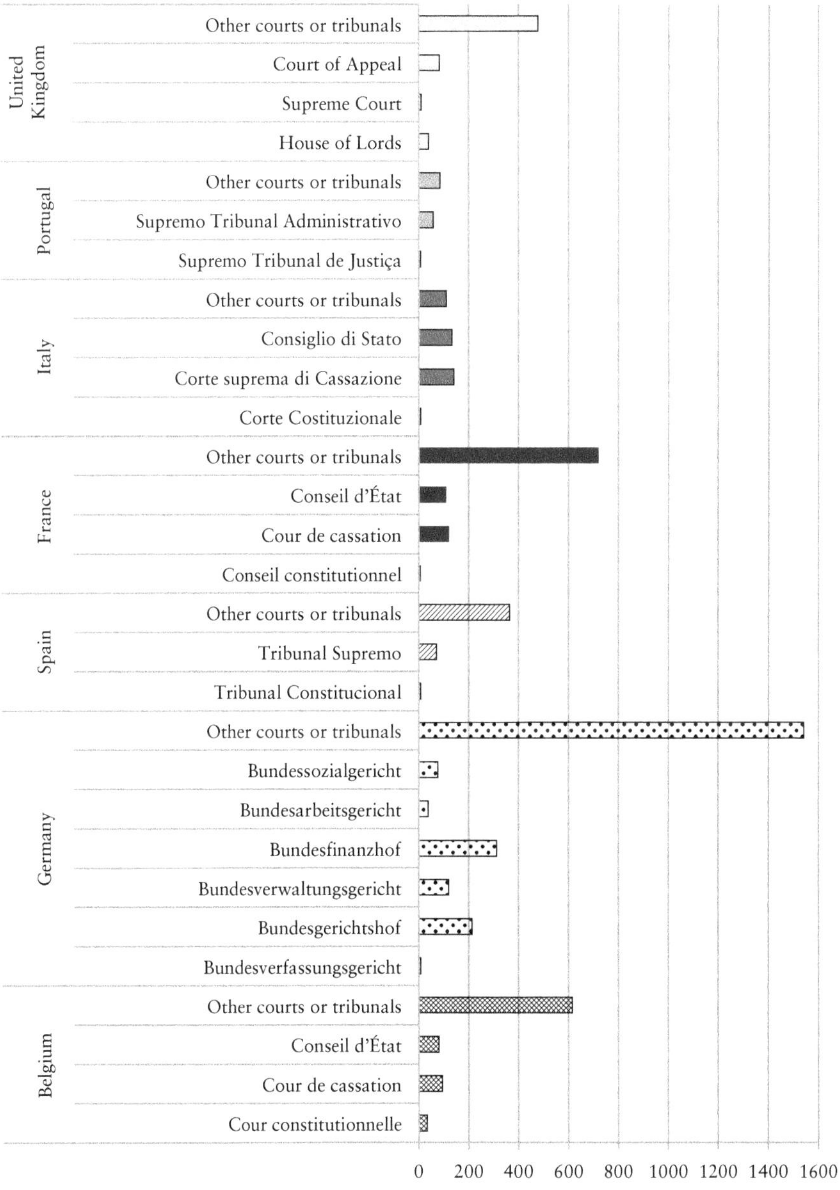

Source: Author's elaboration from Court of Justice of the European Union, Annual Report 2016, Judicial Activity.

unions' strategies in seeking to intervene in political processes during a period of austerity characterised by cutbacks in rights. Thus, despite the limits[20] that the rulings have as instruments for the resolution of grievances, they currently play an important role in conflict over austerity policies and related matters. Unions have been able to exercise their agency in a difficult period of time, partly by participating in the negotiation of EU Directives and partly through efforts to shape the implementation of EU regulation as in the case of preliminary rulings. Preliminary rulings by the ECJ are of great interest for our analysis because from a multilevel perspective they generate spillover dynamics of interactions among courts and unions in the configuration of regulation. In the preliminary rulings the ECJ decides on the validity of national-level outcomes from the standpoint of EU regulation. The immediate trigger for a preliminary ruling is the request of a national court for a ruling from the European Court on the interpretation of EU Directives and their implications for national regulation. However, the national courts issue these requests as a result of earlier initiatives – often from unions – in which the case was brought to their jurisdiction. The result can overturn national law if it is found to be at odds with EU regulation.

In initiating the preliminary ruling process, domestic legal institutions refer a case already under way to the ECJ in order to question it on the interpretation or validity of European law. The ECJ decision has the force of *res judicata*. It is binding not only on the national court on whose initiative the reference for a preliminary ruling was made, but also on all of the national courts of the Member States. Formally, the national court is the point of legal origin of the preliminary ruling process but union representatives have the chance to convince the judge holding domestic jurisdiction to request a ruling from the ECJ on the validity of the Member State's interpretation of EU law. A conflict that begins with a union taking its grievances to court can, in this manner, bring on various legal actions that activate the multilevel dynamics emphasised here. This multilevel process of spillover forges a network of actors that enables unions. This rather complex process makes it possible for unions to participate in validating, interpreting and sometimes transforming national labour law by making use of EU labour law, as well as deliberation and law-making processes.

[20] For example in Case C-117/14, the request for a preliminary ruling was lodged by the Juzgado de lo Social No 23 de Madrid (Spain) on 11 March 2014 with regard to the period of probation. The ECJ held that 'it does not have jurisdiction to answer the questions referred for a preliminary ruling. Firstly, the Charter of Fundamental Rights of the European Union is not applicable, because Law 3/2012 is not implementing EU law. Secondly, the employment contract at issue here, is characterized specifically as "the contract … to be concluded for an indefinite duration" (Article 4(2) of Law 3/2012), and therefore it cannot be categorized as a fixed-term contract under Article 3 of the Clause 3 of the Framework Agreement on Fixed-Term Work'. In Case C-413/13, December, 18, 2014, (FNV KunstenInformatieen Media) the ECJ held first that 'Article 101 TFEU was not applicable in this case, since this case concerns a purely internal situation without impact on intra-Community trade'.

Some case-law decisions have been relevant for generating such spillover consequences, as in the following instance.[21] CCOO, a major Spanish union confederation, took a crucial case to a Spanish labour court asking that travelling time should be treated as working time. The matter went to the Spanish National High Court (Audiencia Nacional) which subsequently referred it to the ECJ for a preliminary ruling. The ECJ ruled that, where workers do not have a fixed or habitual place of work, time spent travelling each day between their homes and the premises of the first and last customers does constitute working time according to the European Working Time Directive. In this instance, unions, national courts, and the ECJ all engaged in a dynamic interaction involving the interpretation of national legislation in the light of the relevant EU Directive. Ultimately, national judges had to apply the new interpretation that emerged from this process, essentially reframing the validity of domestic law in a direction that is more favourable to workers than domestic law had been prior to the preliminary ruling.

In other cases preliminary rulings also provide evidence of how unions can join together in supporting claims initially advanced by one labour organisation at the national level. For example, the request for a preliminary ruling from the Audiencia Nacional (Spain) lodged on 29 January 2018 by the Federación de Servicios de Comisiones Obreras (CCOO)[22] received support from other unions as *interested parties*. A rather disparate coalition of unions, including the Federación Estatal de Servicios de la Unión General de Trabajadores (FES-UGT), the Confederación General del Trabajo (CGT), the Confederación Solidaridad de Trabajadores Vascos (ELA), and the Confederación Intersindical Galega (CIG), joined in supporting CCOO in this case. The confluence of several unions that enjoy official recognition of their 'representativeness' despite their rather significant differences was broad enough to incorporate some pro-independence forces in the Basque Country. The question that brought all these unions together concerns the Working Time Directive[23] and Council Directive 89/391 on the safety and health of workers at work.[24] The case is based also on Article 31 of the Charter of Fundamental Rights.

In numerous ECJ preliminary rulings, unions have been the main actor initiating the case in national courts. Their activism is centred not only on the defence of collective rights, but also on labour conditions. In Case C-396/13 of 17 February 2015,[25] which arose from a dispute between a Finnish trade union

[21] Case 266-14 Unions Workers Commissions (CCOO) v Tyco Integrated Security SL, Tyco Integrated Fire security Corporations Servicios SA (2015), 2015/C, 363/18.

[22] Case C-55/18 *Federación de Servicios de Comisiones Obreras (CCOO) v Deutsche Bank SA* (2018/C 152/10).

[23] Directive 2003/88/EC of the European Parliament and of the Council of 4 November 2003 concerning certain aspects of the organization of working time (OJ 2003 L299).

[24] Council Directive 89/391/EEC of 12 June 1989 on the introduction of measures to encourage improvements in the safety and health of workers at work (OJ 1989 L183).

[25] Case C-396/13 *Sähköalojen ammattiliitto ry v Elektrobudowa Spolka Akcyjna* ECLI:EU:C:2015:86.

and a Polish undertaking, Polish workers agreed to employment contracts with ESA in Poland and were subsequently posted to an ESA branch in Finland. The Polish company ESA did not pay minimum wage rates of remuneration to the employees in accordance with the applicable collective agreements which had been declared universally applicable and thus falling within the scope of Directive 96/71/E.[26]

Another relevant case, Case C-328/13, of 11 September 2014,[27] was based on legal action taken by an Austrian trade union against the Austrian employers' association for bus, aviation and marine companies. In this case, the Austrian Supreme Court decided to refer questions to the ECJ for a preliminary ruling. The ECJ ruled that the terms and conditions laid down in a collective agreement, which, pursuant to the law of a Member State, despite the rescission of that agreement, continue to produce their effects as regards the employment relationship which was governed by them before the agreement was terminated, constitute 'terms and conditions agreed in any collective agreement' so long as that employment relationship is not subject to a new collective agreement or a new individual agreement is not concluded with the employees concerned. Clearly this finding was favourable for unions. In relation to part-time workers, in Case C-476/12, of 5 November 2014,[28] an Austrian trade union in the banking sector started court proceedings against the employers' representatives of the sector. The subject at issue was that part-time workers falling within the scope of the applicable collective agreement in that sector were entitled only to an amount of 'dependent child allowance' that was calculated pro rata on the basis of the number of hours worked.[29] Here it is important to note that unions

[26] In this case the Court ruled that in circumstances such as those of the case before the referring court, Directive 96/71/EC of the European Parliament and of the Council of 16 December 1996 concerning the posting of workers in the framework of the provision of services, read in the light of Article 47 of the Charter of Fundamental Rights of the European Union, prevents a rule of the Member State of the seat of the undertaking that has posted workers to the territory of another Member State – under which the assignment of claims arising from employment relationships is prohibited – from barring a trade union, such as the Sähköalojenammattiliitto, from bringing an action before a court of the second Member State, in which the work is performed, in order to recover for the posted workers, pay claims which relate to the minimum wage, within the meaning of Directive 96/71, and which have been assigned to it, that assignment being in conformity with the law in force in the second Member State.

[27] C-328/13 *Österreichischer Gewerkschaftsbund* ECLI:EU:C:2014:2197.

[28] C-476/12 *Österreichischer Gewerkschaftsbund* ECLI:EU:C:2014:2332.

[29] The ECJ observed that 'the dependent child allowance concerned is not a benefit provided for by law and paid by the State, but is paid by the employer pursuant to a collective agreement, and as such it could not be seen as a "social security benefit", within the meaning of EC Regulation 883/2004; however, it does constitute "pay" to the worker, which is determined by the terms of the employment relationship agreed between the worker and the employer. For part-time workers, the ECJ thus eliminated the pro rata temporis calculation of the dependent child allowance. The ECJ thus concluded that the principle pro rata temporis as laid down in Clause 4.2 of Directive 97/81/EC applies to the calculation of the amount of a dependent child allowance paid by an employer to a part-time worker pursuant to a collective agreement such as that applicable to the employees of Austrian banks and bankers'.

assume an important role defending part-timers and promoting progressive arrangements to accomodate work and family. Unions in this case are solidaristic actors that make effective use of the judicial system – just as this chapter's argument suggests.

To summarise my argument on unions and the courts, although it is important to recognise how the ECJ has tried to limit the collective rights of workers, on balance and if we take into account the overall set of judicial levels and institutions, the primary effect of the judicial system has been to provide unions with an often quite useful instrument for the defence of worker interests. Indeed, I argue that the increasing use of the judicial system to resolve labour demands and conflicts should be seen as reflective of labour's agency and as a form of protest and participation. Variation over time in the use of the judicial system is driven by factors quite similar to those that shape other manifestations of collective action. In the judicial arena the multilevel dynamics that can be found to one degree or another in most types of collective action are especially important.

III. TENTATIVE CONCLUSIONS FOR DEBATE

The last decade has quite clearly been a very hard period for unions. The Green Paper 'Modernising Labour Law'[30] set out the idea that the call for modernisation means focusing labour rights on individual and not collective rights. Unions, in the exercise of workers' collective rights, have designed various collective strategies to defend labour: collective bargaining, strikes, other types of protest and new forms of activism, including boycotts and – as emphasised here – judicialisation. The effort to deny unions a continuing role as relevant political actors has been promoted by an especially neoliberal reading of labour law; this ideological approach tries to essentially expel unions from the political process. In this context, judicialisation as a union strategy has to be analysed not only from the point of view of the judgments of the courts, but also from the perspective of broader political processes. Those processes include those that involve interactions between the national and European levels. In the judicial arena that dynamic is quite evident: unions' legal actions against firms in national-level courts may lead to the request from the national court to the ECJ for a preliminary ruling with spillover consequences in terms of new interpretations of multilevel labour law. From a political theory perspective, judicialisation can be seen to reinforce the institutionalised presence of social conflict in society and the role of unions as representatives of the general interest. Judicial processes incorporate deliberation and interpretation by all the actors who intervene. A clear result is the emergence of new types of law making.

[30] Green Paper, 'Modernising Labour Law to Meet the Challenges of the 21st Century' COM (2006) 708.

Unions' agency is especially important at a time when the ECJ, with the *Viking* and *Laval* cases, has dramatically reduced the possibilities for collective action by unions, favouring instead corporate rights for business. The abusive use of the principle of proportionality by the ECJ imposed restrictions on union rights by placing legal priority on freedoms linked to Europe's internal market instead of prioritising fundamental rights.[31] The Court created a perverse law-making dynamic with the principle of proportionality and the prohibition of secondary boycotts, which is not sustainable under the parameters created by the Charter of Fundamental Rights. Many arguments can be advanced to support a broad spectrum of collective action rights and strategies in the current European context, but the principal one is the solidarity principle in the Charter, constructed by collective and individual rights. Collective action motivated by this perspective should be understood as constituted by union strategies designed to develop and protect individual and collective rights. Much of what unions do fits this perspective as in the case of judicialisation in the defence of labour rights.

The Charter of Fundamental Rights in the Solidarity chapter creates a solid base supportive of types of collective action by unions that serve to promote solidarity and their own agency. The jurisprudence of the ECJ ought to address the proportionality issue and secondary boycotts from the perspective of the Solidarity chapter.

The 2018 EU Justice Score Board[32] includes an indicator of quality of justice systems which addresses the accessibility of legal aid by the level of the court. Unions permit poor people to go further in the defence of rights in a multilevel judicial scenario than would be possible absent this important collective instrument to defend their interests. The full significance of unions' agency in the defence of labour interests and of the rise of judicialisation in labour disputes can only be appreciated when we place these two phenomena alongside one another and examine them from a multilevel perspective that delineates interactions between the global and the national levels.

Understanding the changing reality of labour relations requires the use of conceptual and methodological approaches that are designed to fit the realities of the early twenty-first century and that take cognisance of the significance of unions' agency and of the solidarity principle. Indeed, the actions of lawyers and claimants may be able to contribute to the goal of 'shifting legal visions'.[33]

[31] ACL Davis, A Bogg and C Costello, 'The Role of the Court of Justice in Labour Law' in A Blackett and A Trebilock,.*Research Handbook in European Law* (Edward Elgar, 2016) 128. See also T Novitz, 'The EU and the Right to Strike: Regulation Through the Back Door and Its Impact in Social Dialogue' (2016) 27(1) *King's College Law Journal* 46–66.

[32] Publications Office of the European Union (2018), Luxembourg, 23.

[33] See EA Gonzalez-Ocantos, *Shifting Legal Visions. Judicial Change and Human Rights Trials in Latin-America* (Cambridge University Press, 2016).

In the end, the parameters of labour regulation are broad ones that are very much linked to the state of democracy and governance; the challenge is to avoid neoliberal tendencies that displace 'solidarities of unions and workers consciousness and the politics of struggle with hierarchically organised "teams", multiparty cooperation, individual responsibility and antipolitics'.[34]

[34] W Brown, *Undoing the Demos, Neoliberalism's Stealth Revolution* (Zone Books, 2015) 131.

3

Collective Bargaining and Right to Strike: New Challenges

MARGARITA I RAMOS QUINTANA AND
DULCE MARÍA CAIRÓS BARRETO

I. INTRODUCTION

THIS CHAPTER WILL examine the different models of collective bargaining and the evolution of the right to strike with a view to highlighting the transformations of both institutions today. The first section begins by considering the social conflict that is at the heart of the industrial relations system and which is the basis of labour law. Next, the different models of strike are analysed in relation to the different models of collective bargaining in the continental system, especially, far removed from the British system. Likewise, the processes developed by alternative dispute resolution (ADR) are observed in order to show the anaesthetic effect they have on the right to strike. Finally, the transformations of collective bargaining and their effects on the configuration of the scope of the right to strike are addressed.

II. SOCIAL CONFLICT AT THE HEART OF THE INDUSTRIAL RELATIONS SYSTEM

Social conflict is a notion that is the 'raison d'être of labour law'.[1] The analysis of the origins and evolution of social conflict requires a series of basic or core ideas that must be clearly identified from a historical point of view. Such ideas include the following:

Social conflict arose from the Industrial Revolution, when the development of the economy was built on two fundamental elements: capital and labour.[2]

[1] MC Palomeque López, *Derecho del trabajo e ideología. Medio siglo de formación ideológica del Derecho del trabajo en España*, 7th edition (Madrid, Ed. Tecnos, 2011) 32ff.

[2] The conflict between capital and work is consubstantial to industrial society and therefore to labour relations, P Davis and M Freedland, *O Kahn-Freund's Labour and the Law*, 3rd edn (London, Stevens, 1983) 27ff.

In this context, labour law has been and continues to be the main instrument of the legal order of industrial conflicts, which is the social conflict par excellence of the capitalist economic system. The system of providing work started from the process of industrialisation and is characterised by[3] (a) being performed in a 'factory' – the 'workplace'; (b) using a population defined as a labour force and coming from a new social class – 'the proletariat'; (c) a legal relationship based on a 'contract' to provide work, once all links that were previously based on 'status' are overcome; (d) using an organisational process that corresponds to a 'social division of work'.

On the other hand, labour law creates the category of 'employment contract' to legally channel a new way of providing work:[4] (a) the worker gains access to work in a free or voluntary way, responding to a job offer and without being subject to any ownership by the employer (freedom); (b) the law legitimises the appropriation by the employer of the benefits obtained through the work done by the worker (for the benefit of another); (c) the law recognises the employer has a 'power' that gives supremacy in the contractual relation, obliging the worker to submit to the employer's power of organisation and management of the production process of goods and services[5] (dependence); (d) the provision of work thus configured allows the worker to earn income for his/her survival (salary).

The insufficiency of the legal solution chosen to channel social conflict arising from industrial development was soon revealed: the contractual power attributed to the employer was a unilateral power that gave rise to abuses, exploitation and inhumane working conditions.[6]

From the beginning of the industrialisation process there were diverse manifestations of the basic conflict within the economic system and its most visible consequences: segregation and inequality in wealth distribution. Workers' first reactions were two different forms of opposition to the new economic system: (a) *violent* protests: the process of industrialisation was considered to be the cause of the conditions of exploitation and misery suffered by the working population; (b) *external* protests: in particular strikes through which the subject responsible for the terrible working conditions was identified – the employer or business owner.

The strike was the most characteristic expression of opposition of the working class to the new way of providing work and of the economic consequences

[3] A Baylos Grau, *Derecho del trabajo. Modelo para armar* [Labour Law. Model to Assemble] (Madrid, Editorial Trotta, 1991) 19–28.

[4] G Giugni, 'Diritto del lavoro (voce per un'enciclopedia)', GDLRI, no 1 (1979) 15ff; M Alonso Olea, *De la servidumbre al contrato de trabajo* (Madrid, Tecnos, 1979) 105ff.

[5] The main objective of labour law is to regulate, support and restrict the management and organisational power of the employer and the abstractions contained in these expressions and the material meaning they conceal, P Davis and M Freedland (n 2) 15–16.

[6] G Lyon-Caen, 'Défense et illustration du contra du travail' (1968) T XIII *Archives de Philosophie du Droit* 59.

arising from industrial capitalism.[7] From its beginnings, the strike has shown itself to have a double character: it is an external manifestation of a latent and unresolved labour and economic conflict (functional character), but also it is by nature a conflictive expression, as it constitutes a direct measure of protest, paralysing or interrupting production processes (instrumental character).

The strike constitutes an opposition reaction capable of demonstrating three different dimensions:[8] first, it is an expression of the labour conflict itself (*labour conflict dimension*); secondly, it is an expression of social conflict versus the economic and political system (*social conflict dimension*); finally, the strike is at the beginning of a historical process of 'intervention' of the state in labour relations (*political dimension*).

Law in general, and labour law in particular, have historically observed social conflicts and strikes 'with suspicion', so that three distinct stages can be observed clearly in terms of their regulation: prohibition (*illegality*), tolerance (*permissiveness*) and recognition (*right with guarantees*).

The recognition and scope of the right to strike has historically evolved in parallel with two other inherent rights, freedom of association and collective bargaining. The links between the right to strike and freedom of association show that it is not possible to conceive the exercise of freedom of association and trade union action within and outside the company without the accompaniment of collective action measures, including, and substantially, strikes.[9] The right to freedom of assembly and association includes at its core the possibility to negotiate collectively working conditions in representation of the general interests of workers versus the interests of the company.[10] Without the

[7] For all aspects concerning the meaning and origin of the right/freedom to strike, see KD Ewing, *The Right to Strike* (Oxford, Clarendon Press, 1991) especially 4ff.

[8] MI Ramos Quintana, 'La huelga como derecho fundamental' in W Sanguineti Raymond and E Cabero Morán (eds), *Sindicalismo y Democracia* (Granada, Comares, 2017) 153ff.

[9] The right to strike as an inherent element of freedom of association is based on Article 11(1) of the European Convention on Human Rights (ECHR) and has been interpreted by the European Committee on Human Rights as follows: 'Everyone has the right to freedom of peaceful assembly and freedom of association, including the right to form and join trade unions for the protection of their interests.' Likewise, the same substantial relationship is established in Convention No. 98, as well as in Convention No. 151 of the International Labour Organization (ILO). It is also expressly recognized as such in Article 6.4 of the European Social Charter (ESC). With a view to ensuring the effective exercise of the right to bargain collectively, the parties recognise 'the right of workers and employers to collective action in cases of conflicts of interest, including the right to strike, subject to obligations that might arise out of collective agreements previously entered into'. Certainly, Article 6.4 of the ESC is more specific than Article 11 of the ECHR, but the European Committee of Social Rights has clarified in this respect that although the rights at stake may overlap, it is nevertheless true that it obliges states expressly to protect the right to strike.

[10] Article 5 ESC. Also Article 4 of ILO Convention No 98: 'appropriate measures should be taken in accordance with national conditions to encourage and promote among employers and employers' organizations, on the one hand, and workers' organizations, on the other, the full development and use of voluntary negotiation procedures, with the aim of regulating, through collective agreements, employment conditions'.

instrument of strike as the main measure of collective action to demand fair working conditions, collective bargaining would lack a real counterbalancing power on the part of the workers to compensate for the broad power that the company/employer has in labour relations.[11]

Thus, under these parameters, the configuration of industrial democracy is defined,[12] recognising the legitimate instruments for the defence of interests that each party has within labour relations.[13] Democratic systems of labour relations require that these relations be defined with the participation of workers, with the freedom to form associations or trade unions representing their respective interests, and by means of collective action to counteract the legally binding and recognised corporate powers.[14]

The maximum expression of the threefold composition of the power of workers to counteract the respective corporate power is undoubtedly contemplated in Article 29 of the Charter of Fundamental Rights of the European Union, which, under the title 'Right to negotiation and collective action', states as follows:

> Workers and employers, or their respective organisations, in accordance with European Union law and national laws and practices, have the right to negotiate and conclude collective agreements, at the appropriate levels and to undertake, in the event of a conflict of interests, collective actions to defend their interests, including strikes.

III. THE CONSTRUCTION OF THE STRIKE-RIGHT MODELS ACCORDING TO THEIR RELATIONS WITH COLLECTIVE BARGAINING

In continental labour law, the right to strike has been highly conditioned by its relations with the right to collective bargaining over time. It is not necessary to insist on the essentiality of the processes of collective bargaining in democratic models of labour relations.[15] There are several theoretical models under which

[11] Collective agreements without the right to strike are little more than 'collective begging', KD Ewing, J Hendy and C Jones, *A Manifesto for Labour Law: Towards a Comprehensive Revision of Worker's Rights* (Liverpool, The Institute of Employment Rights, 2016) 2.

[12] Traditionally, it has been considered as part of the legacy inherited by English culture in the field of labour relations, despite the very different paths that the country has taken in recent years, 'I shall argue that direct democracy in labour relations is part of the British heritage', see O Kahn-Freund, *Labour Relations, Heritage and Adjustment* (Oxford, Oxford University Press, 1979) 6.

[13] The recognition of the right to collective bargaining as a means of confronting the imbalance of powers between the interests involved in labour relations, and the close link between it and the legitimate exercise of collective action such as strikes by workers, has been established by a judgment of the Supreme Court of Canada of 2015, *Saskatchewan v Attorney-General of Canada*, 2015. A transcript of part of the legal grounds can be found in Ewing et al (n 11) 9 and note 48.

[14] In Spain there is a close relationship between freedom of association, collective bargaining and strikes, among others, see Constitutional Court rulings number 236/2007 and 659/2007.

[15] They point to this, calling for the application in the United Kingdom of the international instruments that establish it and of which the UK forms a part, Ewing et al (n 11) 51.

the evolution of the relationship between strikes and collective bargaining has taken place. It is possible to detect up to three theoretical models.[16]

A. Classic or Contractual Model

In this model, the collective agreement can be considered as a regulatory instrument of strictly labour/professional conditions signed between the employer and workers' representatives. The collective agreement remains 'stable' over time, setting out the working conditions in force during a period decided by the parties. And, even more, the collective agreement is conceived as an 'instrument of peace'. Thus, during its validity, conflicts cannot be provoked to oppose its provisions.[17]

For its part, the strike can only be a measure to use during the negotiation phase of collective agreements.[18] Collective action can only be brought in relation to the matter of negotiation, so that any demand relating to matters outside the agreement is outside the scope of the right to strike.[19] The sole recipient of the strike is the employer, which limits the subjective scope of the legality of a strike.

B. Labour Model

In this specific model, collective agreements only regulate labour conditions. The agreement is stable in time with duration decided by the parties and the idea of the collective agreement as an immanent bearer of labour peace. However, the parties may enter into temporary peace commitments to strengthen its application during the term of the agreement, linking these pacts only to the parties signing the agreement.[20]

[16] Ramos Quintana, 'La huelga como derecho fundamental' (n 8) 157ff.

[17] Regarding the collective agreement's function of peace, see JC Javillier, *Droit du Travail*, 2nd edn (Paris, LGDG, 1981) 573ff. G Barreiro, 'Ensayo crítico sobre la paz laboral en el convenio colectivo con especial referencia a su carácter inmanente' (1989) 4 REDT 463ff.

[18] 'A contractual strike is understood to be that which is triggered or produced at the time of the negotiation of Collective Agreements in order to press for them, so that the strike is an instrument of the agreement', Judgment by Spanish Constitutional Court 11/1981, 8 April, FJ 14.

[19] So it must be doubted that this model has a place within a strike-right system, MC Palomeque López and M Álvarez de la Rosa, *Derecho del trabajo*, 24th edn (Madrid, Editorial Ramón Areces, 2016) 411.

[20] On the adaptation to the Spanish Constitution of the legality of these clauses that contain waivers to the temporary exercise of the fundamental right of strike, STC 11/1981, FJ 14. A rigorous formulation of the obligations of peace in its double configuration, absolute or relative, can be seen in G Ghezzi, 'Autonomia collettiva, diritto di sciopero e clausole di tregua' in AAVV, *Studi in onore di F Santoro-Passarelli*, volume V (Naples, Jovene, 1972. See the so-called 'duty of peace' as a general theoretical study, MI Ramos Quintana, *El deber de paz laboral (entre la ley y la autonomía colectiva)* (Madrid, Civitas, 1993).

At the same time, the strike is an instrument of defence of the interests of the workers that is not only confined to the negotiation of collective bargaining. The strike continues to be directed at the employer, to whom demands are made through the strike.

C. Multipurpose Model

The collective agreement is shown as a regulatory instrument of labour, trade union or social conditions signed between employers and trade union organisations, preferably with a high degree of implementation. For this reason, the collective agreement presents a certain amount of stability over time but it is open to certain vicissitudes: (a) renegotiation of certain conditions, (b) introduction of new aspects during its period of application and interpretation, and (c) possibility of adaptation to the needs of the employer, allowing disconnection from the contents of the agreement through other negotiated processes. The collective agreement does not contemplate or regulate the resolution of labour disputes (permanent conflict). Conflict resolution is channelled through judicial processes or 'other' predetermined and agreed processes between business and union representatives in the framework of ADR procedures. Conflict is 'separated' from the content of the collective agreement.

On the other hand, the strike becomes an instrument for defending (all) the economic and social interests that workers consider as their own when pertinent and it is based on a right – guaranteed – that can be exercised in any area where the interests of workers are at stake. It is a means of response to any instance of power, whether economic (business) or political (public). In consequence, the strike ceases to be an instrument of vindication exclusively against the employer and in relation to strictly labour issues. Likewise, it can be carried out by public officials and its wider scope explains the legality of solidarity strikes, as well as those of a political nature.

The most advanced models of collective bargaining and strikes continue to reflect a close and inescapable relationship between the two although each of them is capable of being delimited autonomously by presenting its own configuration.

IV. COLLECTIVE BARGAINING AND RESOLUTION OF LABOUR DISPUTES

The transformations undergone by collective bargaining constitute an indispensable field of analysis when observing the high degree of influence that they have had on the changes experienced in the dynamics of exercising the right to strike. Collective bargaining systems today undoubtedly represent the best expression of communication and dialogue between employers and trade union organisations, irrespective of the model and structure of collective bargaining in a given area of labour relations.

Over time, it is possible to observe three distinct stages in the development of industrial relations and collective bargaining, as well as their interactions with labour conflicts: an initial stage of *conflict*, followed by another characterised by *cooperative* relations and, finally, a more advanced stage of *collaboration* and negotiating.[21] The mechanisms for resolving labour disputes and their role not only change as the system of industrial relations evolves from one phase to another, but the mechanisms themselves have contributed to this evolutionary process.

In the first stage of the development of the industrial relations system, collective bargaining starts as a process of dialogue between *opposing parties due to the conflict* that underlies labour relations in the context of the industrial economy. The collective agreement emerges as a figure that departs clearly from other legal categories, such as 'contract' or 'law'.[22] And, on the other hand, the institution of collective bargaining from the outset is openly distinct from what any arbitral formula for resolving conflicts might be.[23]

The transformation of a system of collective bargaining into a system of *cooperation* occurs at a time when collective conflicts reflect the consolidation or 'crystallization of intergroup relations'.[24] However, as the legal recognition of collective bargaining starts to be achieved, it can become an unstable system. It could give rise at any moment to open conflicts through spontaneous actions, among them the strike. Meanwhile, collective agreements continue to be the result of commitments created by agreements between individuals but they still lack guarantees of their application or compliance.

Thus, in order to strengthen the stability of collective agreements, this second phase tends to introduce a set of regulations to ensure non-conflictive negotiation and based on cooperation between the parties. These regulations are the fruit of state intervention in many countries of Europe and the United States, with the exception of Great Britain, where state intervention has traditionally not been accepted and it is the collective agreements themselves that have dealt with the historically produced changes.

The effectiveness of workers' rights established through collective bargaining becomes a legal concern in the complex systems of labour law because legal measures to protect employment and working conditions are dependent on general application of the collective agreements themselves.

In a *cooperative model* of industrial relations, the collective agreement itself finally becomes a direct source of overcoming conflicts and confrontation between the parties. Labour disputes are perceived by negotiators as incentives

[21] Evolution exposed in terms proposed by R Rogowski, 'Industrial Relations, Labour Conflict Resolution and Reflexive Labour Law' in R Rogowski and T Wilthagen (eds), *Reflexive Labour Law* (Boston, Kluwer Law and Taxation Publishers, 1994) 63ff.

[22] Kahn-Freund analysed the original differences between collective bargaining agreement and 'contract' or 'code', see P Davis and M Freedland (n 2) 158, 199.

[23] Rogowski (n 21) 65.

[24] O Kahn-Freund, 'Intergroup Conflicts and their Settlement' (1954) 5 *British Journal of Sociology* 193–227.

to carry out reforms and changes: collective agreements can have positive effects and contribute to shaping relations between negotiating parties, as well as the development of good industrial relations. Nonetheless, the characterisation of conflict as an alternative and opposing situation to cooperation is a constant source of instability, so that, in fact, as such, 'cooperation operates in the shadow of conflict'.[25] Conflict and cooperation coexist as completely opposite realities.

In the third phase of the development of collective bargaining and industrial relations integrated into the social system, collective disputes are dealt with through institutionally separate procedures from collective bargaining and regulation of working conditions (*collaboration model*). The resolution of labour disputes is evicted from the space occupied by collective bargaining, departing from its object and purpose.

Collective bargaining becomes a *codecision process* in which both parties are aware that they are committed to achieving a common goal: regulation of working and social conditions. In addition, negotiators define themselves as members of the industrial relations system. Participating organisations are identified and recognised by the system as intermediaries who provide services to their members through representation, both in collective bargaining and in other forms of collective dialogue and cooperation.

An important fact to note is that in this third stage a business culture is adopted that practises the separation of regulation of working conditions from that of the management of labour conflict. Conflict may appear as an additional burden within the framework of collective bargaining but the parties may well agree and establish mechanisms and procedures to ensure continuity of communication, dialogue and negotiation, even in the event of a conflict.

The allocation of labour dispute resolution to specific (separate) institutions and procedures of collective bargaining can undoubtedly be interpreted as an internal differentiation resulting from the creation of an 'immune system' within the labour relations system,[26] that is, arbitration, mediation and conciliation as mechanisms for resolving labour disputes.

V. ALTERNATIVE SYSTEMS FOR CONFLICT RESOLUTION AND THE RIGHT TO STRIKE: CONSENSUS VERSUS DISSENT

In other branches of law, peaceful systems for the resolution of labour disputes have been proposed as alternatives to the judicial process. This represents their main advantage and positive valuation: they are desirable options compared to

[25] Rogowski (n 21) 66.

[26] ibid 65–66. They would therefore be the mechanisms incorporated into the judicial systems provided by the well-known ADR procedures, according to their terminology in English.

the two characteristics that are usually attributed to the judicial process, which are its long duration and the cost it represents.

Labour law, unlike other legal areas, makes use of extrajudicial systems not only to fulfil the purpose of articulating different channels to the judicial process, but also for a specific added effect: *they contribute decisively to diminishing the external manifestations of labour conflict*. Consequently, they directly and indirectly perform an *anaesthetic* function on exercising the right to strike.

Undoubtedly, the creation and extension of alternative systems for the resolution of labour disputes has had a *mitigating effect* on manifestations and externalisations of the conflict, which seek to provoke damage, such as strikes. In short, these are processes that contribute decisively to achieve environments of 'labour peace' or 'social peace'. Perhaps this aspect has not been sufficiently considered when assessing the countervailing powers in the negotiations leading to agreements for the peaceful resolution of labour disputes: the price of social peace, the value of social peace.

The widespread expansion of ADR procedures highlights the integration of a consensus culture. This explains why, in many cases, the use of alternative systems has been established as a mechanism of last resort prior to the call for a strike. In the labour relations system, ADR represents the prevalence of dialogue and consensus in a legal culture that demonises dissent and confrontation.[27] Paradoxically, in the current historical phase of the recognition of the right to strike at the highest level in many Western countries,[28] that is, even with constitutional guarantees, the dominant political and legal discourse seeks to emphasise the desirability and convenience of a peaceful resolution to labour disputes. The strike diffusely becomes a kind of last resort during a labour dispute that remains unresolved.

However, strikes have now succeeded in becoming integrated into the legal system as a genuine subjective right, particularly in the Member States of the European Union (Article 28 of the Charter of Fundamental Rights of the EU) where workers can directly invoke them before the courts. Nevertheless, it is a true paradox that the dynamics of labour disputes are decisively contributing to set strikes apart from the use of instruments of ADR.

The strike is placed as a right *formally* articulated under imperative legal categories and the maximum level of guardianship (in terms of ownership, content and limits) but *substantially* relegated to the background, giving a material prevalence to peaceful mechanisms of conflict resolution. This is a paradoxical situation that is a consequence of the coexistence of two different ways of confronting labour unrest in a given period of time: a moment 'in transition', typical of the beginning of the twenty-first century. The strike has become

[27] See the work of M Barbera and A Perulli (eds), *Consenso, dissenso e rappresentanza: le nuove relazioni sindacali* (Milan, Cedam, 2014).

[28] With the notable exception of the United Kingdom.

considered as an 'old' way of resolving labour disputes, based on confrontation, which survives formally integrated into the law. On the contrary, ADR expresses 'new ways' of overcoming labour disputes, 'modern' forms based on mutual consensus.

Consequently, the maximum expression of workers' collective action, the strike, acquires the character of 'a product of the past'; a measure to avoid because of the damage it entails. Despite being part of the legal system, it no longer has a special impact on the reality of labour relations. In addition, formally elevated to the category of subjective right, it coexists with other forms of resolving the conflicts that the current reality of labour relations stimulates and prioritises. Only a failure of ADR seems to enable a space in which the strike can continue to make sense and exercise its function of the ultimate expression of conflict and demand.

On the other hand, the scope of the strike is conditioned by the type of collective dispute. When a labour dispute is of an economic nature, only after an attempt and subsequent failure to solve it through ADR is the way open to the initiation of a strike process. Consequently, the right to strike is subject to, and at the expense of, prior exhaustion of peaceful means of resolving labour disputes.

Conversely, in the case of legal conflicts (involving interpretation and application of labour standards), their nature means that their resolution is practised mainly before the labour courts. When dealing with collective disputes of a legal nature, a strike is not usually an appropriate means of resolving them. Consequently, the space reserved for the exercise of a strike is limited to a *specific spectrum of situations and typology of conflicts*. Moreover, it should not be forgotten that the instruments of dialogue between economic and social partners have played a key role in creating and consolidating the widespread use of alternative systems of dispute resolution rather than the use of strikes.

Representations of workers, trade union organisations and, also, business organisations, under a collective bargaining model of *collaboration* have accepted a separate – and peaceful – treatment of labour disputes with respect to collective bargaining itself. In this way, collective bargaining has become a space reserved for the regulation of working conditions, excluding any reference to labour conflict.

The economic and financial crisis has played a decisive role since 2008 in this process of evolving collective bargaining systems, particularly in the countries of Europe. The destruction of 'secure' employment and the process of substitution for 'precarious employment' inevitably forced trade unions to 'negotiate downwards' in the face of increasing unemployment, especially in southern European countries.

The devaluation of wages and the reduction in the cost of dismissal, as measures to encourage the creation of employment, have been part of the austerity solutions to the crisis. These austerity measures have created a discourse of great media power, shared by business, international economic authorities, European institutions and governments themselves though not shared by trade union organisations.[29] Sacrifice was inevitable and scenarios for labour unrest were drastically reduced, except for the large street protests against the labour market reforms undertaken by individual governments.[30]

Is it possible to theorise about the right to strike in a context of severe economic crisis and widespread job destruction and to impute to trade union organisations the responsibility of having abandoned the discourse of dissent? Rather, it would be fair to speak of 'forced consensuses' on the part of the unions as representatives of a working population that observes how it is openly deprived of the labour rights that had been achieved with so much effort, since the fundamental characteristic of the trade union movement throughout its history has been its dissent in the face of an economic system that has installed workers in a position of powerlessness and subjection to economic, managerial and organisational power.

Undoubtedly, the analyses must be contextualised. Each historical time has demanded specific answers. If, at the end of the 1990s, a theoretical discourse began to be elaborated on the benefits of non-judicial or alternative systems of resolution of labour disputes, the crisis has only strengthened its scope of action, displacing the strike as a way of opposing the deterioration of working conditions and the erosion of the regulatory framework of labour relations.

VI. TRANSFORMATION OF COLLECTIVE BARGAINING AND FLEXIBILISATION OF THE FRAMEWORK OF WORKING CONDITIONS

The recent transformations of collective bargaining are fundamentally due to the introduction of new categories in different legal systems. These categories have been created in order to facilitate the *flexibilisation* of the application of collective agreements, and the *adaptation* of their contents to the reality of businesses, circumstances that the economic crisis has only exacerbated. The flexibilisation and adaptation has been carried out through three fundamental procedures:

(a) Attacking the *basic and sector structure* of collective bargaining,[31] allowing collective agreements agreed at the level of the companies to prevail.[32]

[29] 'For ordinary citizens it is difficult to imagine that facilitating dismissal today is the only way to create jobs tomorrow. However, this is the "truth" that neoliberal thought imposes as evident', B De Sousa Santos, *Democracia al borde del caos*, 1st edn (Mexico, Siglo XXI editores, 2014) 89.

[30] Especially, in Spain, France, Greece, Italy and Portugal.

[31] First, the Spanish labour reform of 1994 and subsequent partial reforms of collective bargaining in 2010 and 2011 had begun to alter the basic rules of the structure of collective bargaining that guaranteed the priority of the negotiation of state level sector; also, certain 'flanks' were open to the non-derogability of the agreement by the labour contract, see in general, DM Cairós Barreto, *La articulación y concurrencia de convenios colectivos* (Albacete, Editorial Bomarzo, 2012).

[32] As regards the application of prior agreements and their treatment by case law, see J Gorelli Hernández, *La negociación colectiva de empresa: descuelgue y prioridad aplicativa del convenio de*

This is a strategy promoted by the European institutions to deal with the crisis and its impact on the labour market.[33]

(b) Disfiguring and *stripping the collective agreement of its original legal nature* (agreement with sufficient legal effectiveness and binding force to regulate working conditions by sector or branch of activity) by creating ductile legal tools[34] that allow derogation.[35] And yet, despite the deterioration suffered from neoliberal reforms, collective bargaining remains the most effective instrument to balance the unequal power of workers in the determination of their working relations. Undoubtedly, collective bargaining at the sectoral level is a fundamental and effective tool that contributes to reducing inequality in wealth and health and helps to promote a stable and productive economy.[36]

(c) *Expanding the unilateral power of employers* to establish or modify essential or substantial conditions of the employment relationship. This effect is due to the withdrawal of collective bargaining from certain 'normative territories' in which it was previously used, thus, favouring the employment contract, or even unilateral business decisions, to make individual and collective alterations to the existing work conditions.[37]

VII. TRANSFORMATIONS OF COLLECTIVE BARGAINING AND IMPACT ON THE EXERCISE OF THE RIGHT TO STRIKE

Having reduced collective sectoral bargaining capacity to regulate working conditions, particularly basic and essential conditions such as working time and wages, the position of trade union organisations and, in general, workers' representations, has been greatly weakened. There has been no need to introduce any reform or alter in any way the rules governing freedom of trade union association to achieve the weakening effect of trade unions in general and the erosion of trade union action in the company. And yet, this effect is appreciable if one

empresa (Granada, Ed. Comares, 2013). By the same author, 'Primeras experiencias jurisprudenciales de la prioridad aplicativa del convenio de empresa'(2017) 3 *Trabajo y Derecho* 71–76.

[33] See KD Ewing, 'La Unión Europea, los Estados Unidos de América y la Asociación Transatlántica para el Comercio y la Inversión (TTIP): La Negociación Colectiva y la emergente "'Ley Transnacional de Relaciones Laborales"' (trans DM Cairós Barreto) (2016) 18 *Trabajo y Derecho* 18–25.

[34] In the well-known work by G Zagrebelski, *El derecho dúctil: Ley, derechos, justicia*, 10th edn (Madrid, Editorial Trotta, 2011) 16ff.

[35] The non-application of the collective agreement was initially established with certain limits in the Spanish labour reform of 1994, see W Sanguineti Raymond, *La inaplicación parcial del contenido del convenio colectivo* (Valencia, Tirant lo blanch, 2000); subsequently, the 2012 reform has removed such limits, allowing a virtually universal use of this figure.

[36] Ewing et al (n 11) 1.

[37] See MI Ramos Quintana, *La garantía de los derechos de los trabajadores (inderogabilidad e indisponibilidad)* (Valladolid, Editorial Lex Nova, 2002) 45ff.

takes into account two essential variables, which have influenced the reduction of trade union action in defence of workers' interests:

(a) dismantling collective bargaining by relegating the priority areas of negotiation to the company level.
(b) deregulation in favour of business management, taking as a pretext the economic crisis and the high unemployment rates.

These two circumstances have simultaneously weakened trade union strategies in collective bargaining of working conditions, whose negotiating structure has been 'atomised' in the context of a very high unemployment rate.[38]

The process of 'job replacement' that has been implemented through structural reforms in the labour market, at the request of the global, European and national economic authorities, has led to a labour market characterised by 'short-term jobs',[39] high rates of temporality in recruitment, a high percentage of involuntary part-time work and precariousness in working conditions. The precariousness of working conditions and the deregulation of the normative framework are provoking the erosion of historical conquests that allowed citizens access to the labour force.[40] In the context of these characteristics, it is difficult to avoid relations between collective bargaining and the right to strike not being altered.

In spite of what has been said, there is still a third source of changes and mutations, in particular concerning the collective agreement in its function of regulating working conditions with sufficient ability to create a framework for new relations between collective bargaining and exercise of the right to strike. Such changes have come about because of the Anglo-Saxon model of collective bargaining. As is well known, this model dominates the concept of *continuous or permanent negotiation*, which is carried out either through specifically created bodies for this purpose, or by giving the agreement a continuous 'adaptability' to the changing circumstances of work relationships. The first of these possibilities already existed in continental models.

It has been more difficult to incorporate into the negotiating culture the idea of permeability/ductility of the collective agreement to variations of its content over the period of its validity. It is true that in the continental model there have been experiences of this type in relation to certain working conditions, in particular salary matters, open to renegotiation during the term of the agreement, especially when its duration is lengthy. This idea (which is not incidental because

[38] The unemployment rate in Spain remains very high, above 18% in December 2016, after reaching its highest peak in the second quarter of 2013, 26.3%. Other EU countries have experienced a similar reality: OECD data, 2014: Slovakia (13.9%), Greece (25.9%), Ireland (14.7%), Portugal (12.6%).

[39] R Sennett, *Together. The Rituals, Pleasures and Politics of Cooperation* (New Haven & London, Yale University Press, 2012). The author indicates that short-term work has completely changed the nature of work, pp. 160ff.

[40] See, especially, De Sousa Santos (n 29) especially 87–91.

it affects the stability of its application over time, therefore it is something that is essential), however, has become part of the new type of collective agreement, and has become the 'common' collective agreement.

In Spain, in particular, the current legal framework contemplates the possibility that the collective agreement can be subject to revision during the time of its validity: different periods of validity can be agreed for each subject or homogeneous group of matters within the same agreement. The open and express revision of the agreement while in force can be a category in itself that determines the temporal dynamics of application of the collective agreement. This leads to the possibility of new relations with the exercise of the right to strike.

If the strike is an instrument of collective action by workers to press for better working conditions, precisely in those phases of a renegotiation or modification of the collective agreement, there should be nothing to prevent it from being exercised. This definitively moves away from old models that established the impossibility of calling a strike during the period of validity of the collective agreement to demand working conditions that were already established therein (renegotiation strikes).

The same can be said of the increasingly widespread formulas for changing working conditions agreed upon in collective bargaining (non-application of the agreement for reasons related to the operation of the company). This gives rise to a particularly ductile type of collective agreement that can absorb changes and is derived from the mutant reality of the economy and the organisational dimension of business. If the collective agreement is ductile, modifiable or non-applicable, incorporating all the circumstances that motivate such mechanisms – usually accompanied by situations of conflict and tension on the part of the workers – the coherent action would be for the right to strike to be exercised in such circumstances.

Modification, revision, non-application or, in short, updating the collective agreement during its validity are already realities in continental models of collective bargaining. These are possibilities that are not subject to limits but are now expectations that can happen throughout the validity of the collective agreement. However, changes in the function of adapting the collective agreement to the economic, technical, organisational or productive reality of the company must also produce changes in the understanding of renegotiation strikes, removing any suspicion of illegality.

If the collective agreement is exposed to revisions and modifications *ante tempus*, it is logical to conclude that the exercise of the right to strike is practicable every time the negotiation processes are reopened. This includes any processes in which the alteration of pre-existing working conditions in the collective agreement are discussed or its non-application or any type of innovation or modification. In this scenario, a strike cannot be linked in any way to the validity of the collective agreement. A 'renegotiation' strike, whose purpose is to modify or alter what is agreed in the agreement, can no longer be considered illegal or abusive. It forms part of the logic of the new dynamics of collective bargaining and of the nature of the rules of application of collective agreements.

This reflection also invites us to develop a more far-reaching one. It is necessary to ask whether the states which have signed the European Social Charter (ESC),[41] the European Convention of Human Rights (ECHR)[42] and the Charter of Fundamental Rights of the European Union (CFREU)[43] are obliged to recognise and facilitate the right to strike only when invoked in relation to collective bargaining processes or, on the contrary, the temporal scope of this right goes beyond the period of collective bargaining.

The question then arises as to which strike model signatory member states to such international instruments must operate in their national legal systems: a labour model or a multipurpose model of strikes.

It has been considered that, under the ESC, the right to strike is narrower than in the ECHR since the former guarantees the right to strike only for the purposes of collective bargaining (Article 6.3), while the latter allows the right to strike to be exercised wherever necessary to defend the economic and social interests of workers (Article 11(1)).[44] The same seems to follow from the provisions of Article 28 of the CFREU, when it contemplates separately both realities: on the one hand, it recognises the right of workers and employers or their respective organisations to negotiate and conclude collective agreements and, on the other hand, 'in case of a conflict of interests' it recognises the right to carry out 'collective actions for the defence of their interests, including strike action'.

That being so, states which have signed the ECHR and those which are part of the EU, for which the CFREU has the same value as the Treaties (Article 6 TEU), would be required to ensure in their respective legislation that the right to strike is not circumscribed to the moments of negotiation of collective agreements, but can be exercised when the interests of workers so demand. Thus, the so-called 'renegotiation strikes' would have complete legal coverage. In fact, their illegality cannot be accepted since the collective agreement is no longer considered to be a determinant of labour peace. On the contrary, it is an instrument of regulation of working conditions that can be renegotiated, revised and modified over its term.

Likewise, strikes of 'solidarity' or 'sympathy' – in Anglo-Saxon argot – would be completely integrated within a strike model that is detached from collective bargaining processes. In fact, it is necessary to adopt as a basic conceptual notion that solidarity among workers is lawful in itself and that it is also indispensable for adequate representation by the unions of workers' interests. Trade unions not only articulate and deploy collective strength, but must also support the workers when they need it.[45]

[41] Council of Europe, Turin, 1981.

[42] Council of Europe, 4 November 1950 and its updated protocols.

[43] Since 18 November 2000, adapted in 2007.

[44] Ewing et al (n 11) 83, note 172.

[45] Solidarity is part of the distinctive character of the trade union movement. Not understanding this means not having understood the true nature of freedom of association, ibid 54.

VIII. CONCLUSIONS

The construction and development of the right to strike has always been linked to the development of collective bargaining processes. Thus, different models of the right to strike have been described in accordance with its independent configuration from the negotiation of the collective agreement. Likewise, collective bargaining has developed an important relationship with the configuration of labour disputes. Collective bargaining starts as a process of dialogue between opposing parties in a labour conflict but soon, as the legal recognition of collective bargaining starts to be achieved, this gives rise to open conflicts through spontaneous actions, including the strike. So, the collective agreement ends up being transformed into a direct source of overcoming conflicts. In a new step in the evolution, collective disputes gain independence from collective bargaining, so the regulation of working conditions is separated from the management of labour conflicts.

Extrajudicial and alternative systems for the resolution of conflicts have had an intense development in labour disputes. They contribute decisively to diminishing the external manifestations of labour conflict so they perform an anaesthetic function on exercising the right to strike. It is the case that, having recognised the right to strike at the highest level in many Western countries, even with constitutional guarantees, the dominant political and legal discourse seeks to emphasise the desirability and convenience of a peaceful resolution to labour disputes. The strike becomes the last resort during a labour dispute that remains unresolved. Nevertheless, it is a true paradox that the dynamics of labour disputes are decisively contributing to set strikes apart from the use of instruments of ADR.

The economic and financial crises have had an important impact on the models of collective bargaining. The flexibilisation of the labour market has led to the dismantling of the collective bargaining sectoral structure, relegating the priority areas of negotiation to the company level and deregulation in favour of the business management. In this context, the relations between collective bargaining and the right to strike have to change. If the strike is an instrument of collective action by workers to press for better working conditions, precisely in those phases of a renegotiation or modification of the collective agreement, there should be nothing to prevent it from being exercised. Modification, revision, non-application or updating of collective agreements are legal and possible actions that are not subject to limits, but are now expectations that can happen throughout the validity of the collective agreement.

In this scenario, a strike cannot be linked in any way to the validity of the collective agreement. A 'renegotiation' strike, whose purpose is to modify or alter what is agreed in the agreement, can no longer be considered illegal or abusive. In addition, states which have signed the ECHR and those which are part of the EU, for which the CFREU has the same value as the Treaties, have to ensure in their respective legislation that the right to strike is not limited to the moments of negotiation of collective agreements. Both instruments recognise the right to strike as a different and separate action from the collective negotiation. Thus, so-called 'renegotiation strikes' must now have complete legal coverage since the collective agreement is no longer considered to be a determinant of labour peace. On the contrary, it is an instrument of regulation of working conditions that can be continuously renegotiated, revised and modified. Likewise, strikes of 'solidarity' or 'sympathy' would be completely integrated within a strike model that is detached from collective bargaining processes.

BIBLIOGRAPHY

Alonso Olea, M, *De la servidumbre al contrato de trabajo*, Madrid, Tecnos, 1979.

Barbera, M and Perulli, A (eds), *Consenso, dissenso e rappresentanza: le nuove relazioni sindacali*, Milan, Cedam, 2014.

Barreiro G, 'Ensayo crítico sobre la paz laboral en el convenio colectivo con especial referencia a su carácter inmanente' (1989) 4 REDT.

Baylos Grau, A, *Derecho del trabajo. Modelo para armar* [Labour Law. Model to Assemble] Madrid, Editorial Trotta, 1991.

Cairós Barreto, DM, *La articulación y concurrencia de convenios colectivos*, Albacete, Editorial Bomarzo, 2012.

Davis, P and Freedland, M, *O Kahn-Freund's Labour and the Law.*

De Sousa Santos, B, *Democracia al borde del caos* (1st edn), Mexico, Siglo XXI editores, 2014.

Ewing, KD, *The Right to Strike*, Oxford. Clarendon Press, 1991.

——, 'La Unión Europea, los Estados Unidos de América y la Asociación Transatlántica para el Comercio y la Inversión (TTIP): La Negociación Colectiva y la emergente "Ley Transnacional de Relaciones Laborales"' (trans DM Cairós Barreto) (2016) 18 *Trabajo y Derecho.*

——, Hendy, J and Jones, C, *A Manifesto for Labour Law: Towards a Comprehensive Revision of Worker's Rights*, Liverpool, The Institute of Employment Rights, 2016.

Ghezzi, G, 'Autonomia collettiva, diritto di sciopero e clausole di tregua' in AAVV, *Studi in onore di F Santoro-Passarelli*, volume V, Naples, Jovene, 1972.

Giugni, G, 'Diritto del lavoro (voce per un'enciclopedia)' (1979) 1 GDLRI.

Gorelli Hernández, J, *La negociación colectiva de empresa: descuelgue y prioridad aplicativa del convenio de empresa*, Granada, Ed. Comares, 2013.

——, 'Primeras experiencias jurisprudenciales de la prioridad aplicativa del convenio de empresa' (2017) 3 *Trabajo y Derecho.*

Javillier, JC, *Droit du Travail*, 2nd edn (Paris, LGDG, 1981).

Kahn-Freund, O, 'Intergroup Conflicts and their Settlement' (1954) 5 *British Journal of Sociology.*

——, *Labour Relations, Heritage and Adjustment*, Oxford, Oxford University Press, 1979.

Lyon-Caen, G, 'Défense et illustration du contra du travail' (1968) T XIII *Archives de Philosophie du Droit*.

Palomeque López, MC, *Derecho del trabajo e ideología. Medio siglo de formación ideológica del Derecho del trabajo en España* (7th edn) Madrid, Ed. Tecnos, 2011.

—— and Álvarez de la Rosa, M, *Derecho del trabajo* (24th edn) Madrid, Editorial Ramón Areces, 2016.

Ramos Quintana, MI, *El deber de paz laboral (entre la ley y la autonomía colectiva)*, Madrid, Civitas, 1993.

——, *La garantía de los derechos de los trabajadores (inderogabilidad e indisponibilidad)*, Valladolid, Editorial Lex Nova, 2002.

——, 'La huelga como derecho fundamental' in W Sanguineti Raymond and E Cabero Morán (eds), *Sindicalismo y Democracia* (Granada, Comares, 2017.

Rogowski, R, 'Industrial Relations, Labour Conflict Resolution and Reflexive Labour Law' in R Rogowski and T Wilthagen (eds), *Reflexive Labour Law*, Boston, Kluwer Law and Taxation Publishers, 1994.

Sanguineti Raymond, W, *La inaplicación parcial del contenido del convenio colectivo*, Valencia, Tirant lo blanch, 2000.

Sennett, R, *Together. The Rituals, Pleasures and Politics of Cooperation*, New Haven and London, Yale University Press, 2012.

Zagrebelski, G, *El derecho dúctil: Ley, derechos, justicia* (10the edn) Madrid, Editorial Trotta, 2011.

4

Connecting the Dots: Coordination in Decentralised Trade Union Organising

ASSAF BONDY AND GUY MUNDLAK

I. INTRODUCTION

COLLECTIVE BARGAINING SEEKS to simultaneously achieve several goals, not all of which call for the same strategies. On the one hand, it seeks to provide actual voice to workers' preferences, encourage active participation and provide a mechanism for ongoing dispute resolution.[1] On the other hand, bargaining for small units in which there is active participation suffers from noticeable drawbacks for the workers themselves, to an extent that remains empirically contested.[2] The coverage of enterprise (or smaller) units creates enclaves with higher wages than those in competing organisations and a distinct co-management system that many employers view as a disadvantage. Consequently, the targeting of enclaves may lead to a relative disadvantage of the unionised employer, with potential repercussions for the workers themselves.[3] Adjustments to the bargaining outcomes to offset such a disadvantage may include outsourcing and the incremental diminution of the bargaining unit, or various methods of differentiating between privileged insiders at the expense of outsiders, such as agreements to layoffs or multi-tier agreements.[4] In addition, bargaining targeted at the enterprise (or smaller unit) level is based on a small solidarity basis and may therefore enjoy less leverage; combined with increased resistance from targeted employers, this may risk an ineffective

[1] Richard B Freeman and Robert L Medoff, *What Do Unions Do?* (New York: Basic Books, 1984).

[2] James T Bennet and Bruce Kaufman, *What Do Unions Do? A Twenty-Year Perspective* (New Brunswick, NJ: Transaction, 2007).

[3] Harry C Katz, 'The Decentralization of Collective Bargaining: A Literature Review and Comparative Analysis' (1993) 47 *ILR Review* 3.

[4] Julian Walker, 'Two Tier Wage Systems' (1987) 51 *Research and Current Issues* 2.

bargaining round.[5] Finally, legal instruments that allow the extension of collective agreements are for the most part limited to high-level collective agreements, not enterprise agreements.[6]

Assessing the gains and losses from bargaining at the enterprise level is contingent on the institutional options provided by the industrial relations system.[7] At one end of the continuum, systems that are based on enterprise bargaining, such as the United States or Japan, do not provide a significant alternative, leading to low levels of membership and coverage of collective agreements.[8] At the other extreme, countries with a highly centralised system of bargaining, Austria for example, hardly enable enterprise bargaining and opt for highly coordinated bargaining instead. Consequently, despite declining membership rates, the union wage premium is less relevant and the coverage of collective agreements remains high.[9]

As regards the two stylised extremes – a highly decentralised system on the one hand and a highly centralised system on the other – the assumption is that each needs to compensate for its weaker aspect. A decentralised system needs to engage in some form of coordination, while highly centralised systems need to develop enterprise (or occupational) engagement of workers to satisfy many of the voice advantages that trade unions provide.

This chapter draws on Israel as a case study to demonstrate a 'hybrid' system, positioned in the middle of the de/centralised continuum.[10] In a hybrid system we should expect to observe the two shortcomings described at the outset. Where peak-level coordinated bargaining persists, there is a need to forge a strong presence at lower levels to ensure the advantages of active, organic solidarity, the fulfilment of peak-level agreements by ongoing monitoring and compliance mechanisms, and active labour-management relations.[11] Where enterprise bargaining has emerged, there is a need to develop methods of coordination that transcend the boundaries of the firm. These are required to avoid excessive differentiation between employers and allow the internalisation of public concerns favouring economic sustainability of the individual

[5] The extent of power, whether characterised as voice or monopoly, is dependent on industrial features, such as the level of competition in the sector. David Blanchflower and Alex Bryson 'What Effect Do Unions Have on Wages Now and Would Freeman and Medoff Be Surprised?' in Bennet and Kaufman (eds) (n 2).

[6] Franz Traxler, Sabina Blaschke and Bernhard Kittel, *National Labour Relations in Internationalized Markets* (Oxford: Oxford University Press, 2001).

[7] John Pencavel, 'Unionism Viewed Internationally' (2005) 26(1) *Journal of Labor Research* 65–97.

[8] ICTWSS – Collective Agreements Date Center. Anthony Ferner and Richard Hyman, *Changing Industrial Relations in Europe* (Oxford: Blackwell Publications, 1998).

[9] Ferner and Hyman (n 8).

[10] Guy Mundlak, 'Organizing Workers in "Hybrid Systems": Comparing Trade Union Strategies in Four Countries – Austria, Germany, Israel and the Netherlands (2016) 17 *Theoretical Inquiries in Law* 163.

[11] Guy Mundlak, 'Addressing the Legitimacy Gap in the Israeli Corporatist Revival (2009) 47 *British Journal of Industrial Relations* 765.

enterprise, but also of the industry and of the labour market as a whole (eg, reduction of unemployment, and high levels of inequality between insiders and outsiders).[12]

In the following pages we focus on the latter – the means of coordination. Hybrid systems were previously highly coordinated but are suffering from a continuous loss of membership.[13] Attempts at trade union revitalisation by means of organising workers in greenfield sites are focused on the enterprise level. While the option of sector-level bargaining remains, there is a growing resistance on the part of employers and their associations to negotiating at higher levels.[14] How can trade unions forge a higher level of coordination in times of decentralisation? What could be gained by bringing centralised bargaining back into the trade unions' revitalisation efforts? And under what circumstances could employers acquiesce in bargaining at the sector level?

To answer these questions, this chapter proceeds as follows: in Section II we discuss the importance and prevailing methods of coordination. Section III briefly describes the transformation and hybridisation of the Israeli system of industrial relations. In Section IV we look into clusters of enterprise bargaining in four sectors – cellular phone companies, insurance, public transportation (buses), and fast food chains. In the four sectors, there has been a concentration of organising efforts at the enterprise level, and bargaining followed suit at the enterprise level as well. This empirical part of the study observes organising drives from the last five years, some still pending. It is based for the most part on the study of first collective agreements, with only a few enterprises that have already reached a second round of bargaining. To understand the current patterns of negotiated norms, the study further draws on informants from the trade unions who described the process of bargaining in each of the sectors, as well as the organisational objectives and their personal subjective assessment. Section V concludes, integrating the findings with the objectives of coordination and providing some answers regarding the importance and feasibility of coordination in the context of new organising.

II. COORDINATION: OBJECTIVES AND MEANS

In Marx's manifesto, he declares that the workers of the world should unite.[15] A universal organisation can benefit the labour movement in two ways. First, it

[12] Maarten Keune, 'Decentralizing Wage Setting in Times of Crisis? The Regulation and Use of Wage-related Derogation Clauses in Seven European Countries' (2011) 2 *European Labour Law Journal* 86.

[13] Mundlak (n 10).

[14] Lucio Baccaro and Chiara Benassi, 'Throwing Out the Ballast: Growth Models and the Liberalization of German Industrial Relations' (2017) 15 *Socio-economic Review*.

[15] Karl Marx and Friedrich Engels. *The Communist Manifesto* (London: Penguin, 2004).

increases and multiplies the power of labour. Second, it prevents the shifting of the costs of organising from one group of workers to another. As labour costs increase, following the exercise of labour's collective power, employers may use various strategies to reduce labour costs again – shifting from labour to technology, layoffs or reliance on an international reserve army of (cheap) labour.[16] Universal representation and bargaining is necessary to offset the wide range of strategic responses available to businesses.

As a practical matter, rather than a strict prescription, the trajectory of universalisation is translated into a more pragmatic direction in labour's strategies – namely expanding the bargaining domain and the coordination among multiple bargaining domains. From the global to the enterprise level, increasing coverage and coordination poses both an objective and a challenge. At the global and regional levels, concerns of a 'race to the bottom' and cosmopolitan values point at attempts to raise the floor of rights across countries, despite the Westphalian separation between nationally based industrial systems.[17] At the national level, national pacts, state-wide bargaining that is class-based (blue- or white-collar), the use of extension orders, compulsory measures to ensure extensive membership and sector-wide bargaining are all institutions that cater to extending coverage and coordination across the economy.[18] Enterprise bargaining suffers from the lowest level of coordination, although splitting the enterprise into smaller bargaining units on an occupational level, carving out part-time and temporary workers, outsourcing and fragmentation are all measures that even further marketise and decrease coordination. 'Uberisation' and other forms of fragmented work are therefore the ultimate marketisation of work as a commodity, resistant to collective coordination altogether.[19]

Between marketisation and individualisation on the one hand and the national pact on the other, there is a range of measures that seek to establish coordination. Some are institutionalised, such as sector-wide bargaining. Others are dependent on labour's strategies: for example, when engaging in pattern bargaining, the trade union resorts to a strategy of sequential bargaining, choosing the first establishment, occupation or sector over which to negotiate,

[16] Michael Piore, *Birds of Passage: Migrant Labor and Industrial Societies* (Cambridge: Cambridge University Press, 1979).

[17] Barbara Bechter, Bernd Brandl and Gugliemo Meardi, *From National to Sectoral Industrial Relations: Developments in Sectoral Industrial Relations in the EU* (European Foundation for the Improvement of Living and Working Conditions, 2011). Aristea Koukiadaki, Isabel Tavora and Miguel Martinez Lucio (eds), *Joint Regulation and Labour Market Policy in Europe During the Crisis* (Brussels: ETUI, 2015).

[18] Michael Wallerstein, Miriam Golden and Peter Lange, 'Unions, Employers' Associations, and Wage-setting Institutions in Northern and Central Europe, 1950–1992' (1997) 50 *Industrial and Labor Relations Review* 379. Jelle Visser, *Wage Bargaining Institutions – From Crisis to Crisis*, European Commission – Economic Papers 488 (2013).

[19] Brishen Rogers, 'The Social Costs of Uber' (2017) 82(1) *University of Chicago Law Review Online* 85.

and then replicating, adapting and benchmarking others (establishment, occupation or sector).[20] Hence, pattern bargaining can be used as either an inter- or intra-sectoral form of bargaining, depending on the dominant level of bargaining. In the former case, which is widespread in western and northern European states (eg, Germany, Sweden), bargaining for the labour conditions and wages of metalworkers may be chosen, and then other sectors are arranged in accordance with the gains of the leading sector.[21] In the latter, mainly found in several sectors in the US, a trade union can choose one company in the sector with which to negotiate and then use the bargaining outcomes as the benchmark for the bargaining rounds with other companies in the sector.[22]

Enterprise-level pattern bargaining is not a formal institution, never grounded in law, and rarely found as a formal policy. It does not expand coverage (universalisation) and is focused mostly on coordination between existing bargaining units. It has other variations. Notably, the well-known Japanese practice of labour's 'spring offensive' (Shuntō) is a method of inter-union coordination in what is an otherwise highly decentralised system of bargaining.[23] Similarly, linking collective agreements, so that one agreement adopts arrangements that were negotiated in another and the parties agree that changes in one will automatically affect the other, is another method of coordination.[24] Law can act as a coordinating mechanism when drawing on collective agreements by reference to the most representative agreements as a focal point for statutory and judicial norms, or by drawing on commonly negotiated norms as the 'law of industry'.[25]

Employers may prefer uncoordinated bargaining, mirroring the trade unions' preference for coordination, notably as a means of weakening the power basis of the trade union. In sectors that are exposed to global competition, employers may further object to coordinated bargaining (or to any form of bargaining) if competition extends the local bargaining domain.[26] In areas where there is a labour surplus, employers may see fewer advantages in coordination, as the labour force is easily replaceable.

[20] Bernd Brandl and Franz Traxler, 'Labour Relations, Economic Governance and the Crisis: Turning the Tide Again?' (2008) 52 *Labor History* 1. Stephen Wood, 'The Cooperative Labour Strategy in the US Auto Industry' (1986) 7 *Economic and Industrial Democracy* 415; Robert C Marshall and Antonio Merlo, 'Pattern Bargaining' (2004) 45 *International Economic Review* 239.

[21] Bernhard Ebbinghaus and Bernhard Kittel, 'European Rigidity Versus American Flexibility? The Institutional Adaptability of Collective Bargaining' (2005) 32 *Work and Occupations* 163.

[22] Wood (n 20).

[23] Katheleen A Thelen and Ikuo Kume, 'Coordination as a Political Problem in Coordinated Market Economies' (2006) 19(1) *Governance* 11.

[24] In Israel this was the prevailing method for public-sector bargaining in the past, and it is also extant in some of the private-sector collective agreements, such as in banking.

[25] Edward B Rock and Michael L Wachter, 'The Enforceability of Norms and the Employment Relationship' (1996) 144 *University of Pennsylvania Law Review* 1913.

[26] Baccaro and Benassi (n 14).

However, employers may also have opposing interests that align with the trade unions' interests in coordination: where stronger employers wish to crowd out employers who are undercutting labour costs and driving investment in the labour force downwards; when there is a shortage in the qualified supply of labour (in which case sectoral agreements may be effective in halting upwards pressures and competition among employers); where investment in human capital is of particular importance and workers' retention is a high priority; when other forms of centralised pressures are involved, such as state regulation; when law accords particular privileges to coordinated collective agreements (eg, the permission to derogate or adapt statutory arrangements); and when coordinated bargaining is a key to extension orders that can leverage all of the abovementioned advantages.[27]

The plural forms of coordination in bargaining can be distinguished along several axes: Traxler et al mention two strategies which are particularly important in the present context.[28] First, coordination can be an intentional strategy or merely an outcome of market forces. Second, coordination can be determined by a single agent (for example, the central governing body of a federation of trade unions), or negotiated by several unions. A looser form of coordination is exhibited in sequential, non-linear bargaining rounds, where one union learns and adopts the outcomes of other unions' achievements. Hence, this well-studied form of coordination by means of pattern bargaining can be characterised as an intentional strategy, which is initiated by a single agent on labour's side, who determines the sequence of bargaining and sets the pattern for all subsequent negotiations.[29] However, this common form of pattern bargaining is not the exclusive form of enterprise-level bargaining coordination, as we will demonstrate in the following sections.

III. THE HYBRIDISATION OF THE ISRAELI INDUSTRIAL RELATIONS SYSTEM: THE CHALLENGE POSED BY DECENTRALISATION

Israel's industrial relations system was modelled on corporatist premises.[30] Pre-dating statehood, and later in formalised fashion with the legislation of the Collective Agreements Law (1957), bargaining was recognised at multiple levels. Public-sector bargaining was, and remains, to a large extent

[27] Peter Swenson, 'Bringing Capital Back In, or Social Democracy Reconsidered: Employer Power, Cross-class Alliances, and Centralization of Industrial Relations in Denmark and Sweden (1991) 43 *World Politics* 513. Brandl and Traxler (n 20).

[28] Franz Traxler, Bernd Brandl and Vera Glassner 'Pattern Bargaining: An Investigation into Its Agency, Context and Evidence' (2008) 46(1) *British Journal of Industrial Relations* 33.

[29] Wood (n 20); Marshall and Merlo (n 20).

[30] Arie Shirom, *Introduction to Industrial Relations in Israel* (Tel Aviv: Am Oved, 1983). In Hebrew. Guy Mundlak, *Fading Corporatism in Israel* (Ithaca, NY: ILR Press, 2007).

coordinated – through centralised bargaining and legal (financial) regulation – and usually detached from private-sector bargaining.[31] Private-sector bargaining was more fragmented to begin with, but various methods of coordination existed. State-wide coordination of wages and industrial practice covered areas such as minimum wages (until 1987) and cost-of-living adjustments (COLA) (for some years). State-wide legal norms evolved from separate and distinct collective agreements, later becoming universal standards.[32] Sector-level bargaining developed at different periods, and although it declined in some sectors, notably in industry, it is still a prominent form of bargaining and coordination in the service sectors.

Coordination was never perfect; there were always tensions, in both the public and the private sector. On the one hand, the General Histadrut (the largest federation of trade unions) and the employers' associations wanted to level the playing field across enterprises and sectors (hence intra-sectoral and inter-sectoral coordination). On the other hand, there were pressures from workers' committees at the enterprise level who resisted the outcomes of coordination and from employers who did not realise any gains from coordination.[33] Some of the pressures against coordination were relieved by extension decrees, which imposed uniform outcomes on all employers and their employees. At other times, coordinated bargaining efforts gave way to decentralised and fragmented bargaining, whether formally (attested to by a shift to enterprise bargaining) or informally (local 'wage drift').[34]

Starting from the mid-1980s, and peaking in 1995, the Israeli system transformed considerably, downplaying some of its corporatist features and developing pluralist ones instead. The 'Ghent system', which tied healthcare provision with trade union membership, was removed; the pensions system that had been under the sole control of the General Histadrut was opened to market competition; the General Histadrut sold off its vast economic holdings; and the symbiotic political liaison between the General Histadrut and the ruling political party was terminally disconnected.[35] One of the important implications of the change in the system was the relatively rapid drop in membership rates and, to a lesser extent, in the share of workers who are covered by collective agreements. While in the early 1980s most workers were members of trade unions (more than 80 per cent, with the majority belonging to the General Histadrut) and covered by collective agreements (more than 80 per cent), by 2006 the share

[31] Lev L Grinberg, *Split Corporatism in Israel*, (New York: CUNY Press, 1991).

[32] Mundlak (n 30).

[33] Lev L Grinberg, *The Histadrut Above All* (Jerusalem, Nevo Publishers, 1993). In Hebrew.

[34] Tali Kristal, 'Decentralization of Collective Agreements in Israel, 1957–1998' (2002) 9 *Work, Society and Law*. In Hebrew.

[35] Yitzhak Haberfeld, 'Why do Workers Join Unions? The Case of Israel' (1995) 48 *Industrial & Labor Relations Review* 656. Mundlak (n 30).

of members was down to 31 per cent (two-thirds of them in the Histadrut) and the share of workers who were covered by collective agreements was down to 51 per cent. These figures are indicative of a deep change in the nature of the system, which became more pluralist, decentralised, decentred, conflictual and juridified.[36]

With the removal of the Ghent system, the General Histadrut attempted to organise workers in greenfield sites, but for the most part these organising drives failed.[37] During these initial attempts, the Labor Courts and the legislature developed the law and secured the workers from retaliation and unfair labour practices.[38] However, lack of experience in organising, coupled with a slow judicial response and the unfamiliar terrain for all concerned, can account for the failure of the first wave of enterprise organising attempts.

In 2008 a second wave of organising attempts started. Motivated by the entry of a new trade union ('Power to the Workers') that sought to democratise trade union representation and emphasise grassroots bargaining, the General Histadrut and another veteran federation – the National Histadrut – started developing new strategies for organising and devoted resources accordingly.[39] Unlike the first wave, the second wave can be considered a triumphant success, with a host of organising drives in greenfield sites that were concluded with a collective agreement. Trade unions entered establishments in sectors that were considered to be almost immune to trade union activity. The success of the trade unions was exponential and as more workers succeeded in organising, other workers began to view the trade union as a feasible option they could consider.

According to the Law of Collective Agreements, in order to bargain at the enterprise level a trade union must reach the status of an exclusive bargaining agent, which requires the fulfilment of two major conditions: (a) being the trade union with the most members in the bargaining unit, and (b) with at least a third of the overall number of workers employed in the bargaining unit.[40] The latter condition makes organising difficult as the trade union must achieve a critical mass.

Sector- and national-level bargaining continues and technically remains feasible for greenfield sites as well. From an organising perspective, sector-level bargaining may seem much easier. The Law of Collective Bargaining only requires that the representative trade union be the union with the most *organised workers* in the bargaining domain (ie, that it meet condition (a) for enterprise

[36] Tali Kristal, Guy Mundlak, Yitzhak Haberfeld and Yinon Cohen, 'Union Density in Israel 2006–2012: The Split of the Industrial Relations System' (2015) 14 *Work, Society and Law* 9. In Hebrew.

[37] Mundlak (n 11).

[38] Israel National Labor Court (Appeal) No. 64/09. Israel Law of Collective Agreements (1957. 8th Amendment, 2009).

[39] Kristal et al (n 36).

[40] Israel Law of Collective Agreements (1957).

bargaining, *supra*, but not condition (b)). Hence, if only a handful of workers in a sector are organised in one union, and there are no competing unions, that union has the legal licence to negotiate a sector-level agreement with an employers' association. A sector-level agreement can then be extended to employers who are not members of the employers' association at the request of the negotiating parties.[41]

Despite the legal ease of gaining representative status for sector-level agreements, trade unions do not organise for the purpose of achieving a sectoral agreement. There are several interrelated reasons for the mismatch between organising and coordinated bargaining at a level that extends beyond the single enterprise. First, sector-wide agreements require an employers' association on capital's side. This requires the affirmative interest of employers to coalesce, organise and coordinate. Hence, the association of employers is in fact more important than the organisation of workers. Second, organising workers is based on methods of building solidarity from the bottom up. Enterprise bargaining requires attending to the workers' needs, both as a successful strategy of voice and as an instrument to preserve the necessary support of the workers. Sector-level bargaining is a method of governance that is based on central representation, far removed from the workers' active voice in negotiations. To conclude a sector-wide agreement, the trade union needs to be a good 'social partner' to elicit the cooperation of business, more than it needs to organise the workers.

The new organising wave did not abolish sector-level bargaining altogether. Some sectors, such as hospitality, construction and agriculture, are continuously governed by sectoral agreements. In the cleaning and security sectors, new sectoral agreements play an important role and have been negotiated in tandem with increased responsibility that was placed on employers by the Law on Enforcement of Labor Laws (2011). But in the new sectors, the greenfield sites, where most organising takes place, sector-wide bargaining was never considered an option. This is the result of trade unions' modes of operation, the fascination with new forms of collective action, competition between unions, and employers' reluctance to negotiate at the sectoral level.

The advantages of the new enterprise-based organising are clear. They are an essential ingredient of the labour movement's revitalisation efforts in Israel, highlighting a localised version of industrial democracy, workers' voice and direct participation.[42] At the same time, the new focus on organising and enterprise bargaining risks losing the advantages of coordinated bargaining.

Presenting enterprise bargaining and sectoral bargaining as two diametrically opposed forms of association and bargaining may be a good way to stylise differences, underscoring the challenges facing trade unions in hybrid systems. But is there a continuum between them? The discussion on coordination in

[41] ibid.
[42] Mundlak (n 10).

the previous section suggests there may be. In the following section we seek to describe the clustering of enterprise bargaining in a single sector, asking: to what extent, and by which mechanisms, can a cluster of bargaining rounds in a single sector elevate the level of intra-sectoral coordination, and to what extent can a cluster of enterprise agreements lead to highly coordinated sectoral bargaining?

IV. CONNECTING THE DOTS: THE STUDY OF ENTERPRISE BARGAINING IN FOUR SECTORS

To answer the research question, we chose four sectors in which several new organising drives have succeeded and reached a collective agreement at the enterprise level: cellphone companies, insurance companies, public transportation (bus companies), and the work of youth in the hospitality industry – fast food chains, restaurants and catering. The study traces forms of coordination *within* each of the sectors (and not *between* sectors). The primary source for the study are the collective agreements that were concluded in each of the sectors. To make sense of the comparison between the detailed agreements, interviews were held with relevant union officials.

Collective agreements of the kind studied here are long and detailed, and comparing them is difficult as both differences and similarities appear throughout. To facilitate the comparison, we distinguish two categories:

(a) *Quantitative subjects – wages and benefits*: wage setting, compensation methods (individual, team and corporate-wide bonuses), and fringe benefits; in this category we also observe wage flexibility – the leeway afforded to the employer to change the wage structure.
(b) *Qualitative subjects – organisational aspects*: numerical flexibility – including exclusions from the coverage of the agreement, hiring, the termination of the employment relationship (collective layoffs and individual dismissals), the use of subcontracting and temp workers; functional flexibility, which includes consultation, negotiations and co-determination rights with regard to changes in employment conditions, organisational change (such as mergers and the acquisition of other companies), technological change, and the rights accorded to the trade union (office-space and paid hours for the trade union representatives among the workforce) and the employer (notably industrial peace). To focus the comparison, we demonstrate coordination with regard to protections from various types of dismissals.

A. The Cellphones Sector

Cellphone companies started operating in the mid-1990s, after the removal of the Ghent system, and the newly established companies emerged as part of a new sector that is outside the organised economy. A three-company oligopoly gradually emerged, who remain to date the largest players. In 2010 the Ministry of Communications opened the sector to competition, lowering the price of cellphone services significantly and encouraging the entry of new players.[43] Consequently, there are at present approximately eight small companies beside the big three. Profit margins in the sector have gone down considerably due to the reform.[44]

Shortly after the 2010 reform, the workers in one of the large companies – Pelephone – launched what was one of the most visible and studied organising drives in Israel.[45] Its visibility was due to the size of the company (at the time, over 3,000 employees), the collapse of the common perception that the new industry and services were outside the collective bargaining zone, and the legal precedent that was established during the organising drive – severely curtailing employers' speech against employees' organising. Following a volatile organising drive, a collective agreement was concluded with Pelephone, and shortly thereafter employees in the other two large companies got organised and concluded a collective agreement. In two of the smaller companies a collective agreement had already been concluded at the time of writing, and only a few of the smallest companies remain unorganised at present. All of the agreements in the sector were negotiated on labour's side by the General Histadrut, except for the latest negotiations, which were concluded by the rival National Histadrut. The concentration of organising drives and agreements in the cellphone and ancillary sectors (new telecommunications and internet, high-tech) led to the establishment of a new trade union under the roof of the General Histadrut – representing employees in these fields.

The three major agreements display a high level of similarity. They were negotiated in different years (2013, 2014, 2015) and therefore are to be renegotiated at different times (unlike traditional forms of pattern bargaining). According to the head of the cellphone/internet trade union, the first agreement created the basic platform and consecutive rounds generally matched and topped the previous rounds, thereby achieving incremental improvement. This creates a variation on pattern bargaining whereby the workers' committees in each of the companies on the one side and the human resource managers on the other side emulate previous rounds and negotiate any incremental changes.

With regard to wages, at the time of concluding a first agreement, there is an approximately 10 per cent wage hike, a one-time signing bonus (compensating for the delay in the months of negotiations), and then an annual wage improvement of approximately 3 per cent (2.8–3.1 per cent). While the overall

[43] Jushua D Margolis, Amram Migdal and Kerry Herman, 'Moshe Kahlon: Telecommunications Reform and Competition in Israel's Cellular Market (A)', *Harvard Business School Case* 417-017 (2016).

[44] Interview with the head of the Cellular and IT union.

[45] Pnina Alon-Shenker and Guy Davidov, 'Organizing: Should the Employer Have a Say?' (2016) 17 *Theoretical Inquiries in Law* 63.

wage package, as a whole, is relatively similar, differences are noticeable with regard to its internal distribution among the workers. The wage hike is split in all companies into a flat wage raise and a component that is left to managerial discretion. The overarching principle is that the least compensated workers should not be hurt by inflation, and the wages of the best compensated workers (enjoying the most rewards emerging from managerial discretion) should be contained within bounds. While the trade union respects the employers' demand for differentiation, in return it has negotiated for visibility of the differential reward methods, the criteria and method of administration.[46]

With regard to the qualitative aspects, the agreements provide management much leeway, demanding consultation and negotiation rights that are in line with the general duties of collective labour law in Israel. The qualitative aspect covers all matters from hiring to firing, as well as temporal and functional flexibility. On most matters it provides certain procedural safeguards, but leaves the managerial prerogative intact. To single out an important aspect of the qualitative (or so-called 'organisational') aspect of the agreements, the protection from dismissals is the most significant. The collective agreements translate the general legal duty to act in good faith[47] into a highly detailed protocol, emphasising the trade union's rights in the process. The protocol distinguishes between individual dismissals, for reasons of lacking performance or for disciplinary reasons (with a separate protocol for each of the two), and collective dismissals, notably for the purpose of downsizing. All the agreements refer to each of these situations and construct a similar model. Some variations include an extension or shortening of the period given to the employee for improvement before dismissal hearings can be launched; a distinction between serious and light disciplinary claims in disciplinary dismissals; or a method to overcome an impasse in negotiations over the list of workers to be dismissed at a time of collective layoffs.

Coordination, leading to similarity in the agreements, is fostered by the fact that there is a single hierarchical agent. Since the launch of the new organising drives, the General Histadrut has established a system in which all enterprise-level collective agreements must conform with its guidelines on wages, organisational matters (such as dismissals)[48] and pensions. Deviations from the general

[46] Interview with the head of the economic dept. in the Histadrut.

[47] The Labor Court held that an employee must be provided with the reason for considering the termination of the employment relationship and the necessary facts to substantiate the alleged reason. The employee must be given enough time to prepare and is allowed to be represented at the hearing. The employer must listen to the employee wholeheartedly and consider the employee's claim in good faith.

[48] Other organisational matters that are heavily coordinated by the General Histadrut include the list of occupations that are exempted from the coverage of the collective agreement, priority in hiring from within the internal labour market (promoting the existing workforce), consultation and bargaining rights, and the industrial peace clause.

guidelines must receive the approval of the higher echelons in the relevant trade union and on occasions even the head of the General Histadrut.[49]

The two remaining agreements are in mid-size companies. One was concluded by the General Histadrut and is structured according to the same template that was created in the agreements of the 'big three'. However, it is weaker on the quantitative aspects. By contrast, in one company (Golan) the collective agreement was concluded with the competing National Histadrut. The quantitative aspect is significantly weaker, as no wage supplements are specified at all, and the organisational chapter extends more flexibility to the employer in hiring and firing. This agreement is strikingly different from the others, reflecting either the economic vulnerability of the particular company, which was in a process of acquisition and regulatory supervision at the time the agreement was concluded, or the more business-accommodating position of the trade union representing the workers there.

To summarise, the 'big three' companies, comprising a large part of the sector (in terms of workers employed), exhibit a form of incremental pattern bargaining that was structured from the bottom up. The organising drives were initiated by the workers themselves, but the workers' committees that were established after the recognition of trade unions' representativeness coordinated their demands. The General Histadrut developed a top-down coordinating method, demanding that the workers' committees negotiate on the basis of the General Histadrut's list of essential claims and economic framework. The agreements in the large companies also dictate the benchmark for the smaller companies. Unorganised companies are few and can be organised if workers wish to do so.

The trade unions have not shown any significant interest in sectoral bargaining, despite the similarity of the existing agreements that could be useful in setting an agreed-upon floor in all the companies. The trade union considers the current incremental (pattern) bargaining to offer an advantageous opportunity to raise the wage floor and improve the trade union's involvement in the companies. That, together with the responsiveness to the workers' interests that are confined to their own company and the possibility of covering the whole sector by organising at each company, removes the trade union's interest, even if negotiations for such an agreement are claimed to be easier. The rival National Histadrut clearly does not want a sectoral agreement, which may crowd it out at the enterprise level as well.[50] Without the unions' direct interest in sectoral bargaining, employers are not reacting by means of a business association, and have not shown any particular interest in minimising the effects of enterprise bargaining by switching to the sectoral level.

[49] Interview with the head of the economic dept. in the Histadrut.

[50] Interview with the head of the cellphone and IT union.

B. The Insurance Sector

The insurance sector was previously almost totally unorganised. Following several organising drives that were initiated by workers in the insurance companies themselves, a number of collective agreements were set in place. While the initial organising drives were supervised by high officials in the Histadrut and the head of the Service Workers Union (Maof; belonging to the General Histadrut), the concentration of new organising in the sector led to the establishment of an Insurance Chapter in the Maof trade union (since 2014).[51]

Unlike the cellphone sector, on the employers' side, there are two relevant associations – the Israeli Insurance Association, which organises all the insurance *companies*, and the Association of Insurance Brokers and Agents in Israel, representing the insurance *agents*. Both are well-established organisations with a comprehensive membership but they do not engage in employment matters. In the past, however, they have signed nationwide collective agreements (for example, with regard to COLA). Furthermore, there are insurance agents who are members of the Chamber of Commerce (a recognised and active employers' association). All of these institutions can evolve over time into an employers' association for the purpose of sectoral bargaining but they do not qualify as such at present.

To understand the current coverage of enterprise agreements, it is important to split up the sector according to several parameters: (a) distinguishing insurance companies from insurance agents; (b) distinguishing traditional insurance companies from direct insurance companies that sidestep the need for an agent; (c) distinguishing insurance companies by size, as large insurance companies may employ 3,000 employees, while a small insurance agency may be a family-run business with a few employees. Collective agreements that were already signed or being negotiated at the time of writing concentrate on the larger and medium-sized companies. These agreements reveal similarities along the same pattern as in the cellphone companies. The same coordination methods that were described in the cellphone sector prevail here as well: (a) incremental pattern bargaining, with one workers' committee learning from another; and (b) hierarchical coordination by the General Histadrut.

Two organising attempts among the insurance companies failed. According to the head of the Insurance Chapter, this is because the workers are satisfied with their working conditions. This implies that the union premium is not significant in comparison to the higher bracket of working conditions prevailing in the sector. The coordination of successful organising drives upscaled working conditions in other insurance companies to the level of the more generous employers in the sector but did not surpass them. This indicates that even in enterprise bargaining, coordination is both driven and constrained by market conditions.

[51] Interview with the head of the insurance chapter in the Histadrut.

When asked about the efficacy of a sectoral agreement, given the similarity among the existing agreements (and the working conditions in the non-organised firms), three considerations were articulated by the trade union. First, two agreements provide a lower level of benefits and organisational protections. One agreement was negotiated with a smaller struggling company. That agreement, it was explained, was the best that could be obtained for and by workers without crowding the company out of the market. A sectoral agreement would likely have had a crowding effect. A second agreement that was concluded with a direct insurance company adapts the wages and organisational protections to the unique composition of the workforce. Most of the workers are employed in call centres and work at a low hourly wage, topped by benefits that are tied to performance (eg, the number of insurance policies sold). A sectoral agreement that is modelled on the composition of the workforce in the large full-fledged insurers may inhibit alternative forms of insurance provision.[52] This is considered to be detrimental to coordination through sectoral bargaining.

Second, it appears that one of the agreements in the large insurance companies is considerably more generous to the workforce than the others. It covers non-traditional issues (eg, affirmative action for people with disabilities, or sorting the rights and duties of workers with regard to privacy on the company's computers and email boxes) and extends benefits that are outside the prevailing norm (eg, with regard to severance pay and pensions). The effect of a sectoral agreement on such a company is uncertain. It may be neutral because it is always possible to supplement the sectoral bargaining with additional organisational rights and wages. Just the same, it may also be negative as a sector-wide agreement may serve as a focal point for negotiations and inhibit negotiations for extraordinary arrangements and supplemental rights.

Finally, the coverage of collective agreements in the insurance sector is considerably lower than in the cellphone sector, but the number of insurance companies is still manageable and can still be organised in the future, thereby reaching a comprehensive coverage level on the basis of enterprise bargaining.[53]

As opposed to the limited number of insurance companies, there are a vast number of insurance agents. Despite sporadic organising in a few of the more established agencies, it is recognised that without a sector-level agreement, the coverage of collective agreements will remain spotty at best. The more established agencies will also be reluctant to raise wages over and above the prevailing norm in the small agencies. Hence, a sectoral agreement may be the only feasible method of coordination among insurance agencies. A sectoral agreement may also make it possible to forge a distinct set of organisational rules and wage norms that are suited to the particular nature of the sector. For example,

[52] ibid.
[53] ibid.

insisting on the prevailing template for dismissals that requires six months' trial for improvement may be too demanding for small establishments. Moving to sectoral coordination can open the door to deliberations and rationalise norms that are better adapted to the sector. At present, however, agencies prefer the sector to remain non-organised, and there are no hard incentives for utilising employers' associations to advance the recognition of joint gains from a sectoral agreement.

To summarise, unlike the cellphone companies, the insurance sector illustrates two important aspects: (a) greater heterogeneity between establishments (size, the nature of the work being conducted and the working methods), and (b) partial coverage. The trade union can achieve some gains by moving to a sectoral agreement, particularly where significant coverage of enterprise bargaining is not feasible (small insurance agencies). There is less interest on the employers' side to develop their institutional capacity, currently lacking, for sector-level negotiations. A concern of both sides is that a sectoral agreement may crowd out some companies, and inhibit technological change that affects the means of service provision in the sector. The various interests may explain the relative lack of consideration for the option of coordination through sectoral bargaining. Coordination among organised companies remains partial when the heterogeneous sector is observed as a whole.

C. The Public Transportation (Bus)Sector

Buses account for approximately 90 per cent of the public transportation in Israel. The bus system was never operated directly by the state as the sector was dominated from its inception by two cooperatives, which later underwent a process of degeneration and started recruiting employees. Both co-ops had collective agreements for their workers, and during the 1990s a two-tiered structure was developed, granting the new generation of hired drivers lesser rights.

In 1997 the state opened existing and new bus routes to competition, and by blocking veteran cooperatives from participating in the competition it opened the sector to new companies. A few years later a procurement process commenced and new bus companies competed over lines previously assigned to the two monopolist co-ops (which were banned from participating). The procurement documents detailed the companies' obligations, including minimum wages for bus drivers. Bus drivers can work in either the public transportation system or in private transport firms (providing on-demand bus rides for tourism, schools, the military and the like). While our focus here will be on the public transportation system – which consists of both the established cooperatives and some of the new private companies – we will later compare it to the separate and distinct on-demand transport firms.[54]

[54] Interview with the coordinator of the transportation union in the Histadrut.

Unlike the drivers in the two large co-ops, all the new public transportation companies that were established after the state's decision in 1997 evolved outside the domain of collective relations. All attempts to organise the transport companies and public transportation after the removal of the Ghent system in 1995 failed.[55] Following the organising drive in Pelephone (cellphone), organising drives started gradually in several public transportation companies. However, the current level of coverage by collective agreements in the public transportation sector (including those that are being negotiated at the time of writing), while relatively high, still falls short of the more comprehensive coverage in the cellphone sector. Moreover, this is a sector where three different unions – the General Histadrut, the National Histadrut and Power to the Workers – are somewhat equally active in organising and negotiating. Consequently, inter-union rivalry is common.

The new agreements in the sector, and to some extent the collective agreements that were concluded in the two large cooperatives, share one important similarity in common – the drivers' wages. This is because the minimum wage established by the procurement system has become the de facto maximum wage as well. Because the public transportation companies compete for bus routes, their offers are assessed according to several measures of quality and costs. The cost factor is crucial and a company cannot realistically compete if it raises the drivers' wages. At the time of writing the wages that appear in all the collective agreements, as well as in individual contracts in the non-unionised companies, are 39 NIS per hour (equivalent to 145 per cent of the statutory minimum wage). All other wage components are standardised as well and are equivalent to the minima in the procurement documents or the statutory minima (overtime, working hours on days of rest, convalescence pay).[56] Non-regulated benefits (subsidised meals, holiday gifts and other company welfare benefits) are at relatively negligible sums, with slight differences between the companies. The trade unions have little or no leverage to raise labour costs over and above the minima that are established in the procurement documents and in statute.

With regard to the qualitative (organisational) aspects in the collective agreements, there are variations. As regards protection from dismissals, some of the agreements allow a flexible and easy dismissal process, while others are more in line with the General Histadrut's common protocol for the three types of dismissal. There are variations between trade unions, and over time. However, current negotiations adhere to the General Histadrut's protocol and there is a recognisable process of incremental emulation.

The identical wages and labour costs in the different companies could justify a sectoral agreement. Despite their strong competition, the public transportation companies also have shared interests. Because of a state-wide shortage of

[55] Alon-Shenker and Davidov (n 45).

[56] Interview with the coordinator of the transportation union in the Histadrut.

drivers, the public transportation companies, usually in competition with each other, established in 2015 a business association to pressure the state to raise the wages established in the procurement documents as a means of attracting new drivers. The association's efforts (backed by drivers' organising) to raise the wages and subsidies were successful, enabling a wage hike from 32 NIS per hour (123 per cent of the minimum wage at the time) to 39 NIS per hour (145 per cent of the minimum wage at present).[57]

Despite what seems to be fertile ground for coordination and joint action on both sides, there is no discussion of a sector-level agreement. Several explanations can be inferred indirectly from the interviews. First, there is a sense that the sector is gradually reaching comprehensive coverage similar to that of the cellphone sector. Although organising drives in the sector on an enterprise basis drains the trade unions' resources due to employers' resistance and inter-union rivalry, collective agreements are becoming the norm of the sector. Moreover, the trade union informants explained that they view the procurement process as the major target for change. This, they explain, they can achieve as political lobbyists, together with the employers, and do not need the coordinating method of sectoral bargaining. The workers' committees in the various companies, despite rivalry between the trade unions, sought to draw on their joint industrial power but as they prepared for a state-wide strike the procurement wages were raised at the last moment, rendering further coordinated action unnecessary. Hence, the trade unions concede the benefits of formal coordination but exhibit optimism as regards alternative and available strategies such as enterprise bargaining and political lobbying.

Another tension that accounts for the hesitant attitude towards a sectoral agreement is rooted in two conflicting interests. On the trade union side there is an interest in creating a continuity of employment rights when drivers move from one company to another, particularly when one company loses its routes to another company. The uniform wage in the sector allows easy transitions of drivers from one company to another. Such coordination can only be achieved by means of a sector-level agreement as it requires arrangements that are external to any particular company.[58] At the same time, the shortage of drivers leads to increased investment in bus companies that offer driving courses and entry bonuses to attract new drivers. Consequently, on the employers' side, there is an interest in retaining workers and preventing transitions, and they are therefore opposed to sector-wide coordination. Hence, the uniform wages in the sector serve not only as an incentive for sectoral bargaining, but also as a deterrent to it.

[57] ibid.

[58] For example, sectoral seniority was recently negotiated in the cleaning and security sector-level agreements and has appeared for a long time in the construction sector agreement.

The deterrents to formalised sectoral coordination in the public transportation sector can be highlighted by a different dynamic in the on-demand transport sector. A few hundred companies operate transport services, operating different types of vehicles – from minivans to luxury tour buses. The wages and working conditions are generally at a lower level than those of the public transportation sector. The working schedules are also different. However, despite the variance, which may seem to be a deterrent to sectoral bargaining, a sector-wide agreement was concluded.[59] This exceptional agreement in a previously unorganised sector was the result of distinct interests. On the trade union side, the number of companies and their diverse sizes render them more difficult to organise. On the employers' side, there is an interest of the larger transport companies to self-regulate the field and to crowd out the smaller companies that discount on labour costs, inter alia by means of avoiding minimum statutory standards.

To summarise, the regulatory basis to which the public transportation companies are bound serves as the primary coordinating mechanism in the sector. The existing organising drives operate within very strict margins, and differences in the content of agreements are due to competing trade unions but have a lesser impact on the payroll. The homogeneity of the primary occupation in the sector (bus drivers), severe shortage of bus drivers, and the need for labour–management coordination vis-à-vis the government are all considered to be an incentive for sector-level cooperation. Coordination among the trade unions and employers is mostly at the political level and not at the bargaining table. The option of sectoral bargaining is deterred by competition and rivalry over drivers. By contrast, coordination is sought in the adjacent sector of on-demand transport companies. The fragmentation and heterogeneity created an incentive for coordination in an effort to secure workers' rights as part of the joint interest of some employers and the trade unions to prevent a race to the bottom.

D. Youth in the Hospitality (Fast Food, Restaurant and Reception Halls) Sector

The fast food sector was chosen for the study because of the trade union's purposeful and proactive consideration of moving from enterprise bargaining to the sector level. The relevant trade union is the youth branch of the Histadrut. It is a unique trade union that operates at a distance from the central headquarters, and is also part of a youth movement (Study and Work Youth) that was

[59] Following primary interviews with the coordinator of the transportation union in the Histadrut, a sectoral agreement was signed in the transport sector, in July 2017.

established alongside the state's apprenticeship system in the 1950s.[60] Over the years, the apprenticeship system was dissolved and the youth movement now deals mostly with social organisation of youth throughout the country. Sticking to its original objective, it also offers individual aid and legal representation to working youth and engages in lobbying regarding working youth in the Knesset, Israel's parliament.[61]

The leading assumption motivating organising was that a stronger presence of the trade union in establishments that commonly employ youth can increase compliance – through a joint mechanism of rights enforcement. To that extent, the major target was the fast food chains which commonly employ high-school students and young adults. These chains were not organised until recently. At the same time, other attempts at organising were made in catering services that are operated by reception halls, grocery chains and restaurants.[62] In all of these economic fields, employment is usually on an hourly basis, short term and unskilled, with few opportunities for advancement. The few existing collective agreements that have been negotiated, as well as the sector-level agreement at the reception halls, can be described as 'minimum plus' agreements. They guarantee minimum wage and a slight improvement in wages after several months of work. The agreements address common problems that youth face in these jobs, such as being 'on call' and the requirement that they show up for work on short notice; the number of shifts they are assigned; and a guarantee of a minimum number of hours for which they must be compensated. Other issues include a subsidised meal at work, social activities and a reward programme. At the qualitative level, the agreements provide for respecting the law on good faith in dismissals and leave intact the managerial prerogative on all matters. They also provide several side-benefits, such as the opportunity for the employers to hire by using an internet-based employment service that is managed by the trade union.

Interviews revealed that the agreements' purpose is to enable the trade union to set a foot in the workplace and provide an opportunity to act from within to improve compliance. To that end, the agreements establish a parity commission that is responsible for periodic inspection of wages and complaints. The trade union's actual presence in such establishments is unprecedented and viewed as a necessary stepping stone towards greater representational power in the future.[63]

From the employers' point of view, there are two components to the costs associated with these agreements: (a) the marginal progression of wages and welfare benefits, and (b) the costs of increased compliance with the minimum legal standards. From the unions' point of view, the effects of greater compliance are claimed to be twofold: within the collective domain and outside it.

[60] https://noal.org.il/about/noal.
[61] https://noal.org.il/about/avoda.
[62] Interview with the head of the trade union dept. in the Work and Study Youth Movement.
[63] ibid.

The secured and formalised access of employees to the trade union explains the former. These agreements also impact non-union establishments as the result of a spillover effect. First, youth who are moving from one workplace to another take with them the knowledge they have gained and the sense of entitlement to their wages and benefits. Second, employers who are concerned that they may become the target of an organising drive may try to demonstrate compliance with minimum rights, thereby refuting the trade union's claim that organising is necessary to satisfy the workers' rights.[64]

Given the numerous employers in the hospitality and restaurant sectors and the similar problems encountered by young workers in the various sectors, there is a significant advantage to a broad sectoral agreement. To overcome the employers' resistance, the union deliberately chose to organise the biggest fast food chains first. High public visibility should encourage these employers to act as leaders in the field, subsequently to be emulated by smaller employers. This strategy succeeded with two employers, but the attempts to negotiate an agreement in two others failed, including the symbolic attempt at organising at McDonalds, which is the largest and most visible chain.

A sector-wide agreement with an extension order is the only way to forge new norms for the sector. Enterprise bargaining can only serve as a launching pad or a model for others to follow. There are, however, two complications with such a strategy. First, there already is a sector-wide agreement with an extension order for reception halls (last negotiated in 2006). The 'minimum plus' agreement has the advantage of directly addressing some of the contested problems in the sector – the relationship between tips and wages, number of hours (minimum and maximum), night work and the like.[65] As noted at the outset, however, when the major problem in the sector is slack compliance, then the negotiations at the sectoral level are too far removed from daily practices to address the problem. Second, coordinating for the purpose of extending protection for youth requires a very broad notion of a sector that cuts across various establishments but with no tradition of being recognised as an industrial sector to target. The variations among the relevant establishments extend beyond just the focus on the employment of youth. Indeed, the current state of organising demarcates between fast food chains, coffee chains, reception halls and restaurants.

To summarise, as regards the work of youth, the hospitality sector is one in which enterprise bargaining is scarce and the main mechanism of coordination is the minimum statutory wages and benefits towards which agreements gravitate. There are no real substitutes for the coordination offered by sector-wide agreements in these sector(s). Coordination is visible in the programme

[64] ibid.

[65] Such sectoral agreements in the past had one major advantage – the guarantee of pension. However, since 2008 there has been a state-wide collective agreement with an extension order that secures pension for all employees in the country. The contribution of the sectoral agreement in this respect is therefore no longer of much importance.

developed by the trade union, but problems in carrying out the actual organising have not enabled it to carry out the strategy. Moreover, even if sectoral agreements can be concluded, they will not solve the overarching problem of lacking compliance.

V. CONCLUSION: INSERTING COORDINATION IN DECENTRALISED BARGAINING

With the decline in membership, trade unions are constantly seeking ways to extend their influence. There is a growing interest in organising workers in countries where such practices were neglected in the past, partially because of the broad coverage of collective agreements. Trade unions relied on the convenience of coordinated bargaining and were not sufficiently active in the field. But as trade unions are starting to correct past practices, organising drives are happening at the enterprise level.[66] It has been claimed that these organising drives contribute to the revitalisation of trade unions and considerably change the meaning of membership in and identification with the trade union as an agent that aids workers in actively pursuing shared goals. But with the enthusiasm over new enterprise bargaining, the advantages of coordinated bargaining across firms, within sectors and across sectors are being neglected. The current study has sought to identify partial coordination mechanisms in sectors where there are clusters of enterprise agreements, and to understand whether they can substitute for the traditional coordination of a sector-level agreement.

The strongest forms of coordination, leading to an almost complete substitute for a sectoral agreement, was found in the cellphone and insurance (providers, as opposed to agencies) sectors. These are characterised by:

(a) Coverage: almost full coverage of the sector and potentially even fully comprehensive coverage, given the finite number of establishments.
(b) Vertical coordination: the largest union dominates organising in the sector and is therefore responsible for most of the agreements. Internal hierarchy, a newly established policy on the General Histadrut's demands in bargaining and de facto organisational oversight of the negotiations all lead to a high level of uniformity.
(c) Horizontal coordination: workers' committees that are active in the organisation drives share information; workers are informed through Facebook groups and are well aware of what workers in competing firms receive. There is an incremental pattern bargaining, although not in the American

[66] Mundlak (n 10). Paul De-Beer and Maarten Keune, 'Dutch Unions in a Time of Crisis' in Steffen Lehndorff, Heiner Dribbusch and Thorsten Schulten (eds), *Rough Waters: European Trade Unions in Time of Crisis* (Brussels: ETUI, 2016).

sense, or in the form of a strategically organised Blitz (ie, simultaneous proactive organising by the trade union), because the trade union does not push to cover the sector and remains responsive to local initiatives.

(d) Market mechanisms serve for the purpose of coordination. Market-related institutions, such as a private company that provides detailed information on the prevailing wage levels (for a fee), and market constraints (level of competition, labour supply) prescribe the brackets that define the space for negotiations.

Another form of coordination was found in the public transportation sector, which adds to some of the above-listed components another option:

(e) Strong state regulation of the sector limits the space of negotiations, leading to a greater level of coordination in bargaining.

The forms of coordination are compared in Table 4.1.

Table 4.1 Comparison of the forms of coordination in the four sectors

	A Coverage	**B Vertical coordination**	**C Horizontal coordination**	**D Market mechanisms**	**E State regulation**
Cellphone sector HIGH	Comprehensive	One dominant union	Emulation by strong workers' committees	Information on wages on both the labour and management sides	No
Insurance companies MEDIUM-HIGH	Partial, but potentially comprehensive	One dominant union, but this may be changing	Emulation by strong workers' committees; variations between companies due to different modes of operation and size	Information on wages on both the labour and management sides	Strongly regulated sector that requires transparency, although not necessarily with regard to labour conditions of most workers. A 'culture of response' to regulation

(continued)

Table 4.1 *(Continued)*

	A Coverage	B Vertical coordination	C Horizontal coordination	D Market mechanisms	E State regulation
Insurance agencies LOW	Very low and with no potential for full coverage	One dominant union, but this may be changing	Unknown at present	General market conditions. No particular method of coordination	Not regulated
Public transportation HIGH	Gradually becoming comprehensive	Multiple and competing unions	Some coordination, but partially inhibited by inter-union rivalry	Heavily regulated market	
Transport companies LOW	None → a sector agreement was concluded				
Fast food chains LOW	Low	One union, but concentration and fragmentation are applied	Weaker workers' committees. Major role is that of vertical coordination	Mostly around minimum wages and employment standards	None
Reception halls HIGH but slack enforcement	Scarce at the enterprise level **but there is a sector-level agreement**	One union	Weaker workers' committees. Major role is that of vertical coordination	Mostly around minimum wages and employment standards	None

The effects of the various mechanisms are difficult to quantify with precision. To the extent that coordination is expected to govern and equalise working conditions in the sector, there are indirect effects of enterprise bargaining, with partial coverage in the sector as a whole. For example, despite low levels of organising in the fast food sector, there is a spillover effect on employers who seek to improve compliance with prevailing norms to prevent further organising attempts. Similarly, in the public transportation sector, where there is a shortage of drivers, unorganised companies cannot avoid the norms that have developed in the organised segment because drivers will prefer alternative employment opportunities.

To summarise, coordination that evolves from enterprise bargaining ranges from low to high, and is usually based on a conjunction of several factors. The more factors that are operating together, the higher is the level of coordination that can be reached.

Where the level of coordination is high, a sector-level agreement may be redundant. It may reduce transaction costs and relieve some of the tension between employers and employees that characterises enterprise bargaining (cellphone and insurance companies). It can also aid in establishing a strong political basis that brings together employers and employees to lobby for political change (public transportation). But nonetheless, a sectoral agreement will not increase coordination levels in these sectors.

At the other extreme, where coordination is low, a sectoral agreement is necessary. The major factor responsible for the low levels of coordination and uniformity in the sector is the low level of coverage. Hence, this is crucial for insurance agencies, on-demand transport companies, and the fast food chains (and similar fields). These sectors feature at least some of the following characteristics: multiple employers, differentiation in employers' sizes and modes of operation, constrained profit margins and a surplus of labour supply. Another gain that can be achieved in sectoral agreements is when there is a need to coordinate employment standards across the boundaries of the firm, particularly in sectors where the workforce is highly mobile. This was demonstrated with regard to the public and on-demand transport sectors.

While sectoral agreements remain a useful form of coordination, they also have some disadvantages that can be partially addressed through enterprise bargaining. For example, a sectoral agreement may inhibit the development of new forms of service provisions (eg, the direct insurance companies, or the smaller and leaner cellphone companies); it may crowd out weaker companies (eg, insurance); and cannot function without a strong organisational basis at the enterprise level that ensures compliance (reception halls). Even as we recommend reconsidering the neglect of sectoral bargaining, it is important to be remindful of its drawbacks. Mirroring the challenge of coordination is the challenge of creating an active culture of solidarity and activism at the shop floor level.

5

Unions and On-demand Work in the United States

KATHERINE V.W. STONE

I. WORKING TIME STRUGGLES IN AMERICAN LABOUR HISTORY

WORKING TIME HAS been an animating issue for the American labour movement since its early days. From the 1820s until the 1850s, the animating goal of labour organisations was the Ten Hour Day. After the Civil War, labour unions began to rally around demand for the Eight Hour Day. In 1884, the Federation of Organized Trades and Labor Unions, which later became the American Federation of Labor (AFL), proclaimed that 'eight hours shall constitute a legal day's labour from and after May 1, 1886'. Two years later, the bloody Haymarket massacre in Chicago 1886 began as a rally to support workers striking for the eight-hour day. By the end of the nineteenth century, the AFL and many of its largest affiliated unions called for the eight-hour day and, by the early twentieth century, some had achieved it. The issue continued to be a rallying cry for organised labour until 1938, when the US Congress enacted the Fair Labor Standards Act, implicitly adopting the eight-hour day by requiring time-and-a-half pay for overtime after 40 hours of work per week.

Working time again became controversial in the 1990s in the US and Europe when women began to demand flexible hours in order to accommodate child care and other care work needs. Some countries in Europe, particularly the Netherlands, instituted reforms to enable women to move in and out of part-time work as their family situations so demanded, and to ensure that they received parity in pay and benefits when they did so.[1] And in some countries, labour unions have relaxed contractual restrictions on working hours and requirements

[1] See Jelle Visser, 'Flexibility and Security in Post-Standard Employment Relations: The Netherlands' in Katherine VW Stone and Harry Arthurs (eds), *Rethinking Employment Regulation: Beyond the Standard Contract of Employment* (Russell Sage Foundation, 2013).

to pay overtime and made working time regulations more flexible in order to accommodate workers' family needs.

Working time flexibility has proven to be a two-edged sword. For example, in the 1990s in Germany, some of the largest unions agreed to 'time corridors' by which local unions, and in some cases individual workers, could negotiate for working time arrangements that deviated from the contractually set overtime rules.[2] While it proved beneficial to some workers, many commentators warned that, by relaxing working time restrictions, these time corridors enabled employers to undermine hard-won rights to overtime pay.[3]

In Japan, changes to working time legislation to provide more flexibility have been a boon for employers more than for workers. From 1947, Japan, like all industrialised countries, had working hours legislation that mandated a set number of hours in the work week and that overtime be paid for time worked over the statutory maximum. In 1987, a new law introduced a flex-time scheme by which workers could determine their hours flexibly and overtime would be calculated on the basis of hours worked in a statutorily set accounting period rather than on a daily basis. Under this provision, employers are required to pay an overtime premium for hours worked over the maximum during the accounting period, which can be defined as a month or even longer. Since 1990, the number of firms adopting the flexible hours system has increased dramatically. As of 2006, nearly 70 per cent of firms with 1,000 employees or more had a flex-time system in place, covering nearly 50 per cent of their workforce.[4] The Japanese flex-time scheme enabled employers to avoid paying overtime premiums.

II. CURRENT CONTROVERSIES OVER WORKING TIME

In the past few years, controversies over working time have erupted again, but in a new form. Today the concept of a 'working day' as having a defined period of time and a work week having fixed schedule has been up-ended as employers have instituted 'on-demand' work. In one sense, most US workers are already 'on demand' in that they can be hired or fired anytime at the whim of their employer. That is, the American at-will employment contract has no fixed duration but is rather a minute-to-minute arrangement that is subject to renewal or

[2] See Harry Katz and Owen Darbershire, *Converging Divergences* (Cornell University Press, 2000) 177–80.

[3] See eg, Reinhard Bispinck, 'Germany: Working Time and Its Negotiation' in Maarten Keune and Béla Galgóczi (eds), *Collective Bargaining on Working Time: Recent European Experiences* (ETUI, 2006).

[4] See, Japan Institute for Labour Policy and Training, 'Discretionary Labor System' in *Labor Situation in Japan and Analysis: Detailed Exposition 2005/2006*, at 59. The Ministry of Labor found that the percentage of firms adopting the simpler flex-time scheme had increased from 13 per cent in 1990, to 40.5 per cent in 1996, to 58.5 per cent in 2006.

cancellation at every moment of the working day.[5] But the current controversies about 'on-demand' work centre not on the circumstances of hiring and firing, but on the question of who determines the time for the performance of the work itself. Rather than having fixed hours, on-demand workers have hours that vary from day to day, sometimes at their choice and sometimes at their employer's command. An additional development that confounds conventional notions of working time arises from the fact that work today often takes place outside the employer's premises – at home, coffee shops, one's own car, etc. – thereby blurring the line between work time and non-work time.

There are two types of on-demand workers, each of which has distinctive characteristics and raises distinct problems for labour regulation. First, there is on-demand work that an employer imposes on a worker who would prefer a fixed, regular schedule. This is *involuntary* on-demand work, and it is becoming increasingly common in the retail, restaurant and hospitality industries. Employers that utilise just-in-time staffing inform workers on a day-to-day or week-to-week basis of which hours they will work on the following day or week. The other type of on-demand work is *voluntary* in the sense that workers choose their own hours, working as many as they want each day. Most voluntary on-demand work is coordinated by computer platforms such as Uber, Task Rabbit, Mechanical Turk and the like. Voluntary on-demand workers typically work on their own time and in their own spaces, whether their homes, cars or local coffee shops.

On the surface, just-in-time work and digital platform work are very different from each other. The former workers have involuntary variable schedules while the latter workers relish their voluntary time flexibility. However, they are both aspects of a larger phenomenon – the radical transformation of work.

The recent explosion of both types of on-demand work represents an extreme form of the larger trend toward the casualisation of work. In the past, when you had a job, you expected it to last indefinitely and expected your employer to provide a steady income, predictable advancement opportunities and a reasonable package of benefits that included health insurance, sick days, some paid vacation time and retirement benefits. Jobs today are very different. They are provisional, not in the legal sense, but in the practical sense that lifetime job security has vanished. Moreover, while jobs in the past offered fixed pay rates, with a regularised system of wage increases and clear paths for promotion, they do not do so today. Today pay is likely to be variable, dependent on one's weekly or monthly performance. And most jobs offer few, if any, benefits.[6]

[5] For an explication and analysis of the American at-will employment relationship, see Katherine VW Stone, 'Revisiting the At-Will Employment Doctrine: Imposed Terms, Implied Terms, and the Normative World of the Workplace' (2007) 36(1) *Industrial Law Journal* 84–101.

[6] For a history, description, and analysis of the changing nature of work, see Katherine VW Stone, *From Widgets to Digits: Employment Regulation for the Changing Workplace* (Cambridge University Press, 2004).

Moreover, many jobs today no longer fit the mould of a simple bilateral employment relationship defined by an explicit and implicit set of terms. Many workers have multiple employers, often with ad hoc schedules. Many work off site, or move from site to site, and never even see or know who is their putative 'employer'. Many work for subcontractors on a long and complex supply chain. Others are regularly on site at a particular workplace and have specified hours but are classified as 'independent contractors'.

In addition, many jobs today do not take the form of a direct relationship between a worker and an employer. Rather, a firm may hire a worker to be part of a team for a particular project, with the explicit understanding that the job only lasts until the project is completed. Firms have also increased their use of temporary workers through agencies and other third-party intermediaries, even for tasks that extend over a lengthy period of time. And many firms have replaced regular 'employees' with 'independent contractors' – ie workers who are not considered employees at all. Even when firms hire for an open-ended position, today they are usually explicit, at the time of hire, that the position is at will and the worker can be let go at any time. And many jobs have no fixed period of working time.

Workers in these new employment arrangements face problems that are not easily addressed by existing labour and employment laws. Below I describe the problems posed by new flexible forms of work and then turn to the question of how unions and public policies might address them.

A. Involuntary Flexible Work and Just-in-time Scheduling

Firms in the retail and hospitality industry utilise complex algorithms that enable them to predict staffing needs based on predicted customer flow at every point in time. They use these algorithms to minimise personnel costs. Thus, instead of giving their workers a fixed schedule, they give them schedules that can change on short notice. A *New York Times* editorial in 2015 reported that, 'According to federal data, 66 percent of food service workers, 52 percent of retail workers and 40 percent of janitors and house cleaners have at most a week's notice of their schedules'.[7] Under variable scheduling, individual in any given week could work five hours on a Monday, four hours on Tuesday, none on Wednesday, seven on Thursday, none on Friday or Saturday, and four on Sunday. Moreover, that individual might not know until the prior week what her schedule will be for the week coming up.

Retail giants use complex software, often provided by specialty workforce management firms, to predict their staffing needs so that they never have more employees than necessary on any given day. One leading firm boasts that it can

[7] Editorial, 'When Bosses Schedule Hours That Just Don't Work', *NY Times* (1 September 2015).

predict staffing demand in 15-minute intervals so that there are never excess staff, even for a few minutes.[8] Just-in-time scheduling has become widespread in restaurants, hotels and retail establishments.

Just-in-time scheduling is brutal for employees. Employees in the retail sector complain that they cannot plan their lives. They report that it is impossible to arrange child care when one does not know what hours one will be working. Moreover, because most retail work is part time and extremely low paid, those workers who want to take second jobs or enrol in training programmes cannot do so because of their constantly shifting and unpredictable hours.

B. Voluntary Flexible Work: The Rise of Digital Platform Workers

Voluntary flexible workers provide on-demand services to customers in accord with parameters established by digital platforms. The workers usually decide themselves, on a daily or hourly basis, when to work and when not to. Workers for digital platforms provide transportation, deliver goods or perform tasks such as household chores or dog walking, usually on a one-off basis. Typically, the workers, many of whom work for more than one digital platform, do not get the customers themselves, nor do they determine the pricing for their services. Rather, the digital platform sets the fees, charges the customers and provides the workers with their remuneration. The workers, however, frequently use their own tools and equipment, and decide which hours and how many hours they want to work each day. Some of the familiar on-demand platform services are Uber, Lyft, Task Rabbit, InstaCart, Handy, GetMaid, ZingyPet and Postmates. Hundreds of new ones spring up daily in cities around the globe. The outer boundary of the category is fuzzy – some observers include Airbnb and Ebay as part of the 'On Demand economy'.[9]

On-demand work for digital platforms raises many difficult issues under the labour and employment laws. Most prominently, platform work poses the question of whether the workers are 'employees' under the labour and employment laws. Because platform workers typically choose their hours and provide their own materials, the companies that utilise them claim that they are independent contractors, not employees under the labour laws. Yet, platform workers differ from conventional independent contractors because they are subject to the selection, direction, monitoring and discipline of an employing entity.

There has been litigation in many states about how on-demand platform workers should be classified. In 2015 the California Commissioner of Labor found that an Uber driver was an employee and entitled to the benefit of state

[8] www.kronos.com/Scheduling-Software/Labor-Forecasting-Software.aspx.

[9] 'There's an app for that – Freelance workers available at a moment's notice will reshape the nature of companies and the structure of careers', *The Economist*, 30 December 2014.

labour laws regarding expense reimbursement.[10] Not long thereafter, the New York Labor Department ruled that two Uber drivers were entitled to workers' compensation under New York law.[11] Also, the National Labor Relations Board (NLRB) has several cases that pose the question of whether Uber or Post-mate drivers are entitled to the National Labor Relations Act's (NLRA) protection for engaging in collective action.

At stake in the on-demand employee status litigation is whether Uber, Lyft and other platform workers will be entitled to the benefits and protections of federal and state laws guaranteeing overtime pay, minimum wages, expense reimbursement, rest breaks, workers' compensation, unemployment compensation, social security, protection against discrimination, or the right to form a union, should the drivers win. Moreover, if they are found to be independent contractors, then any collective action they might take to improve their working conditions could expose them to antitrust liability.

i. The Threshold Question: Are Gig Workers Employees?

Under US law there is no uniform test for distinguishing employees from independent contractors. Different employment statutes and different courts apply different variants of either an agency test or an economic realities test. Both approaches lead to inconsistent and unpredictable results.

For example, the federal minimum wage law is famously circular. It defines an 'employee' as 'any individual employed by an employer',[12] and it defines 'employer' as 'any person acting directly or indirectly in the interest of an employer in relation to an employee'.[13] It further states that 'employ' is meant 'to include to suffer or permit to work'.[14] Despite the linguistic circularity, the Supreme Court has stated that definitions under the Act are to be construed broadly and that employee status is determined by an 'economic realities test' rather than the narrower common law agency test.[15] Specifically, courts look beyond the question, central to the common law agency test, of who controls the employee's work, and look instead to whether, as a matter of economic reality,

[10] *Barbara Ann Berwick v Uber Corp.*, 2015 WL 4153765 (CA.Dept.Lab., 2015). Uber filed an appeal, and then in November 2016, the case was settled without an admission of fault or liability by either party. Order Granting Stipulation to Dismiss Case with Prejudice, San Francisco County Superior Court, November 22, 2016.

[11] Noam Scheiber, 'St. Rules 2 Uber Drivers Eligible for Jobless Pay', *NY Times*, 12 October 2016, www.nytimes.com/2016/10/13/business/state-rules-2-former-uber-drivers-eligible-for-jobless-payments.html.

[12] 29 USC 203(e)(1).

[13] 29 USC 202(a).

[14] 29 USC 203(g).

[15] *Rutherford Food Corp. v McComb*, 331 US 722, 728–29 (1947). See also, *Nationwide Mut. Ins. v Darden*, 503 US 381, 326 (1992) (recognising the 'striking breadth' of definition of 'employ' under Fair Labor Standards Act).

the individual is dependent on the entity.[16] In applying the 'economic reality test,' courts have stated that the following factors are relevant to determine whether an employment relationship exists for purposes of the Fair Labor Standards Act (FLSA): whether the putative employer has the right to hire, fire and set daily working conditions; whether the worker is paid by the hour, week or month, instead of a set amount for completing a specific job; whether the worker receives benefits; the extent to which the work was a part of an integrated process; the degree of skill required to perform the work; the permanence of the working relationship; whether the worker has invested in the business; whether the putative employer owned the premises and equipment where the work was performed; whether the services are integral to the business; the putative employer's amount and degree of control over the work process; the employee's liability for loss or profit; the employee's initiative, judgement or foresight in open market competition; and the degree that the work is an independent operation.[17] No one factor is dispositive – the totality of the circumstances is considered and courts must engage in a 'particularized inquiry into the facts of each case'.[18] In practice, as with all multi-factor tests, the FLSA test for employee status is applied in different ways by different courts depending upon which factors are emphasised and how the factors are weighted.

Some state courts, in interpreting their state labour laws, use an agency test rather than an economic realities test that looks at who has the right to control the work. But there too, the outcome is usually uncertain. For example, until 1989, the California Supreme Court applied a right-to-control test but it elaborated the test to require not just control, but 'control of the details'. Thus, in California, a worker was an independent contractor only if the worker had the right to 'control the manner and means of accomplishing the desired result'.[19] The California Court also added additional factors, such as whether the putative employer has the right to hire and fire at will, which party provides the tools and place of work, the skill required and whether the person performing services is engaged in a distinct occupation or business.[20] Then, in 1989, in *Borello v Department of Industrial Relations*, the California Supreme Court modified its expanded agency test by proclaiming that the test must be applied in a manner that was consistent with the remedial and protective purposes of the statute under consideration.[21] The new approach broadened the category of employee

[16] See generally, *Bartels v Birmingham*, 332 US 126, 130 (1947) (describing multi-factor economic realities test for determining employee status); *US v Silk*, 331 US 704, 716 (1947).

[17] *Rutherford*, 331 US at 729–30; *Baker v Flint Engineering & Construction Co.*, 137 F.3d 1439 (10th Cir. 1998). See also *Herman v RSR Security Services, Ltd.*, 172 F.3d 132 (2d Cir. 1999) (adopting a four-factor economic realities test).

[18] *Goldberg v Whitaker House Corp.*, 366 US 28, 33 (1961). See also, *Danneskjod v Hausrath*, 82 F.3d 37, 39 (2d Cir. 1996), *Carter v Dutchess Community College*, 735 F.2d 8 (2d Cir. 1984).

[19] See, eg, *Tieberg v Unemployment Insurance*, 949. App. Bd., 2 Cal.3d 943, 946 (1970).

[20] ibid at 949.

[21] *Borello v Dept. of Industrial Relations*, 48 Cal,. 3rd 341 (1989).

by adding factors such as the degree of permanence of the job, the investment of the alleged employee, and the opportunity for having a profit or loss. It also adopted a presumption that 'any person "in service to another" is a "covered employee."'[22] *Borello* thereby expanded the category of employee and hence the reach of the state labour laws.

In 2018 the California Supreme Court again modified the test for terming employee status in a case that has direct relevance to workers utilised by on-demand platforms. In *Dynamex Operations v Superior Court*,[23] a case involving drivers for a package delivery service, the Court adopted what has been termed the 'ABC test', which it barrowed from Massachusetts. Under the ABC test, for a hiring entity to successfully claim that a worker is an independent contractor, it must establish:

(A) that the worker is free from the control and direction of the hiring entity in connection with the performance of the work, both under the contract for performance of the work and in fact:
(B) that the worker performs work that is outside the usual course of the hiring entity's business; *and*
(C) that the worker is customarily engaged in an independently established trade, occupation, or business of the same nature as the work performed.[24]

Although *Dynamex* did not involve on-demand workers, the ABC test adopted by the California Court has important implications for the gig economy. Under the test, the hiring entity must establish all three prongs. The second prong – that the 'work that is outside the usual course of the hiring entity's business' – will prove to be problematic for most on-demand companies. The California Court itself gives as an example of a situation that satisfies the prong a case in which a retail store hires a plumber to repair a leak in a bathroom on its premises. Clearly, in that case, the plumber is not part of the company's usual course of business. But for Uber, drivers are the centrepiece of its business so that, under the ABC test, the drivers would be classified as 'employees'. *Dynamex* was a recent case so it is too soon to know how courts will apply the new test to on-demand platform workers, but it is likely to change outcome in a many situations.[25]

ii. Do We Need a Third Category?

Some analysts have argued that workers who get their task assignments from computer platforms represent a new type of worker that fits neither

[22] ibid at 354.
[23] *Dynamex Operations v Superior Court*, 416 P.3d 1 (Cal. 2018).
[24] ibid at 7.
[25] In a post-*Dynamex* case, the California District Court ruled that a gig worker for the online food delivery company was likely to succeed on the merits in his claim that he was an employee, based on the ABC test adopted in *Dynamex*. *Lawson v Grubhead, Inc.*, 2018 WL 2735400 (2018). The issue is currently on appeal to the Ninth Circuit Court of Appeals. *Lawson v Grubhub*, Case No. 15-CV-05128 JSC.

the category of employee nor independent contractor.[26] For example, Seth Harris and Alan Kruger argue that there should be a new category called 'independent worker', comprised of individuals who would be entitled to some of the rights but not all the protections available to employees.[27] Others have objected to these proposals, claiming that to add a new category would compound the problem of misclassification and uncertainty by encouraging even more deceptive efforts by hiring entities to manipulate the categories. If there were three categories instead of two, sceptics contend, there will be more disputes and litigation about which of the categories any individual working relationship fits.[28]

Several countries have adopted a third category with mixed results. It has proven to be difficult to define a new category with sufficient precision to avoid manipulation or to achieve consensus about which employment rights to give independent workers.[29] In the US it would take legislation to create such a category and it is unlikely that such legislation can be enacted in light of today's political realities.

III. ADDRESSING THE PROBLEMS OF FLEXIBLE WORKERS

As discussed above, involuntary on-demand workers have serious problems stemming from their unpredictable schedules and fluctuating incomes. Voluntary on-demand workers also have fluctuating incomes. They also lack any protections for safety, industrial accident protection, social insurance, protection against discrimination or guarantee of a minimum wage. Both groups have uncertain incomes, no job security and no stable package of benefits. Below I discuss some approaches that could ameliorate these problems.

A. Involuntary Flexible Workers

Just-in-time workers in the retail, restaurant and hospitality fields are considered 'employees' and are hence eligible for the benefits and protections of the labour

[26] See generally, Miriam A Cherry and Antonio Aloisi, 'Dependent Contractors' in the Gig Economy: A Comparative Approach' (2017) 66 *American University Law Review* 635, 646–50 (recounting proposals for adopting a third category between employee and independent contractor to address issues involving non-standard workers).

[27] Seth A Harris and Alan B Kruger, *A Proposal for Modernizing Labor Laws for Twenty-First-Century Work: The 'Independent Worker'*, Hamilton Project Discussion Paper 2015-10, December 2015. Available at www.hamiltonproject.org/assets/files/modernizing_labor_laws_for_twenty_first_century_work_krueger_harris.pdf. See also, Lauren Weber, 'What if There were a New Type of Worker?' *Wall Street Journal* (28 January 2015).

[28] See eg, Ben Sachs, 'Do We Need an "Independent Worker" Category?' *On Labor* (8 December 2015). See generally, Cherry and Aloisi (n 26).

[29] See Cherry and Aloisi (n 26).

laws. However, at present, no law requires an employer to provide regular or predictable hours. Some retail workers have organised protests in their efforts to obtain fair scheduling legislation at the state and federal level to address their concerns. For example, in New York City, the Retail Action Coalition, affiliated with the Retail, Wholesale, and Department Store Union (RWDSU), has demonstrated to promote a Fair Scheduling Practices law in New York State. Legislation has also been proposed at the federal level. Although these efforts have not yet been successful, they have publicised the issue and put it on the radar screen of progressive politicians.[30]

Some just-in-time workers are attempting to address the problem of irregular and unpredictable hours through unionisation. Because they are employees, they have a right to organise under the labour law. However, unions have been slow to address the issue of irregular and unpredictable scheduling, even though for many retail and hospitality workers, the problems stemming from variable hours may be more important than traditional issues of pay and seniority.

One promising approach to the problem of irregular work and unpredictable scheduling can be found in the collective bargaining model pioneered by flight attendants' unions over 50 years ago. Those workers achieved, through collective bargaining, an effective system by which the workers bid on their preferred work schedule each month and the bids are awarded by seniority. In this way, flight attendants have been able to achieve predictability in their schedules and plan their lives accordingly, even when the employers' staffing needs were unpredictable and variable due to factors like weather delays and equipment failures. The flight attendant union contracts also limit on-call work and require a minimum-hours guarantee for those workers who are on call. If workers who suffer from variable hours and short shifts were to unionise, they could negotiate an arrangement akin to the flight attendant model that could provide them with stability and a reliable income.

B. Voluntary Flexible Workers

i. Unions for On-demand Workers?

Because of their uncertain status under the labour laws, it is unclear whether or not on-demand workers have a right to unionise. If they are determined to be 'independent contractors', they would not have a right to unionise under the labour law. Moreover, as independent contractors, any collective action they take to improve their wages could subject them to liability and substantial damages

[30] See, eg, Annamaria Duran, *Fair Scheduling Laws: The Newest Employment Law Trend in the USA*, in Swipeclock Workforce Management, at www3.swipeclock.com/blog/fair-scheduling-laws-the-newest-employment-law-trend-in-the-usa/; National Women's Law Center, *Schedules That Work Act*, at nwlc.org/resources/schedules-work-act-giving-workers-tools-they-need-succeed/.

under the antitrust laws. However, even in the face of that uncertainty, some on-demand workers have been attempting to take collective action and form organisations to improve their working conditions.

Some on-demand platform workers are forming associations that are not full-fledged unions but which provide them with some rights and protections. For example, some Uber drivers in New York City have formed the Independent Drivers Guild, which meets regularly with Uber management and seeks to advocate for the drivers over discipline and other complaints.[31] Other Uber drivers in New York have joined the rival New York Taxi Workers Alliance, an organisation that offers services such as assistance with traffic citations, and lobbies the Taxi and Limousine Commission on behalf of drivers.

In Seattle, Uber drivers joined with local unions to press for a city Ordinance that would give them a right to representation. In December 2015, the City of Seattle enacted an Ordinance to permit for-hire drivers to unionise and bargain collectively for driver compensation rates and other terms of their contracts.[32] The stated goal of the Ordinance is to 'level[] the bargaining power between for-hire drivers and the entities that control many aspects of their working conditions'.[33] The Ordinance declared that

> business models wherein companies control aspects of their drivers' work, but rely on the drivers being classified as independent contracts, render for-hire drivers exempt from minimum labor requirements that the City of Seattle … undermine Seattle's efforts to create opportunities for all workers in Seattle to earn a living wage.[34]

The Seattle Ordinance does not take a position on whether the drivers are independent contractors or employees. Rather, it establishes a procedure for drivers to select an exclusive driver representative (EDR) who will be the sole representative of for-hire drivers operating in the city for a particular on-demand company, called a 'driver coordinator'. The Director of the city's Finance and Administrative Services Department is designated to receive petitions from groups seeking to be designated the EDR and to determine whether a particular group has sufficient support amongst drivers for that company to be so named. Once an EDR is certified, the EDR and the company hiring those drivers – the 'driver coordinator' – are required to meet and bargain over vehicle standards, safe driving practices, the nature and amount of payments to be made, minimum hours of work and other conditions of work. After reaching an agreement, the parties transmit the agreement to the Director for review and if it is found

[31] Emma G Fitzsimmons, 'Uber Drivers Are Barely Making Ends Meet, Too', *New York Times* (18 June 2018) p. A16.

[32] For an official description of the Seattle Ordinance, see *For Hire Driver Collective Bargaining*, Seattle Department of Finance and Administrative Services, at www.seattle.gov/business-regulations/taxis-for-hires-and-tncs/for-hire-driver-collective-bargaining.

[33] Seattle Ordinance, Section 1J.

[34] Seattle Ordinance, Section 1H.

to be compliant, it is final and binding on all parties. If the parties fail to agree, then the Ordinance provides for interest arbitration.

On 3 March 2016 the US Chamber of Commerce challenged the Seattle Ordinance in federal court. In its Complaint, it contended that the Ordinance violates the Sherman Antitrust Act by authorising for-hire drivers to form illegal cartels, and that it violates the NLRA by regulating matters that lie within the exclusive jurisdiction of the NLRB. After preliminary rulings by lower courts upholding the Ordinance, the Ninth Circuit Court of Appeals ruled in favour of the Chamber of Commerce in May 2018. The Court held that the Ordinance violated the antitrust laws and thus could not be enforced. At the same time, however, the Court stated that it would not violate the NLRA for states to permit unionisation by independent contractors. Both issues are currently on appeal.[35]

If the ruling concerning the NLRA is upheld, it could open the door for a new form of unionism that could prove to be meaningful for on-demand workers.

ii. Other Forms of Organisations for On-demand Workers

Although on-demand workers may not have the legal right to form unions, there are other forms of association that could provide them with protection and representation. For example, workers can form associations that do not bargain or attempt to set wages, but rather attempt to provide assistance with work-related problems. The New York Taxi Worker Alliance mentioned above provides these types of benefits for its members. In addition, it trains workers to assist others. Because many employers have established institutions at the workplace to promote fairness at work such as grievance procedures, open door policies and, increasingly, arbitration, a workplace association that helps individuals utilise these procedures would be very valuable.

Where unions exist, union representatives have often become de facto 'workplace lawyers' to help individual resolve their problems informally or help steer them to the right place within the legal system. This is an important role that unions play and it is one that a workplace association could do as well. That is, even without being 'certified' as a union, an association of on-demand workers could work with volunteers and train them to be effective worker advocates in their place of work.

The role of workplace lawyer has become increasingly important because the Supreme Court has approved efforts by employers to impose mandatory arbitration on workers for adjudicating their employment rights.[36] In arbitration

[35] Linda Chiem, *States, DC Seek Full 9th Circ. Redo Of Uber Union Law Fight*, Law360 (6 July 2018) at www.law360.com/articles/1060673/states-dc-seek-full-9th-circ-redo-of-uber-union-law-fight.

[36] See Katherine VW Stone, 'The Bold Ambition of Justice Scalia's Arbitration Jurisprudence: Keep Workers and Consumers Out of Court' (2017) 21 *Employment Rights & Employment Policy*

individuals usually need a lawyer in order to prevail. However, most employment lawyers will not take individual arbitration cases because the stakes are too small to make it worthwhile. Thus individual workers would benefit tremendously from having lay advocates, trained by a workplace organisation, help them present their case.

An organisation of on-demand workers could operate to provide assistance and support to workers on multiple and various platforms. In recent years, there has been a proliferation of organisations called workers' centres, which act in conjunction with community groups to achieve benefits for workers on a regional basis. These are locally based groups that assist workers in their efforts to improve their conditions. Some direct themselves towards a specific group such as immigrant workers, Korean workers or contingent workers. The centres provide information to their constituents about relevant regulations, collect information about labour law violations, pressure local employers to improve conditions, train workers to stand up for their rights, and lobby local authorities for improvements in legislation. For example, contingent worker centres have lobbied state legislatures for laws that would compel companies to pay travel and meal time for contingent workers and requiring them to post the pay rates. A worker centre that focused on issues involving on-demand workers could play a similar role.

In addition, there have been effective alliances between community groups, worker centres and local unions in many cities to address the problem for workers in flexible labour markets. The coalitions advocate measures such as living wages, regional benefit funds and job training programmes to offer lifetime learning so that displaced workers can learn new skills. Los Angeles has been at the forefront of the labour–community alliance movement. Over the past 25 years, a strong labour– community coalition in LA has achieved many victories, including securing the enactment of several broad living-wage ordinances that mandate not only decent wages, but also health benefits for many groups of public and private sector workers. The coalition also got the City Council to enact a 'worker retention ordinance' that prevents firms that contract with the airport from discharging their workers each time a sub-contract changes hand, a 'sweat-free procurement ordinance' that requires the city's contractors to provide decent working conditions and pay a living wage, and a 'Clean Trucks ordinance' requiring trucking firms at the ports to hire drivers rather than utilise independent contractors.[37] An on-demand worker centre could contribute to these alliances.

Journal 189; Katherine VW Stone, 'Procedure, Substance, and Power: Collective Litigation and Arbitration Under the Labor Law' (2013) 61 *UCLA Law Review Discourses* 164, available at www.uclalawreview.org.

[37] See generally Katherine Stone and Scott Cummings, 'Labor Activism in Local Politics: From CBAs to "CBAs"' in Guy Davidov and Brian Langille (eds), *The Idea of Labour Law* (Oxford University Press, 2011) 273–92 (describing achievements of Los Angeles labour–community alliances).

iii. A Political Agenda for On-demand Workers

Associations of on-demand workers could also help restore labour's voice in politics. In the United States, the role of big money in politics has mushroomed in the wake of the Citizens' United ruling in 2010.[38] And, with widening income inequality, the very rich are becoming even richer, and thus have more money than ever to spend. Today most of the funding for electoral candidates is provided by the 'super-pacs' of a small number of billionaires. Thus it is no surprise that the candidates who win with support from the super rich turn around and write legislation and regulations that benefit their benefactors. As Jacob Hacker and Paul Pierson have shown in their best-selling book *Winner Take All Politics*, the rise of money in politics has gone hand in hand with banking deregulation, tax code changes, relaxation of the antitrust laws, and other legislative measures that have benefitted the rich.[39]

In the past, unions used their political clout to ensure that tax burdens were fairly imposed, that social benefits – healthcare, old age assistance – were available to the 'middle class', that higher education was accessible to everyone who wanted it, and that Congress provided economic stimulus to create jobs and improve physical, economic and social infrastructure. Now, in light of changes in the nature of work and the decline of unions, these programmes are being dismantled or severely diluted. Workers need to form new organisations to protect their interests in the political domain.

What would a political programme of associations of on-demand workers? On-demand workers are but one type of precarious worker in today's labour market. Because so many workers today move frequently between jobs, and into and out of the labour market, we need to restructure social programmes that currently rely on long-term job attachment and replace them with programmes tailored to the new labour market realities. That is, we need to refocus social policies on workers in transition. We need programmes that provide income maintenance as people move between jobs, lifetime learning opportunities so they can qualify for new jobs, relocation assistance, child care assistance, portable benefits, and even new housing policies that enable people to move in and out of the labour market throughout their working life.

There are proposals currently under discussion to address the problems workers face today. For example, in 2015 President Obama proposed a system of wage insurance to provide pay protection for workers who lose jobs and cannot find new ones at their former pay level.

A more comprehensive proposal was made by Nick Hanauer and David Rolf in an article in *Democracy Journal* in 2016. They proposed a programme

[38] *Citizens United v Federal Election Commission*, 558 US 310 (2010).

[39] Jacob S Harker and Paul Pierson, *Winner-Take-All Politics: How Washington Made the Rich Richer – and Turned Its Back on the Middle Class* (Simon & Shuster, 2011).

they called 'Shared Security' in which all employment would carry with it prorated, portable and universal benefits. Under their proposal, all employers of an individual – whether the employee is part time or full time – would be required to make deposits into its worker's Shared Security Account. Over time, the worker's account would accumulate funds to provide sick leave, paid vacation leave, 401(k) pension contributions, and health insurance premiums. It would also provide social insurance, including unemployment compensation, workers' compensation, and paid maternity, paternity, family, and medical leave.

These programmes deserve serious consideration. However, they do not necessarily benefit on-demand platform workers who are designated independent contractors. But with the spread of the ABC test, they could redound to their benefit as well.

Another proposal that would supplement both wage insurance and the Shared Security programme and assist both employees and independent contractors is what I call a 'workplace sabbatical'. It would be a new social program to enable workers to accumulate time in the labour market – whether for one employer or multiple ones, and whether as an employee or as an independent contractor – that they could use to take paid time off in order to improve their position in the labour market. Workers could use their sabbatical to engage in training, entrepreneurial activity, changing jobs, public service work or care work for dependents. It could also help cushion a bout of involuntary unemployment. The workplace sabbatical would enable workers to navigate career transitions, thereby giving flexibility and security in an era of uncertainty.

While the workplace sabbatical idea may sound utopian, the US military adopted a similar policy in 2015. It developed a programme it termed 'career intermission leave', by which servicemen and servicewomen who served a certain period of time could take up to three years off and keep their jobs and rank when they returned. During their career intermission, they would receive a percentage of their pay as well as retain their health insurance and other benefits. The military adopted this policy to encourage service members who have young children to remain in the service. But intermissions could also be used to engage for education, training or other projects.

The proposals for wage insurance, shared security, and a workplace sabbatical are not incompatible. Rather, they are the kinds of public policy measures we need to address the problems of today's on-demand and other precarious workers.

IV. CONCLUSION

On-demand and just-in-time workers represent a further step away from the stable standard employment relationships of the past. And they have made workers ever more precarious. The challenge today is to find a way to empower precarious workers and enable them to protect their livelihoods and enjoy stable and meaningful lives. This will require new forms of collective action and new types of organisations – be they called associations or unions – to empower, sustain and amplify these efforts. I have suggested some forms that such organisations could take and some policies they could advocate. There are certainly others that could be developed. We are in an era where the nature of work has totally changed so imagination, experimentation and invention are not fanciful – they are imperative.

Part II

Collective Action and Multi-Level Agency

6

Exploring Multi-Level Collective Bargaining: Transnational Legal Frameworks that Promote Worker Agency

TONIA NOVITZ

I. INTRODUCTION

THIS CHAPTER WILL examine the scope for transnational freedom of association and multi-level collective bargaining. Section II begins by considering why examination of the transnational dimension of trade union activity is timely, highlighting how worker agency is being undermined by precarity constituted through employment and immigration status at the national level. Section III then turns to the scope for transnational worker solidarity, in particular through international (or global) framework agreements. These agreements could be regarded as extra-legal, but it will be argued in Section IV that their content, negotiation and operation remain shaped by various international and transnational (especially European) legal regimes relating to labour standards and human rights. The capacity of transnational law to promote or obstruct transnational collective agency (and agency for workers at the national level) will be evaluated.

II. PROBLEMS FOR WORKER AGENCY IN DOMESTIC LABOUR MARKETS: EMPLOYMENT AND IMMIGRATION STATUS

There are two contemporary aspects of the contemporary domestic labour market, identifiable in the UK, Spain and elsewhere, which can be identified as significant 'problems' for worker agency. One problem is the decline in access to standard forms of employment, resulting in what have been described as 'precarious jobs'.[1] This has repercussions in terms of access to protection under national employment laws, but also has the potential to silence voice in the workplace. The other problem is an increase in discrimination and exploitation linked to the actual or perceived immigration status of the worker, such that it is not only jobs but 'particular people who are precarious'.[2] It is argued here that this is an attempt to divide the workforce in ways that enable greater access for employers to cheap labour, but which in so doing affects access to employment and terms and conditions for everyone. A key recipe for placing a check on these forms of precarity and prejudice is domestic solidarity, most obviously in the form of a trade union, but also in other modes of worker organisation, with scope for organisation and effective opposition, for example in the forms of collective bargaining and industrial action. The barrier however is the domestic enactment of increasingly repressive trade union laws which limit workers' collective bargaining power. As a result, there are renewed attempts to build cross-border solidarity between workers. While the later sections of this chapter consider such attempts and the preconditions for their success, this section seeks to identify the dimensions of these two emergent constraints on worker agency.

A. Precarity Associated with Employment Status

For at least two decades, it has been possible to detect what Collins has described as 'the vertical disintegration of the employment relationship', designed to evade formal legal protections.[3] Examples include use of subcontractors, agency workers, casual workers, temporary migrant workers and those hired on 'zero hours contracts'.[4] Women tend to be over-represented in atypical work, given that their involvement in the labour market may need to be organised around caring responsibilities that do not accord with the conventional parameters of a standard employment relationship (SER).[5]

Others have observed that supply chain regulation and complex corporate links have made it difficult not just to identify an employee but who might be

[1] Identified initially by G Rodgers and J Rodgers, *Precarious Jobs in Labour Market Regulation: The Growth of Atypical Employment in Western Europe* (Brussels, ILO, 1989).

[2] H Lewis, P Dwyer, S Hodkinson and L Waite, 'Hyper-precarious Lives: Migrants, work and forced labour in the Global North' (2015) 39(5) *Progress in Human Geography* 580, 585.

[3] H Collins, 'Independent Contractors and the Vertical Disintegration of the Employment Relationship' (1990) 10 *Oxford Journal of Legal Studies* 353.

[4] V De Stefano, 'Non-standard Work and Limits on Freedom of Association: A Human Rights-based Approach (2017) 46 *Industrial Law Journal* 185.

[5] L Hayes, *Stories of Care: A Labour of Law – Gender and Class at Work* (London, Palgrave, 2017); L Rodgers, *Labour law, Vulnerability and the Regulation of Precarious Work* (Cheltenham, Edward Elgar, 2016); L Vosko, *Managing the Margins: Gender, Citizenship and the International Regulation of Precarious Employment* (Oxford, OUP, 2010).

the employer,[6] so that even if one has employment law rights it is difficult to identify the person or entity that should be the target of their enforcement. It has been argued that contemporary use of 'franchises' blurs these boundaries even further,[7] as does the use of technological devices which distance payment for work from the beneficiary and the organiser of the supply of labour.[8] Use of the 'gig' economy, which offers a platform, such as an 'app' to enable the delivery of services, has become very popular. In part, this is designed to offer flexibility to workers, but also enables lower prices for consumers for example of courier, delivery or taxi services.[9] The danger in all these scenarios is that the 'precariat' (identified by Guy Standing) are not only placed outside employment law experiencing consequent exposure to dismissal and income insecurity, but experience forms of deprivation of voice alongside social and political isolation, such that they may have no investment in the labour markets or even the legal systems of the states in which they live.[10]

The financial crisis and accompanying austerity policies have arguably exacerbated the declining coverage of employment law, particularly in Europe. Public sector workers are increasingly designated as independent contractors outside an 'employment relationship' to facilitate dismissal and reduction of wages in ways that restrict public spending.[11] Further, the desire to attract foreign direct investment (FDI) would seem to have influenced state designation of employment status. Private employers are encouraged to invest on site in a country on the basis that they will have at their disposal a flexible and easily expendable workforce, including one that will no longer be covered by collectively bargained wages or offer significant resistance to restructuring.[12]

A letter of the European Central Bank (ECB) to the Spanish government of 5 August 2011 recommended on economic grounds the introduction of temporary work contracts, reducing the costs of severance pay and expectations

[6] J Prassl, *The Concept of the Employer* (Oxford, OUP, 2015).

[7] D Weil, *The Fissured Workplace: Why Work Has Become So Bad For So Many And What Can Be Done To Improve It* (Cambridge, Mass., Harvard UP, 2014).

[8] K Bales, A Bogg and T Novitz, '"Voice" and "Choice" in Modern Working Practices: Problems with the Taylor Review' (2018) 47 *Industrial Law Journal* 46; J Prassl, *Humans as a Service: The Promises and Perils of Work in the Gig Economy* (Oxford, OUP, 2018).

[9] V De Stefano, 'The Rise of the "Just-in-Time Workforce": On-demand Work, Crowd Work and Labour Protection in the 'Gig-Economy' (2016) ILO Working Paper available at: http://www.ilo.org/travail/whatwedo/publications/WCMS_443267/lang--en/index.htm.

[10] G Standing, *The Precariat: The New Dangerous Class* (London, Bloomsbury, 2014).

[11] J Peters, 'Neoliberal Convergence in North America and Western Europe: Fiscal Austerity, Privatization, and Public Sector Reform (2012) 19(2) *Review of International Political Economy* 208; T Novitz, 'Changes in Employment Status under Austerity and Beyond – Implications for Freedom of Association' (2016) 39 *Dublin University Law Journal* 27; and J P Bohoslavsky, *Report on Structural Adjustment and Labour Rights* A/HRC/34/57 (Geneva, UN, 2017).

[12] S Clauwaert and I Schömann, *The Crisis and National Labour Law Reforms: A Mapping Exercise* (Brussels, ETUI Working Paper 2012.04, 2012); and A Koukiadaki, I Tavora and L M Martinez (eds), *The Transformation of Joint Regulation and Labour Market Policy in Europe During the Crisis: Comparative Project Report* (Manchester/Brussels, University of Manchester/The European Commission, 2014).

of renewal.[13] The Royal Decree Law 3/2012 on Urgent Measures to Reform Labour Market confirmed by Parliament as Law 3/2013 therefore introduced a new type of 'entrepreneur contract', for employers with fewer than 50 employees offering unrestricted possibilities for dismissal in the first year.[14] This is in addition to increased use of outsourcing and temporary agency work in the Spanish public sector,[15] and further elaboration and application of the Code of the Autonomous Worker initially introduced in 2007,[16] creating an intermediate employment status known as *Trabajador Autonomo Economicamente Dependiente* or a 'TRADE' worker.[17] Further, the Spanish reform entailed measures privileging company over sectoral collective agreements, diminishing access to wages agreed at higher levels.[18]

Even without ECB intervention, UK austerity objectives led to the legislative creation of an 'employee-shareholder' who is able to exchange key employment rights (such as protection from unfair dismissal) for an uncertain £2,000 share in the company for which they work.[19] The number of independent contractors or 'micro-businesses' in operation in the UK labour market is increasing as are rates of atypical hiring (such as temporary agency work, one person companies or zero hours contracts) together with in-work poverty.[20] This suggests that workers' insecurity in employment reduces their confidence in asking for higher pay and improved terms and conditions, enabling employers to deny that there is any need for them to make such concessions.[21]

In a number of UK cases, those offering services through 'gig' platforms, such as Uber drivers, have been deemed by the tribunals and courts to be 'workers'. In *Uber v Aslam*, the Employment Appeal Tribunal upheld a decision that Uber drivers should have access as 'workers' to the national minimum wage

[13] M Luz Rodriguez, 'Labour Rights in Crisis in the Eurozone: The Spanish Case' in C Kilpatrick and B De Witte (eds), *Social Rights in Times of Crisis in the Eurozone: The Role of Fundamental Rights' Challenges* EUI Working Paper LAW 2014/5 (Florence, European University Institute, 2014), 108–9.

[14] Rodriguez (n 13) 109.

[15] C Chacartegui, 'Segmentation of Public Employment in the Frame of Austerity Policies: Precariousness as a Consequence' (2014) 36 *Comparative Labor Law and Policy Journal* 203, 208–9.

[16] J Lopez, 'Formalizing the Segmentation of Workers' Rights: Tensions among Regulatory Levels (2014) 36 *Comparative Labor Law and Policy Journal* 281, 286.

[17] M A Cherry and A Aloisi, '"Dependent Contractors" in the Gig Economy: A Comparative Approach' (2017) 66(3) *American University Law Review* 635, 671–675.

[18] Koukiadaki et al (n 12) 516–517.

[19] By virtue of the Growth and Infrastructure Act, section 31 inserting section 205A into the Employment Rights Act 1996.

[20] A Henley, *The Post Crisis Growth in the Self-employed: Volunteers or reluctant recruits?* (IZA Discussion Papers, No. 9232, 2015); Joseph Rowntree Foundation Report, *Monitoring Poverty and Social Exclusion 2016* available at: https://www.jrf.org.uk/report/monitoring-poverty-and-social-exclusion-2016?gclid=CMymjo2yq9QCFUKVGwodvk4A2Q.

[21] Also discussed in a US context by A M Lofaso, 'The Vanishing Employee: Putting the Autonomous Dignified Union Worker Back to Work' (2010) 5 *Florida International University Law Review* 497; and M Finkin, 'Employee Self-representation and the Law in the United States (2013) 50(4) *Osgoode Hall Law Journal* 937.

and working time protections.[22] While apparently offering relief from precarity, but this also amounts to inferior protection under UK law as they are not deemed to be 'employees' who could claim statutory protection from dismissal protection.[23] In the case of *Independent Workers' Union of Great Britain (IGWB) and RooFoods Limited TA/Deliveroo*,[24] an application for trade union recognition of food delivery couriers failed. This was due to the insertion of a 'substitution' clause by Deliveroo into the couriers' contracts after the application had been made, so as to prompt a finding that they were not 'workers' entitled to representation by a trade union, but instead independent contractors on business on their own account free to arrange for others to perform any work subcontracted to them. It is to be hoped that this finding will be overturned following the more recent findings of the UK Supreme Court in the *Pimlico Plumbers* case,[25] where it was indicated that it would be more helpful to consider whether personal service is a 'dominant feature' of the terms of hiring, rendering substitution clauses less relevant than previously thought to the determination of whether there is an employment relationship. The judicial review being pursued now by the IGWB is significant because one effective approach to these new platform-based modes of work (which generate such precarity) may not be individual claims as a worker around wages and working time, but rather solidarity through trade union representation and collective bargaining.[26]

The difficulty of course is the increasing constraints placed on collective action by the Trade Union Act 2016.[27] Bogg has commented that this legislation involves 'the systematic undermining of political opposition both in the sphere of party politics and in wider civil society, the State's increasing recourse to the direct use of coercion and criminal penalties to pacify workers and trade unions, and the elevation of unity and social order over agonistic expressions of industrial and political dissent'.[28]

Adams and Deakin argue that the SER may withstand temporary temptations to undermine established legal forms of reciprocity and legal protection, and prove durable. They note that developing and emergent economies tend to use the SER as a legal form by which to achieve economic gains from labour.[29] Durable too, one might argue, is the collective response of workers to erosion of their rights through organisation in a trade union. Although the demise of

[22] [2017] IRLR 4, ET; UKEAT/0056/17/DA, 20 November 2017.

[23] Under sections 96 and 98 of the Employment Rights Act 1996.

[24] 14 November 2017 (TUR1/985(2016).

[25] *Pimlico Plumbers Ltd and another v Smith*, judgment of 13 June 2018 [2018] UKSC 29.

[26] See https://iwgb.org.uk/2018/02/12/iwgb-applies-for-judicial-review-of-deliveroo-worker-rights-decision/.

[27] Summarized in M Ford and T Novitz, 'Legislating for Control: The Trade Union Act 2016' (2016) 45 *Industrial Law Journal* 277.

[28] A Bogg, 'Beyond Neo-Liberalism: The Trade Union Act 2016 and the Authoritarian State' (2016) 45 *Industrial Law Journal* 299, 300.

[29] Z Adams and S Deakin, 'Institutional Solutions to Precariousness and Inequality in Labour Markets (2014) 52 *British Journal of Industrial Relations* 779.

trade unions has been predicted for a long period of time now, there remains a strong desire to be a trade union member and to be represented in collective bargaining even when obstructed by law and again this is evident in emergent as well as so-called 'developed' states.[30]

Adams and Deakin see a role for international regulation, when sovereign states pool their resources so as to resist erosion of the SER.[31] My suggestion is that protection against precarity may best be achieved by broader transnational worker solidarity, with the support of public authority in the form of international and transnational legal interventions. Before going on to explore this possibility, I would like to investigate further the other worrying trend alongside precarity within domestic labour markets, namely immigration-based discrimination and exploitation.

B. Discrimination and Exploitation Relating to Immigration Status

A resurgence in nationalism would now seem to be affecting the potential for discrimination in the labour market. A prime example is Donald Trump's brazen 'America First Job Plan', which gives American priorities over other nationals for jobs.[32] This is presumably created on the basis that foreign nationals were generally being paid less than existing workers and pricing them out of local jobs, which may well be the case for lower-skilled workers and temporary guest-workers who enter the country only for short periods as has been the case in the UK. Longer term migration does not seem to have such effects, as standard requirements of non-discrimination apply and have more potential to be meaningfully enforced.[33] Short term migration is increasingly common, whereby the stay in a host country for work purposes is lawful, but the worker's precarity is enhanced by reason of the temporary nature of their entitlement to live and work there. They may also enter as workers whose employment status is simultaneously also precarious, being hired as agency workers or subcontractors on contractual arrangements designed to limit their employment law entitlements during their stay.[34]

[30] B Abbott and S Williams, 'Widening the 'Representation Gap'? The implications of the 'lobbying act' for worker representation in the UK' (2014) 45(6) *Industrial Relations Journal* 507; and B Balsmeier, 'Unions, Collective Relations Laws and R&D Investment in Emerging and Developing Countries' (2017) 46(1) *Research Policy* 292.

[31] Adams and Deakin (n 29).

[32] Announced 17 February 2017 and available at http://www.express.co.uk/news/world/766378/US-President-America-First-job-growth.

[33] T Novitz, 'Collective Bargaining, Equality and Migration: The journey to and from Brexit' (2017) 46 *Industrial Law Journal* 109 and A Burstein, G Hanson, L Yian and J Vogel, 'Tradability and the Labor-Market Impact of Immigration: Theory and Evidence from the US' (2017) NBER Working Paper No. 23330 available at: http://www.nber.org/papers/w23330.

[34] See E Tucker, 'Intra-Company Transfers and Fissured Workplaces: *CS Wind* and the challenge of union organizing in Canada' (2016) Paper prepared for ReMarkLab Final Conference: New Foundations of Labour Law in the Globalised Market Economy? Stockholm, May 2016. He discusses

In the UK, there has been ongoing concern that immigration status feeds into precarity at work. There has long been awareness of the role of 'gangmasters' in bringing 'guest workers' to the country where they live in situations of extreme isolation and vulnerability, prompting the then 'New' Labour Government to set up a licensing scheme (and what is now an underfunded investigation apparatus) to address the issue.[35] It is not necessary, under this scheme, for those working for a gangmaster to be lawfully resident in the UK; the protections of the legislation are to apply regardless. Modern slavery, including trafficking, is now criminalised under the Modern Slavery Act 2015, although only minimal assistance is given to victims and visa-related problems continue to arise. The difficulty with such an approach is that it addresses only the extremity of the 'hyper-precarious' worker and those forms of exploitation, neglecting the 'continuum' in a decline in human agency within the labour market, which can also be affected by more stringent immigration controls.[36] A recent matter of concern in the industrial action taken by the University and College Union (UCU) in 2018 was the potential for striking academics to be reported by a university employer to the Home Office and sanctioned (or even deported) for participating in industrial action.[37] Under pressure from UCU, the Home Secretary has now changed the rules to prevent this kind of exposure for taking lawful industrial action.[38]

This is far from being a purely UK phenomenon, for these cases of geographical isolation of temporary immigrants in the agricultural and construction sectors would seem to be rife across Europe. Examples include recent cases before the European Court of Human Rights, such as the Greek case of *Chowdury and Others v. Greece*[39] and before the European Court of Justice in the *Elektrobudwa* case.[40] In *Chowdhury*, what was notable was the attempt by the illegal immigrants, the Bangladeshi migrant fruit pickers, to act collectively, taking strike action, but without transnational support (as other immigrants were trafficked in to take their jobs). The *Elektrobudwa* case did not involve illegality or trafficking, but demonstrated how in situations of isolated temporary posted work, (here electrical contractors on a construction site), a trade union may be helpful in representing and securing justice, at least in the form of unpaid wages.

the issues concerning collective bargaining in this context. See also J Howe and R Owens (eds), *Temporary Labour Migration in the Global Era: The regulatory challenges* (Oxford, Hart, 2016).

[35] See the Gangmasters (Licensing) Act 2004 and subsequent amendments.

[36] Lewis (n 2) 586–7.

[37] See http://www.ucu.org.uk/media/9302/Strike-and-Tier-2-staff---letter-to-the-Home-Secretary-Mar-18/pdf/uculetter_amberrudd_tier2staff_strikes.pdf.

[38] See https://www.ucu.org.uk/article/9575/Home-secretary-changes-rules-to-ensure-migrant-workers-can-take-strike-action.

[39] (2016) application no. 21884/15.

[40] Case 396/13 *Sähköalojen ammattiliitto ry v Elektrobudowa Spółka Akcyjna*, judgment of 12 February 2015.

Indeed, solidarity between guest workers and local unions in a host state arguably offers a route capable of taming exploitative conditions associated with immigration status (or its absence). This is important because of the doubtful scope of individual legal redress. For example, in the UK, contractual relief will be difficult to achieve where the worker is in breach of national immigration rules (contractual enforcement precluded in *Zarkasi v Anandita*[41] and still uncertain when weighing policy considerations by virtue of the Supreme Court decision in *Patel v Mirza*).[42] Further, it seems that claims that discrimination on grounds of precarious (but lawful) immigration status will not be regarded as discrimination on grounds of nationality, closing off an important route to compensation.[43]

Hobsbawm once observed that 'nationalism by definition excludes from its purview all who do not belong to its own "nation", ie the vast majority of the human race'.[44] He suggested that a 'supra-national restructuring of the globe' through European and international legal structures which could offer scope for a complete change in perspective and, even, greater wisdom. To achieve this, workers would need meaningful access to freedom of association at international and regional levels, in pragmatic terms enabling organising in solidarity.[45] Section III considers how workers' organisations are operating transnationally to promote such solidarity and thereby move away from a discriminatory protectionist impulse, while Section IV considers the adequacy (or otherwise) of the legal apparatus transnationally which could offer support for their activities.

III. EXISTING EXTRA-LEGAL MECHANISMS FOR TRANSNATIONAL SOLIDARITY

The challenges arising in domestic labour markets do not arise so much in imitation of each other, but because such markets have connections that span conventional national boundaries. Multinational enterprises (MNEs) and their corporate subsidiaries subcontract and franchise across territorial borders. In doing so, their business opportunities are enabled by contemporary modes of manufacture and service provision which enable transnational cross-border sites of production and delivery. In this way, commercial enterprise is often distanced from the labour from which it profits, while similar working arrangements (precarious due to employment or immigration status) may well be replicated in numerous sites.

[41] [2012] ICR 788.
[42] [2016] 3 WLR 399; [2016] UKSC 42.
[43] Joined cases *Onu v Akwiwu and Taiwo v Olaigbe* [2016] IRLR 719.
[44] E J Hobsbawm, *Nations and Nationalism since 1780*, 2nd ed. (Cambridge, CUP, 1992), 176.
[45] Hobsbawm (n 44) 184–192.

We have seen that there can be efficacy in domestic solidarity between (and collective action by) workers who do not fit within the same categories for employment law protection or who possess different immigration status. Indeed, this may be a reason why countries are increasingly adopting more draconian collective labour laws which place limits on trade union activities. In response to the relative weakness of national level workers' organisations, trade unions have taken on international or 'global' dimensions so as to enhance collective bargaining and its benefits.

Trubek and others have observed the formation of alliances between unions in the fields of telecommunications and car manufacture.[46] More recently, Bernaciek has explained how Solidarnosc's international office has placed Polish posted workers in touch with Norwegian trade unions, so that they can become members and supported boycotts by Danish unions in response to the undercutting of wages.[47]

One facet of transnational solidarity was the creation of international framework agreements (IFAs). The first documented was an agreement between Accor and the International Union of Food, Agricultural, Hotel, Restaurant, Catering, Tobacco and Allied Workers' Associations (IUF) in 1994. A Code of Practice adopted in 1998 by the International Confederation of Free Trade Unions (ICFTU) gave impetus to this practice. 'International Trade Secretariats', now known 'Global Union Federations' (GUFs), used this resource as a basis to conclude agreements with MNEs. Platzer and Rüb have estimated that of the with 113 IFAs concluded by 2012, coverage has been extended to at least 65,000 MNEs with more than 850,000 subsidiaries.[48]

IFAs, now more commonly known as global framework agreements (GFAs), are intended to be revised, usually after a fixed term of anywhere between one to five years, but sometimes will operate for an indefinite period, which has yet to be subject to 'review', especially where their operation is largely 'dormant'.[49] A list of GFAs, which may be signed by more than one GUF, is to be found on the 'Global Unions' website which keeps a collated archive.[50] The European Commission also keeps a list of international and European framework agreements accurate up until 2015.[51]

[46] D M Trubek, J Mosher and J S Rothstein, 'Transnationalism in the Regulation of Labor Relations: International regimes and transnational advocacy networks' (2000) *Law and Social Inquiry* 1187.

[47] M Bernaciek, 'Polish Trade Unions and Social Dumping Debates: Between a rock and a hard place' (2016) 22(4) *Transfer* 505, 513.

[48] H-W Platzer and S Rüb, *International Framework Agreements: An instrument for enforcing social human rights?*(2014) Friedrich Ebert Stiftung Working Paper, 3–4.

[49] K Papadakis, 'Globalizing Industrial Relations: What role for International Framework Agreements?' in S Hayter, ed., *The Role of Collective Bargaining in the Global Economy: Negotiating for social justice* (Geneva, ILO, 2011), 281.

[50] See http://www.global-unions.org/-framework-agreements-%20.html?lang=en.

[51] See http://ec.europa.eu/social/main.jsp?catId=978&langId=en.

Defining features of GFAs/IFAs have been identified by various commentators since the 1990s[52] and are usually understood to include provisions stating that:

- they are global in reach;
- they have one (or more than one) GUF as a signatory;
- ILO core labour standards under the 1998 Declaration and/or ILO Conventions are a source of reference;
- freedom of association and the right to collective bargaining are protected under the agreement;
- the MNE will exercise influence over supply chains and subsidiaries/franchises etc.;
- trades unions or other representative workers' bodies (such as staff councils or works councils) are to be involved in implementation whether at a local or regional level; and
- workers are to be informed that they have a right to bring complaints and they can do so if the agreement is not honoured.

Sometimes a more general overarching declaratory instrument or 'Charter' is agreed with more detailed agreements on specific issues, such as health and safety, sustainability, employer codetermination and/or education and training to follow.[53]

IFAs (and now GFAs) have offered a departure from codes of conduct unilaterally designed by MNEs. Combination, not only nationally, but through an affiliation with a trade union of global reach, allows workers to potentially shape the terms on which their labour is purchased, when this might otherwise be impossible. In this respect, IFAs have been regarded 'a key trade union tool for addressing the growth of corporate power',[54] although Ewing has himself expressed concern that 'it is an initiative without any legal support and from which US corporations have largely excluded themselves'.[55]

[52] N Hammer, 'International Framework Agreements: Global industrial relations between rights and bargaining' (2005) 11(4) *Transfer* 511; O E Herrnstadt, 'Are International Framework Agreements a path to corporate social responsibility?' (2007/8) 10 *University of Pennsylvania Journal of Business and Employment Law* 187; D Miller, 'Preparing for the Long Haul: Negotiating International Framework Agreements in the Global Textile, Garment and Footwear Sector' (2004) 4(2) *Global Social Policy* 215 and L Riisgaard, 'International Framework Agreements: A New Model for Securing Workers Rights?' (2005) 44(4) *Industrial Relations* 707.

[53] M Whittall, M Martinez Lucio, S Mustchin, V Telljohann and F Rocha Sanchez, 'Workplace trade union engagement with European Works Councils and transnational agreements: The Volkswagen Europe' (2017) *European Journal of Industrial Relations* 1.

[54] This was a UK Trade Union Congress statement, cited by K D Ewing, 'International Regulation of the Global Economy – The role of trade unions' in B Bercusson and C Estlund (eds), *Regulating Labour in the Wake of Globalisation: New challenges, new institutions* (Oxford, Hart, 2008), 205.

[55] K D Ewing, 'Transnational Labour Law' (2016) 27 *King's Law Journal* 132, 133.

The GUFs do not confine their operations to the negotiation of GFAs, which have not been concluded with the same frequency since the financial crisis of 2008, as is evident from the GUF database. Instead, GUFs continue to utilise their entitlements to freedom of association and collective bargaining to act in solidarity in a variety of cross-border ways, a recent example being the action taken by Belgian dockers in June 2017 support of Spanish colleagues when European-level social dialogue broke down.[56] This kind of action depends for its legality in the given country in which it takes place, subject to the broad recognition by the International Labour Organisation (ILO) Committee on Freedom of Association that 'a general prohibition of sympathy strikes could lead to abuse and workers should be able to take such action provided the initial strike they are supporting is itself lawful'.[57] For this reason, the next part goes on to examine the extent of 'legal support' for trade unions at the global level and the significance of its absence with reference to IFAs and GFAs.

IV. THE SIGNIFICANCE OF TRANSNATIONAL LAW FOR WORKER AGENCY

Ewing is correct that any lack of legal support for IFAs and GFAs will be relevant to the realisation of their objectives.[58] For example, hard law can obstruct the conclusion and implementation of a framework agreement. If independent trade union activity is prohibited by legislation in the state hosting MNE production or delivery of services, the scope for new GFA terms protecting freedom of association seems likely to be minimal and if imposed from abroad (e.g. another state such as Spain or Sweden), the effectiveness of the agreement is cast in doubt. There will be no representatives on the ground to raise concerns to MNE representatives or GUFs abroad. Further, if collective action by trade unions is viewed as an illegitimate encroachment on the lawful freedoms of employers to supply goods or services or to invest, the balance of power in collective bargaining will be affected and the capacity to provide an incentive for compliance with the GFA may be undermined.[59]

Also, in more positive ways, hard law can shape the content, negotiations and enforcement of IFAs. Practical examples here are taken from the IFAs and GFAs concluded (or revised) since 2010.[60] It will be evident that there is further

[56] See http://www.itfglobal.org/en/news-events/news/2017/june/itfetf-dockers-take-action-to-back-spanish-colleagues/.

[57] ILO *Digest of Decisions of the Committee on Freedom of Association* 5th ed. (2006), para. 534; and 6th ed. (2018) para. 770.

[58] Ewing (n 55).

[59] Papadakis (n 49).

[60] See agreements discussed in T Novitz, 'Multi-level Collective Bargaining – Connections with legal frameworks?' in B J Mulder, M J Hotvedt, M Nesvik and T L Sundet (eds), *Sui Generis: Festskrift til Stein Evju* (Oslo, Universitetsforlaget, 2016), 495. Other more recent texts are also the subject of scrutiny in this chapter.

scope for refinement and improvement of the legal support offered, which seems to be under threat at multiple levels.

A. Hard Law as Content

While IFAs (and now GFAs) can be regarded as merely 'gentlemen's agreements',[61] having regulatory effects which are not strictly 'legal', they do draw on norms established in 'hard' international law. For example, the labour standards included in GFAs, as noted above, tend to consist of explicit reference to ILO Conventions.[62] The core ILO Conventions, especially those relating to freedom of association and collective bargaining (Nos 87 and 98) are almost invariably included. An illustration is the IFA signed between ICEM, BWI, PSI and GDF SUEZ (2010), where there is specific mention of these instruments and also Convention No. 135:

> There is agreement on full respect for trade union rights based on the principles in ILO conventions 87, 98, and 135. The rights of workers who wish to form or join trade unions are to be respected and there shall be no discrimination against such workers or against trade union or other employee representatives ... GDF SUEZ will provide information on its operations to trade unions in order to facilitate the practice of collective bargaining. (clause 1.2)

All the so called 'fundamental' or core Conventions (nos 87, 98, 29, 105, 138, 182, 100 and 111) are listed in clause 1 of the IFA between ThyssenKrupp AG, the Group Works Council of Thyssenkrupp AG, IG Metall and IndustriALL Global Union (2015). The core Conventions have also been listed in clause 1 of the very brief GFA between Aeon Co Ltd, UNI Global Union, UA Zenzen and the Federation of Aeon Group Workers' Unions (2014), which also makes reference to ILO Convention No. 155 on Occupational Health and Safety, as well as the UN Global Compact.

However, by way of contrast, certain IFAs contain only a 'clause of neutrality of union organizing' that falls notably short of ILO standards.[63] There have been instances when 'neutrality' has arisen because there were no recognised trade unions. For example, the revised UNI-Telefonica Code of Conduct (2007) stated that: 'where no trade union exists, the company shall adopt a neutral view and shall not prevent workers from organising. It shall also respect the right of trade unions to organise employees'.[64] However, such a reference to 'neutrality' can also be taken to indicate that workers are free to join – or not to

[61] R Bourque, 'International Framework Agreements and the Future of Collective Bargaining' (2008) 12 *Multinational Companies Just Labour: A Canadian journal of work and society* 30, 37.

[62] Hammer (n 52).

[63] Papadakis (n 49), 281.

[64] Discussed by C Niforou, 'International Framework Agreements and the Democratic Deficit of Global Labour Governance' (2014) 35(2) *Economic and Industrial Democracy* 352, 367.

join – a trade union. Arguably, this reflects the jurisprudence of the European Court of Human Rights, also adopted by other international supervisory bodies, indicating external normative pressure on the content of these agreements.[65]

In the IFA between Siemens AG, the Central Works Council of Siemens AG, the IG Metall and the IndustriAll Global Union (2012), the following is said:

> The right of employees to form labour unions, join existing labour unions and conduct collective negotiations, is acknowledged. Members of employee organizations or unions will be neither advantaged nor disadvantaged on account of their membership (see principles of ILO Conventions 87 and 98). (clause 2.4)

Another example consists of the GFA on social, societal and environmental responsibility between the Renault Group, the Renault Group Works' Council and IndustriALL Global Union (2013), which states that:

> Every employee is free to join a trade union or not. The Renault Group also undertakes to respect the terms of the ILO convention no. 98 on the right to organise and collective bargaining. As such, the Renault Group respects the right of its employees to organise themselves collectively, and remains strictly neutral. The signatories undertake to respect the choice of each employee on this matter.

Further, some IFAs eschew detailed reference to ILO Conventions but instead refer more generally to 'principles'. A good recent example is the IFA between Ford Motor Company and Global IMF/Ford Global Information Sharing Network (2012):

> The Principles are based on a thorough review of labor standards espoused by various groups and institutions worldwide, including those outlines by the International Labour Organization and stand as a general endorsement of the following human rights frameworks and charters:
>
> - The UN Universal Declaration of Human Rights
> - The ILO Tripartite Declaration of Principles Concerning Multilateral Enterprises and Social Policy
> - OECD Guidelines for Multinational Enterprises
> - The Global Sullivan Principles of Social Responsibility' (Preamble)

Notably the Siemens IFA (2012) refers to the ILO Conventions and also:

> explicitly supports and acknowledges the ten principles of the Global Compact: fundamental employee and human rights, environmental protection and anti-corruption. The Global Compact builds on the UN's Universal Declaration of Human Rights, the International Labour Organization's Declaration on Fundamental Principles and Rights at Work and the Rio Declaration on Environment and

[65] V Mantouvalou, 'Is There a Human Right not to be a Trade Union Member? Labour rights under the European Convention on Human Rights' in C Fenwick and T Novitz, (eds), *Human Rights at Work: Perspectives on Law and Regulation*. (Oxford, Hart/Oñati, 2010).

> Development. These elementary principles are also reflected in the Siemens Business Conduct Guidelines.

In this way, soft law declaratory instruments as well as ratified ILO Conventions offer a frame of reference (see also the Aeon GFA (2014) above).

Eligibility to claim rights under IFAs and GFAs differs between and even arguably within agreements. It is not clear how developments in various countries regarding the creation of precarious forms of labour or the peculiarities of eligibility for statutory protection under labour laws are to be understood in this context.

For example, the framework agreement between Banco Itau-Unibanco SA and Union Network International for the Americas (2014), suggests that the core labour standards under the ILO Declaration on Fundamental Principles at Rights of Work of 1998 are to be respected and protected 'in good faith and in accordance with the laws of each country' making no obvious distinction as to employment status regarding access to

> I. Freedom of association and the effective recognition of collective bargaining
> II. The elimination of all forms of forced and compulsory labour
> III. The effective abolition of child labour, and
> IV. The elimination of discrimination in respect of employment and occupation.'

This would be consistent with an understanding of these norms as human rights. However, elsewhere in the same document it seems that leaders of workers' organizations are only be to protected from discrimination to the extent that they are 'employees' (clauses 12 and 14) and that only 'workers' can claim equal wages under national laws or the national collective agreement. By way of contrast, the IFA between Salini-Impreglio and BWI, Feneal-UIL, Filca-CISL and Fillea-CGIL (2014) refers only to the interests and entitlements of 'workers', but makes specific reference under a 'non-discrimination' clause for 'migrants and posted workers' to 'enjoy at least the conditions applicable to the local national workers', which would seem to be a development to be applauded, given what we have seen of exploitation of migrant and posted workers transnationally to date (as discussed above).

In this context, we are also seeing the terms in IFAs and GFAs linked generally to the notion of 'sustainable development'. For example, the Ford (2012) agreement refers to 'sustainable development' in the context of environmental protection. The Renault (2013) agreement is titled 'Committing Together for Sustainable Growth and Development'. Notably the Salini-Impreglio (2014) agreement acknowledges at the outset that 'industrial sustainable development of the construction industry is in the interest of both the company and its workers'.

This may reflect the increasing dominance of 'sustainable development' rhetoric on the international stage, so that it now encompasses labour standards. But concerns have been expressed regarding what consequences this may have for protection of workers. Do labour standards become subsumed by other over-arching environmental concerns in this context?[66] Or is this a dynamic approach which could highlight the significance of labour rights in a new setting?[67] Arguably sustainability can mean 'durability' in the sense of intra-generational as well as inter-generational justice.[68] Much may turn on the design of these norms at the international, as well as the regional and national levels.

The United Nations Sustainable Development Goals (SDGs) of 2015[69] arguably indicate the significance of three key pillars of sustainable development policy: economic, environmental but also social. The latter is evident in the mention of 'decent work' in SDG 8. It is at least arguable that a focus on sustainability, rather than individual workers' rights, and the role of trade unions in promoting policy-based mutually beneficial decisions could have a positive effect. Further, the 2015 SDGs stress the importance of protecting those rendered vulnerable by migration. For example, the UN General Assembly SDG Resolution states:

> We recognize the positive contribution of migrants for inclusive growth and sustainable development. We also recognize that international migration is a multi-dimensional reality of major relevance for the development of countries of origin, transit and destination, which requires coherent and comprehensive responses. We will cooperate internationally to ensure safe, orderly and regular migration involving full respect for human rights and the humane treatment of migrants regardless of migration status. (paragraph 29)

As noted above, it is difficult to access texts of GFAs negotiated since the SDGs were adopted, but we might well expect some transformation in their content accordingly. At least there is potential to enable transnational solidarity around migrant workers' treatment.

B. Hard Law for Negotiation

The ILO does not broker framework agreements, nor does the European Union. Nevertheless, IFA and GFA bargaining processes (and any later enforcement

[66] L Bartels, *Human Rights and Sustainable Development Obligations in EU Free Trade Agreements*, Legal Studies Research Paper No. 24/2012, 18–19; and L van den Putte and J Orbie, 'EU Bilateral Trade Agreements and the Surprising Rise of Labour Provisions' (2015) 31(3) *International Journal of Comparative Labour Law and Industrial Relations* 263, 281.

[67] T Novitz, 'Labour standards and Trade: Need we choose between "Human Rights" and "Sustainable Development"?' in H Gött (ed) *Labour Standards in International Economic Law* (Cham: Springer, 2018).

[68] T Novitz, 'The Paradigm of Sustainability in a European Social Context: Collective Participation in Protection of Future Interests?'(2015) 31(3) *International Journal of Comparative Labour Law and Industrial Relations* 243.

[69] A/Res/70/1 available at: https://sustainabledevelopment.un.org/post2015/transformingourworld/publication.

of an IFA or GFA) depend on national level mobilisation of workers' organisations, regional lobbying by organisations like the European Trade Union Confederation (ETUC) and international communications by GUFs. Multi-level campaigns are needed to bring MNEs to the bargaining table, needing local level and 'bottom-up' activism.[70] The ability to engage in such campaigns depends in turn on the connection to legal regimes at national, regional and global levels.

For example, there are strong links between GFAs, IFAs and European MNCs, but also European unions and works councils. Currently, only just under 18% of IFAs (or GFAs) involve enterprises based outside Europe.[71] The efficacy of enforcement of labour standards in certain European countries, at least prior to the austerity measures of the financial crisis, may also explain why European companies may be accustomed to complying with norms which are rejected by US corporate interests. Herrnstadt has observed that the absence of many legislative rights for US workers (otherwise familiar to those in Europe) meant that for US workers issues such as healthcare, retirement security, job security and benefits took priority over IFAs in discussion with employers.[72] Approximately three-quarters of IFAs and GFAs have been co-signed by European Works Councils (EWC) representatives.[73] EWCs are also used as a model for World Employee Councils (WECs) or Global Works Councils (GWCs), which can assist in the negotiation of future IFAs and in the IFA's implementation.[74]

In turn, this means that the regime for EU-level social dialogue depends also on the protections given by EU Member States to trade unions at the domestic level. As Ewing observed, 'although legal support is not a precondition for the concluding of an IFA, it is hard to escape the conclusion that it is helpful'.[75] His view was that the existence of a 'structured environment allows unions to raise issues of this kind, even if there is no obligation on the part of management to respond, far less conclude an agreement'.[76] Therefore, as noted above, changes to European labour laws linked to austerity,[77] could limit the potential for European trade unions to agitate for European based MNEs to negotiate. Similarly, it has been demonstrated that eligibility for information

[70] T Novitz, 'Big Unions and Big Business: Can international framework agreements promote sustainable development at a local level?' in T Novitz and D Mangan (eds.), *The Role of Labour Standards in Development: From theory to sustainable practice?* (Oxford, OUP/British Academy, 2011).

[71] Platzer and Rüb (n 48) 6.

[72] Herrnstadt (n 52) 191.

[73] As is illustrated by the series of agreements involving Volkswagen documented by Whittall et al (n 53).

[74] Papadakis (n 49) 282 and 286–7; and S Sciarra, 'Collective Exit Strategies: New Ideas in Transnational Labour Law' in G Davidov and B Langille (eds), *The Idea of Labour Law*. (Oxford, OUP, 2011), 417.

[75] Ewing (n 54) 224.

[76] Ewing (n 54) 224.

[77] Discussed in Clauwaert and Schömann (n 12), Koukiadaki (n 12) and Novitz (n 11).

and consultation rights under EU law can be contingent on access to standard forms of employment, which in the wake of redesign of labour markets and public sector employment can pose particular problems.[78] While it is possible for extra-legal framework agreements to transcend the narrow confines of employment status as it is locally defined it may be hard to overcome the ways in which workers have become accustomed to such forms of disempowerment.

The recent dispute at the ILO regarding the scope of the right to strike also has the capacity to undermine the sense of workers' organisations that they are entitled to mobilise to address working conditions at local and global levels.[79] It would be dangerous to see collective agreements as operating in some kind of 'autonomous' system of industrial relations unshaped by legal norms and controls.[80] Rather, these industrial relations and labour law systems speak to each other and interact in important ways. IFAs and now GFAs enable employers and workers to negotiate in 'the shadow of the law',[81] not only in terms of the legal norms that inform their content but the very capacities (or capabilities) that enable the parties to engage in any form of bargaining.

C. Hard Law for Effectiveness and Enforcement

Further, hard law is significant in terms of how it affects the enforcement of IFAs or GFAs. These agreements tend to contain detailed information regarding the proposed dissemination of their content, which is to be publicised amongst the workforce. There is usually also reference to 'the creation of concrete mechanisms for monitoring the implementation of the agreement'.[82]

The Ford (2012) agreement, for example, contemplates discussion of compliance in a 'Global Sharing Forum', while the Siemens (2013) agreement contemplates engagement through a 'Central Works Council'. The Thyssenkrupp (2016) agreement (clause 12) sets up an 'International Committee' composed of the chair and two deputies of Global Works Council created by the company, the chairperson of the European Works Council and two representatives of GUFs. Members of the International Committee are to be informed of violations

[78] See Case C-176/12 *Association de mediation sociale (AMS) v CGT*, Judgment of 15 January 2014, where an NGO hired only eight employees on indefinite contracts, but over a hundred on what were termed 'accompanied-employment contracts' and could use this to evade appointment of a union representative for information and consultation purposes.

[79] K D Ewing, 'Myth and Reality of the Right to Strike as a "Fundamental Labour Right" (2013) 29(2) *International Journal of Comparative Labour Law and Industrial Relations* 145; C La Hovary, 'Employers' Group 2012 Challenge to the Right to Strike' (2013) 42 *Industrial Law Journal* 338; J Bellace, 'The ILO and the Right to Strike' (2014) 153(1) *International Labour Review* 29.

[80] Cf. R Rogowski, *Reflexive Labour Law in the World Society* (Cheltenham, Edward Elgar, 2013).

[81] G Teubner, 'Substantive and Reflexive Elements in Modern Law' (1983) 17 *Law and Society Review* 242; cf. D Ashiagbor, 'Evaluating the Reflexive Turn in Labour Law' in A Bogg, C Costello, A Davies and J Prassl (eds), *The Autonomy of Labour Law* (Oxford, OUP, 2015), 128.

[82] Platzer and Rüb (n 48) 11.

of the agreement and propose appropriate measures to remedy these, including preventative measures and can visit sites accordingly at Thyssenkrupp's expense. The agreement between Industriall and Aker ASA (2012) goes further in detailing annual review and complaints procedures, explicitly involving 'shop stewards' in dispute procedures.

The establishment of such committees and dispute procedures allow worker voice access to the senior management of the company in unprecedented ways, which Riisgard has described as an opportunity 'to override union-hostile local management'.[83] That tactic was utilised in relation to enforcement provisions set out in the IFA with Accor (1995), so that when strike leaders were sacked in Indonesia, the IUF could intervene directly by contacting the MNC human resources department based in Paris.[84] Similarly, Stevis reported that the DaimlerChrysler IFAs (from 2002–2007) assisted in the resolution of disputes in Brazil and Turkey.[85]

Framework agreements are predominantly a feature of corporate governance by European-based MNEs, so it is perhaps not surprising that not only Global Works Councils but also European Works Councils (EWC) play a key role in their implementation.[86] This is likely to be the case where the IFA provides for formal review at every annual meeting of the EWC, such as under the Accor (1995) agreement. Other examples abound in the analysis offered by Papadakis who points to the way in which the Leoni (2002) declaratory IFA enabled meetings between management and German works councils which led to assistance for workers in unorganised plants in Romania[87] and the Bosch (2004) 'Basic Principles' IFA led to solidarity and assistance for US workers taking industrial action.[88] In this way, the inclusion of EWCs in IFA enforcement processes enables non-organised and 'non-European concerns' to find their way onto the agenda.[89]

Just as the British system of collective *laissez faire* was maintained by an 'indirect' pattern of auxiliary support,[90] so Sciarra has reminded us that European Works Councils legislation in the EU constitutes 'transnational

[83] Riisgaard, (n 52) 727.

[84] Miller (n 52) 696.

[85] D Stevis, *International Framework Agreements and Global Social Dialogue* (2010) ILO Employment Sector Working Paper No. 47/2010, 4.

[86] I Schömann, A Sobczak, E Voss and P Wilke, *Codes of Conduct and International Framework Agreements: New forms of governance at company level* (Dublin/Luxembourg: Official Publications for the European Communities, 2008), 50.

[87] Papadakis (n 49) 288.

[88] Papadakis (n 49) 291.

[89] J Wills, 'Bargaining for the Space to Organize in the Global Economy: A review of the Accor-IUF Trade Union Rights Agreement' (2002) 9(4) *Review of International Political Economy* 675.

[90] See O Kahn-Freund, 'Intergroup Conflicts and their Settlement' (1954) 5 *British Journal of Sociology* 193; A Bogg, *The Democratic Aspects of Trade Union Recognition* (Oxford, Hart, 2009), 3 et seq.

auxiliary legislation'.[91] Sciarra sees the EWCs as foundational for the conclusion and enforcement of IFAs and other normative non-binding agreements, but also associated provisions for training and planning for skills requirements.[92] In this context, we may need to reflect on why and how EWCs have provided these opportunities for collective voice (trade union and otherwise). This, in turn, indicates that the protection of human rights such as freedom of speech and freedom of association, as protected by the European Convention on Human Rights 1950, could be a vital legal prop to the workings of the EWCs and thereby contemporary framework agreements.[93]

One further question relating to enforcement is not only the efficacy of legally constructed institutions which might influence compliance, but also the role that national laws can play in giving IFAs or GFAs legal effect. For example, Coleman has argued that framework agreements could be regarded as contracts suitable as a basis for claims in national courts.[94] This is controversial because, as observed by Papadakis, 'IFAs were not intended to produce legally binding consequences let alone legal sanctions'.[95] His view is subject only to the proviso that terms in these agreements can become legally binding when incorporated into the national collective agreement in a particular jurisdiction and given effect through that means. This would require 'negotiations at national level in accordance with national laws and practices',[96] such that straightforward contractual enforcement seems unlikely. Even if converted into national level collective agreements, one returns again to the scope there is under national law to enforce these types of procedural terms, given the failure of the European Court of Justice to recognise the potential viability of dynamic clauses in collective agreements.[97] Last, but not least, the obvious mechanism for 'enforcing' collective agreements is the threat of industrial action and, without

[91] Sciarra (n 74) 418. See Council Directive 94/45/EC of 22 September 1994 on the establishment of a European Works Council or a procedure in Community-scale undertakings and Community-scale groups of undertakings for the purposes of informing and consulting employees and Directive 2009/38/EC of the European Parliament and of the Council of 6 May 2009 on the establishment of a European Works Council or a procedure in Community-scale undertakings and Community-scale groups of undertakings for the purposes of informing and consulting employees (Recast).

[92] Discussed also by Bourque (n 61) 39.

[93] Fenwick and Novitz (n 65).

[94] S Coleman, 'Enforcing International Framework Agreements in US Courts: A contract analysis' (2010) 41 *Columbia Human Rights Law Review* 601, 610.

[95] Papadakis (n 49) 282.

[96] R F Hoekstra, *The Legal Regulation of a living wage through International Framework Agreements* (2014), paper presented at the IREC in 2014, 11 available at: https://www.eurofound.europa.eu/el/events/irec-2014-abstracts-and-papers.

[97] In the case of Case C-426/11 *Alemo-Herron and others v Parkwood Leisure Ltd,* Judgment of 18 July 2013, as discussed by J Prassl, 'Freedom of Contract as a General Principle of EU Law? Transfers of Undertakings and the Protection of Employer Rights in EU Labour Law' (2013) 42 *Industrial Law Journal* 434, 444–445.

the entitlement to take transnational solidarity action, for example under the ECHR,[98] the scope for enforcement of IFAs remains limited.

V. CONCLUSION

Collective solidarity has the potential to challenge new patterns of work and migration that undermine labour standards in many countries. Twin difficulties then arise. Mobilisation within national borders, such as in the *Chowdury* case,[99] is unlikely to be successful without broad transnational support. Effective mobilisation is also dependent on the competence of regional and global workers' organisations to organise and bargain. The very existence of international (or global) framework agreements is indicative of the potential for multi-level collective bargaining. This chapter has considered the preconditions for the effectiveness of such attempts to promote worker agency.

It might be possible to see IFAs (and their development into GFAs) as part of a trend towards soft law or reflexive governance,[100] but this disguises the multi-level regulation which determines their content and efficacy. Rather, I have sought to demonstrate how international, regional and national laws and legal regimes may influence the norms set out in framework agreements, alongside the capacities of the parties to engage in bargaining and enforcement. Such agreements draw on international (ILO and other) labour standards and utilise institutions for worker voice constructed under EU law, such as European works councils. They also depend on European and international human rights standards, relating to freedom of association and the right to strike, and will be limited in conjunction with the perceived legitimate exceptions to their exercise recognised by human rights adjudicators. These norms operate alongside one another, but also interact in ways that are not so much hierarchical as transnational.

Accordingly, we need to look more towards enabling laws. We may not need a precise international law aimed at countering the activities of Uber, but rather initiatives concerning labour norms and human rights which connect transnationally through a variety of mechanisms operating simultaneously. Together these have the potential to offer workers voice in solidarity to defend themselves. If we forget the significance of this legal matrix and allow this plurality of multi-level labour standards to be eroded, then it is unlikely that framework agreements can be sustained or more significantly regenerated. That, in turn, would affect the potential for current national labour market trends regarding precarious and migrant workers to be addressed or reversed.

[98] See *RMT v UK* (2015) 60 EHRR 10, also commentary from A Bogg and K D Ewing, 'The Implications of the RMT Case' (2014) 43 *Industrial Law Journal* 221.

[99] (2016) application no. 21884/15.

[100] G Meardi and P Marginson, 'Global Labour Governance: Potential and limits of an emerging perspective' (2014) 28(4) *Work, Employment and Society* 651.

BIBLIOGRAPHY

Abbott, B and S Williams, 'Widening the 'Representation Gap'? The implications of the 'lobbying act' for worker representation in the UK' (2014) 45(6) *Industrial Relations Journal* 507.

Adams, Z and S Deakin, 'Institutional Solutions to Precariousness and Inequality in Labour Markets (2014) 52 *British Journal of Industrial Relations* 779.

Ashiagbor, D 'Evaluating the Reflexive Turn in Labour Law' in A Bogg, C Costello, A Davies and J Prassl (eds), *The Autonomy of Labour Law* (Oxford, OUP, 2015).

Bales, K, A Bogg and T Novitz, '"Voice" and "Choice" in Modern Working Practices: Problems with the Taylor Review' (2018) 47 *Industrial Law Journal* 46.

Balsmeier, B 'Unions, Collective Relations Laws and R&D Investment in Emerging and Developing Countries' (2017) 46(1) *Research Policy* 292.

Bartels, L *Human Rights and Sustainable Development Obligations in EU Free Trade Agreements*, Legal Studies Research Paper No. 24/2012.

Bellace, J 'The ILO and the Right to Strike' (2014) 153(1) *International Labour Review* 29.

Bernaciek, M 'Polish Trade Unions and Social Dumping Debates: Between a rock and a hard place' (2016) 22(4) *Transfer* 505.

Bohoslavsky, J P *Report on Structural Adjustment and Labour Rights* A/HRC/34/57 (Geneva, UN, 2017).

Bogg, A *The Democratic Aspects of Trade Union Recognition* (Oxford, Hart, 2009).

—— 'Beyond Neo-Liberalism: The Trade Union Act 2016 and the Authoritarian State' (2016) 45 *Industrial Law Journal* 299.

Bogg, A and K D Ewing, 'The Implications of the RMT Case' (2014) 43 *Industrial Law Journal* 221.

Bourque, R 'International Framework Agreements and the Future of Collective Bargaining' (2008) 12 *Multinational Companies Just Labour: A Canadian journal of work and society* 30.

Burstein, A, G Hanson, L Yian and J Vogel, 'Tradability and the Labor-Market Impact of Immigration: Theory and Evidence from the US' (2017) NBER Working Paper No. 23330 available at: http://www.nber.org/papers/w23330.

Chacartegui, C 'Segmentation of Public Employment in the Frame of Austerity Policies: Precariousness as a Consequence' (2014) 36 *Comparative Labor Law and Policy Journal* 203.

Cherry, M A and A Aloisi, '"Dependent Contractors" in the Gig Economy: A Comparative Approach' (2017) 66(3) *American University Law Review* 635.

Clauwaert, S and I Schömann, *The Crisis and National Labour Law Reforms: A Mapping Exercise* (Brussels, ETUI Working Paper 2012.04, 2012.

Coleman, S 'Enforcing International Framework Agreements in US Courts: A contract analysis' (2010) 41 *Columbia Human Rights Law Review* 601.

Collins, H 'Independent Contractors and the Vertical Disintegration of the Employment Relationship' (1990) 10 *Oxford Journal of Legal Studies* 353.

De Stefano, V 'The Rise of the "Just-in-Time Workforce": On-demand Work, Crowd Work and Labour Protection in the 'Gig-Economy' (2016) ILO Working Paper available at: http://www.ilo.org/travail/whatwedo/publications/WCMS_443267/lang--en/index.htm.

—— 'Non-standard Work and Limits on Freedom of Association: A Human Rights-based Approach (2017) 46 *Industrial Law Journal* 185.

Ewing, K D 'International Regulation of the Global Economy – The role of trade unions' in B Bercusson and C Estlund (eds), *Regulating Labour in the Wake of Globalisation: New challenges, new institutions* (Oxford, Hart, 2008).

—— 'Myth and Reality of the Right to Strike as a "Fundamental Labour Right" (2013) 29(2) *International Journal of Comparative Labour Law and Industrial Relations* 145.

—— 'Transnational Labour Law' (2016) 27 *King's Law Journal* 132.

Finkin, M 'Employee Self-representation and the Law in the United States (2013) 50(4) *Osgoode Hall Law Journal* 937.

Ford, M and T Novitz, 'Legislating for Control: The Trade Union Act 2016' (2016) 45 *Industrial Law Journal* 277.

Hammer, N 'International Framework Agreements: Global industrial relations between rights and bargaining' (2005) 11(4) *Transfer* 511.

Hayes, L *Stories of Care: A Labour of Law – Gender and Class at Work* (London, Palgrave, 2017).

Henley, A *The Post Crisis Growth in the Self-employed: Volunteers or reluctant recruits?* (IZA Discussion Papers, No. 9232, 2015); Joseph Rowntree Foundation Report, *Monitoring Poverty and Social Exclusion 2016* available at: https://www.jrf.org.uk/report/monitoring-poverty-and-social-exclusion-2016?gclid=CMymjo2yq9QCFUKVGwodvk4A2Q.

Herrnstadt, O E 'Are International Framework Agreements a path to corporate social responsibility?' (2007/8) 10 *University of Pennsylvania Journal of Business and Employment Law* 187.

Hobsbawm, E J *Nations and Nationalism since 1780*, 2nd ed. (Cambridge, CUP, 1992).

Hoekstra, R F *The Legal Regulation of a living wage through International Framework Agreements* (2014), paper presented at the IREC in 2014, 11 available at: https://www.eurofound.europa.eu/el/events/irec-2014-abstracts-and-papers.

Howe, J and R Owens (eds), *Temporary Labour Migration in the Global Era: The regulatory challenges* (Oxford, Hart, 2016).

Kahn-Freund, O 'Intergroup Conflicts and their Settlement' (1954) 5 *British Journal of Sociology* 193.

Koukiadaki, A, I Tavora and L M Martinez (eds), *The Transformation of Joint Regulation and Labour Market Policy in Europe During the Crisis: Comparative Project Report* (Manchester/Brussels, University of Manchester/The European Commission, 2014).

La Hovary, C 'Employers' Group 2012 Challenge to the Right to Strike' (2013) 42 *Industrial Law Journal* 338.

Lewis, H, P Dwyer, S Hodkinson and L Waite, 'Hyper-precarious Lives: Migrants, work and forced labour in the Global North' (2015) 39(5) *Progress in Human Geography* 580.

Lofaso, A M 'The Vanishing Employee: Putting the Autonomous Dignified Union Worker Back to Work' (2010) 5 *Florida International University Law Review* 497.

Lopez, L 'Formalizing the Segmentation of Workers' Rights: Tensions among Regulatory Levels (2014) 36 *Comparative Labor Law and Policy Journal* 281.

Luz Rodriguez, M 'Labour Rights in Crisis in the Eurozone: The Spanish Case' in C Kilpatrick and B De Witte (eds), *Social Rights in Times of Crisis in the Eurozone: The Role of Fundamental Rights' Challenges* EUI Working Paper LAW 2014/5 (Florence, European University Institute, 2014).

Mantouvalou, V 'Is There a Human Right not to be a Trade Union Member? Labour rights under the European Convention on Human Rights' in C Fenwick and T Novitz, (eds), *Human Rights at Work: Perspectives on Law and Regulation.* (Oxford, Hart/Oñati, 2010).

Meardi, G and P Marginson, 'Global Labour Governance: Potential and limits of an emerging perspective' (2014) 28(4) *Work, Employment and Society* 651.

Miller, D 'Preparing for the Long Haul: Negotiating International Framework Agreements in the Global Textile, Garment and Footwear Sector' (2004) 4(2) *Global Social Policy* 215.

Niforou, C 'International Framework Agreements and the Democratic Deficit of Global Labour Governance' (2014) 35(2) *Economic and Industrial Democracy* 352.

Novitz, T 'Big Unions and Big Business: Can international framework agreements promote sustainable development at a local level?' in T Novitz and D Mangan (eds.), *The Role of Labour Standards in Development: From theory to sustainable practice?* (Oxford, OUP/British Academy, 2011).

—— 'The Paradigm of Sustainability in a European Social Context: Collective Participation in Protection of Future Interests?' (2015) 31(3) *International Journal of Comparative Labour Law and Industrial Relations* 243.

—— 'Changes in Employment Status under Austerity and Beyond – Implications for Freedom of Association' (2016) 39 *Dublin University Law Journal* 27.

—— 'Multi-level Collective Bargaining – Connections with legal frameworks?' in B J Mulder, M J Hotvedt, M Nesvik and T L Sundet (eds), *Sui Generis: Festskrift til Stein Evju* (Oslo, Universitetsforlaget, 2016).

—— 'Collective Bargaining, Equality and Migration: The journey to and from Brexit' (2017) 46 *Industrial Law Journal* 109.

—— 'Labour standards and Trade: Need we choose between "Human Rights" and "Sustainable Development"?' in H Gött (ed) *Labour Standards in International Economic Law* (Cham: Springer, 2018).

Papadakis, K 'Globalizing Industrial Relations: What role for International Framework Agreements?' in S Hayter, ed., *The Role of Collective Bargaining in the Global Economy: Negotiating for social justice* (Geneva, ILO, 2011).

Peters, J 'Neoliberal Convergence in North America and Western Europe: Fiscal Austerity, Privatization, and Public Sector Reform (2012) 19(2) *Review of International Political Economy* 208.

Platzer, H-W and S Rüb, *International Framework Agreements: An instrument for enforcing social human rights?* (2014) Friedrich Ebert Stiftung Working Paper.

Prassl, J 'Freedom of Contract as a General Principle of EU Law? Transfers of Undertakings and the Protection of Employer Rights in EU Labour Law' (2013) 42 *Industrial Law Journal* 434.

—— *The Concept of the Employer* (Oxford, OUP, 2015).

—— *Humans as a Service: The Promises and Perils of Work in the Gig Economy* (Oxford, OUP, 2018).

Riisgaard, L 'International Framework Agreements: A New Model for Securing Workers Rights?' (2005) 44(4) *Industrial Relations* 707.

Rodgers, G and J Rodgers, *Precarious Jobs in Labour Market Regulation: The Growth of Atypical Employment in Western Europe* (Brussels, ILO, 1989).

Rodgers, L *Labour law, Vulnerability and the Regulation of Precarious Work* (Cheltenham, Edward Elgar, 2016).

Rogowski, R *Reflexive Labour Law in the World Society* (Cheltenham, Edward Elgar, 2013).

Sciarra, S 'Collective Exit Strategies: New Ideas in Transnational Labour Law' in G Davidov and B Langille (eds), *The Idea of Labour Law*. (Oxford, OUP, 2011).

Schömann, I, A Sobczak, E Voss and P Wilke, *Codes of Conduct and International Framework Agreements: New forms of governance at company level* (Dublin/ Luxembourg: Official Publications for the European Communities, 2008).

Standing, G, *The Precariat: The New Dangerous Class* (London, Bloomsbury, 2014).

Stevis, D *International Framework Agreements and Global Social Dialogue* (2010) ILO Employment Sector Working Paper No. 47/2010.

Teubner, G 'Substantive and Reflexive Elements in Modern Law' (1983) 17 *Law and Society Review* 242.

Trubek, D M, J Mosher and J S Rothstein, 'Transnationalism in the Regulation of Labor Relations: International regimes and transnational advocacy networks' (2000) *Law and Social Inquiry* 1187.

Tucker, E 'Intra-Company Transfers and Fissured Workplaces: *CS Wind* and the challenge of union organizing in Canada' (2016) Paper prepared for ReMarkLab Final Conference: New Foundations of Labour Law in the Globalised Market Economy? Stockholm, May 2016.

van den Putte, L and J Orbie, 'EU Bilateral Trade Agreements and the Surprising Rise of Labour Provisions' (2015) 31(3) *International Journal of Comparative Labour Law and Industrial Relations* 263.

Vosko, L *Managing the Margins: Gender, Citizenship and the International Regulation of Precarious Employment* (Oxford, OUP, 2010).

Weil, D *The Fissured Workplace: Why Work Has Become So Bad For So Many And What Can Be Done To Improve It* (Cambridge, Mass., Harvard UP, 2014).

Whittall, M, M Martinez Lucio, S Mustchin, V Telljohann and F Rocha Sanchez, 'Workplace trade union engagement with European Works Councils and transnational agreements: The Volkswagen Europe' (2017) *European Journal of Industrial Relations* 1.

Wills, J 'Bargaining for the Space to Organize in the Global Economy: A review of the Accor-IUF Trade Union Rights Agreement' (2002) 9(4) *Review of International Political Economy* 675.

7

Trade Unions' Action for Refugees and Asylum Seekers: Mapping the Process to Agency

CONSUELO CHACARTEGUI*

I. WORK AND WAR-TO-PEACE TRANSITIONS

IT IS A fact that European institutions are failing to comply with international duties to protect refugees: the cases of Aquarius and Lifeline are paradigmatic.[1] The European Council on Thursday 28 June 2018 focused on migration, security and defence. After hours of frantic negotiations, the EU leaders finally agreed to share out refugees arriving in the bloc on a 'voluntary basis' and create 'controlled centres' inside the European Union to process asylum requests.[2] According to Eurostat, the 28 Member States of the European Union granted protection status to 538,000 asylum seekers in 2017, a number significantly down compared with 2016 (when almost 1,200,000 first-time applicants were registered).[3] The highest number of persons granted protection status in 2017 was registered in Germany (325,400), ahead of France (40,600),

* This work was first discussed at a workshop held at the International Institute for the Sociology of Law in Oñati, Spain on 22–23 June 2017. Supported by the Spanish Ministry of Economy and Competitiveness, Grant DER2015-69652-P and FEDER, UE. I am grateful to Professor Julia López López for inviting me to take part and for her and the participants' helpful suggestions.

[1] European Parliament–Press Release, EU Summit/Migration: Parliament calls for joint solutions based on solidarity (Brussels, 27 June 2018), www.europarl.europa.eu/news/en/press-room/20180627 IPR06709/eu-summit-migration-parliament-calls-for-joint-solutions-based-on-solidarity.

[2] Council of the European Union–Press Release, European Council Conclusions (Brussels, 29 June 2018), www.consilium.europa.eu/en/press/press-releases/2018/06/29/20180628-euco-conclusions-final/pdf. The European Council reconfirms that 'a precondition for a functioning EU policy relies on a comprehensive approach to migration which combines more effective control of the EU's external borders, increased external action and the internal aspects, in line with our principles and values' www.consilium.europa.eu/en/meetings/european-council/2018/06/28-29/.

[3] Eurostat, 'Asylum in the EU Member States' (2017) 46 *News Release* 1, ec.europa.eu/eurostat/en/web/products-press-releases/-/3-16032017-BP.

Italy (35,100), Austria (34,000) and Sweden (31,200). In relation to the nationality of applicants, Syrians (175,800 persons, or 33 per cent), Afghans (100,700, or 19 per cent) and Iraqis (64,300, or 12 per cent) remained the main citizenships of people seeking international protection in the EU Member States in 2017.[4] However, the response of national authorities is disheartening.[5] At the end of 2017, the rate of recognition for humanitarian status, i.e. the share of positive decisions in the total number of decisions, was 46 per cent for first instance decisions in the EU. For final decisions on appeal, the recognition rate was 36 per cent.[6] The United Nations High Commissioner for Refugees (UNHCR) has pointed out that Europe is dramatically failing to comply with its international obligations to protect refugees. The UNHCR will continue to engage in the review of ILO Recommendation 71, which explains how the labour market can contribute to peace and security.[7]

Taking into account this reality, having a job arises as a key element of social integration that supports the peace of societies, and trade unions are one important vehicle to achieve this aim. ILO Recommendation 71 (1944) underlines that the character and magnitude of the employment adjustments required during the transition from war to peace will necessitate special actions. These actions are more particularly oriented towards facilitating the re-employment of all persons whose usual employment has been interrupted as a result of war, enemy action or resistance to the enemy or enemy-dominated authorities, by assisting persons concerned to find without delay the most suitable employment.

As will be analysed in the following, it is crucial to help refugees and asylum seekers to integrate into the labour market as an important part of the holistic integration into our societies. The trade union movement is already playing an active role in this regard as well as with other categories of 'recent migrants',[8] such as environmental refugees.[9] The ETUC statement on the European refugees

[4] Eurostat, 'Asylum decisions in the EU' (2018) 67 *News Release* 1, ec.europa.eu/eurostat/web/products-press-releases/-/3-19042018-AP.

[5] United Nations High Commissioner for Refugees, *Global Appeal 2018–2019* (Geneva, UNHCR, 2018) www.unhcr.org/publications/fundraising/5a0c05027/unhcr-global-appeal-2018-2019-full-report.html.

[6] Eurostat, 'Asylum decisions in the EU' (2018) 67 *News Release* 4, ec.europa.eu/eurostat/web/products-press-releases/-/3-19042018-AP.

[7] United Nations High Commissioner for Refugees, *Global Appeal 2018–2019* (Geneva, UNHCR, 2018) www.unhcr.org/publications/fundraising/5a0c05027/unhcr-global-appeal-2018-2019-full-report.html. According to this report, since 2014, approximately 208,150 asylum seekers have arrived in the EU by sea. During the first three quarters of 2017, over 2,600 refugees and migrants perished or went missing in the Mediterranean, 94 per cent of whom were trying to cross from Libya to Italy.

[8] S McKay, 'The Future of Work of Recent Migrants and Refugees' in S McKay (ed), *Refugees, Recent Migrants and Employment: Challenging Barriers and Exploring Pathways* (London, Routledge, 2009) 233. The author theorises about the commonalities of experience between the categories of refugees and 'recent migrants'.

[9] D Keane, 'The Environmental Causes and Consequences of Migration: A Search for the Meaning of Environmental Refugees' (2004) 2 *The Georgetown International Environmental Law Review* 209. The author maintains that climate conditions are not the sole and substantial cause of large-scale migrations.

and asylum seekers emergency, adopted at the Executive Committee on 25 and 26 June 2018,[10] and the emergency motion of the European Trade Union Confederation (ETUC) regarding the refugee crisis, adopted at the ETUC 13th Congress on 30 September 2015, remarked on the role of collective bargaining in respecting the dignity of refugees as opposed to their 'marketisation'.[11] On the other hand, local unions are concerned about the consequences of unfair working conditions for refugees and vulnerable workers, and they claim to ensure that applicable collective bargaining agreements are guaranteed to the refugees and asylum seekers in their respective countries. A representative number of refugee practices based on solidarity are engaged in by trade unions. Domestic initiatives from unions of Germany, France, Spain, Sweden and Denmark are some examples of humanitarian practices applied to the field of collective bargaining processes. Following the idea of agency embedded in an open-ended practice, the action of unions contributes to consolidating democratic power in a democracy.[12]

Refugees' protection in international law developed after World War II in response to the Holocaust.[13] The 1951 United Nations Convention relating to the Status of Refugees (Refugee Convention of Geneva) defined a refugee as a person who is outside his or her country of nationality or habitual residence; has a well-founded fear of persecution because of his or her race, religion, nationality, membership in a particular social group or political opinion; and is unable or unwilling to avail himself or herself of the protection of that country, or to return there, for fear of persecution. Refugees and asylum seekers should be treated on terms equal to those in the domestic workforce; this is the basic principle advocated by the International Labour Organization (ILO) and United Nations (UN) Conventions, but the reality is very different.[14]

Peace and work coexist as two sides of the same coin. The employment contract could play an essential role in helping refugees rebuild their lives and

[10] European Trade Union Confederation, *Statement on the European refugees and asylum seekers emergency, and on integration of migrants in European labour markets* (Sofia, 25 June 2018) www.etuc.org/en/document/etuc-statement-european-refugees-and-asylum-seekers-emergency-and-integration-migrants.

[11] J López López, 'The Regulation of Temporary Immigration as Part of New Forms of the Supply Chain: Segmenting Labour Rights For Workers' in RM Owens and J How (eds), *Temporary Labour Migration in the Global Era: The Regulatory Changes* (Oxford, Hart Publishing, 2016) 241, 259. The author analyzes the concept of dignity and its worth in the process of agency of temporary migrant workers.

[12] G O'Donnell, *Democracy, Agency, and the State: Theory with Comparative Intent* (Oxford, Oxford University Press, 2010) 133.

[13] G Noll, *Negotiating Asylum. The EU Acquis, Extraterritorial Protection and the Common Market of Deflection* (The Hague, Martinus Nijhoff Publishers, 2000) 3.

[14] T Novitz, 'Collective Bargaining, Equality and Migration: The Journey to and from Brexit' (2017) 46 *Industrial Law Journal* 109, underlines that 'effective representation in trade unions, especially where there is sectoral bargaining, has the capacity to foster solidarity, flattens wage inequalities and assists in productivity'.

can provide critical support to adapt to new and challenging circumstances. The aim of this chapter is to outline a trade union strategy for dealing with the right to work of refugees and what policies trade unions can carry out to remain relevant to the social integration of asylum seekers. For refugees, the practical consequences of an employment contract go beyond the simple existence of job protection. The aim of this work is to know whether this law 'on the books' is a true reflection of law 'in action',[15] and what is the role of the trade unions in a frame in which the situation of refugees and asylum seekers is a highly politicised issue in the European Union.

In the historical development of these tendencies, the task of the ILO has been crucial in the twenty-first century, with institutional actions and consolidated programmes promoting access of refugees to employment and labour markets; creation of immediate jobs and improvement of economically critical infrastructure through employment-intensive investment programmes; improving access to and capacities to deliver market-based vocational and technical education and training for refugees and host communities; investing in capacity and ownership by local actors of the identification and implementation of local economic development; enhancing employment services, and supporting business development and livelihoods projects; improving the regulatory framework for Syrian workers in the labour market through innovative approaches; and promoting better linkages between national and humanitarian responses to Syrian child labour. The ILO also recommends regular dialogue with national policy makers, trade unions and employers' organisations as well as development partners on how to provide access to work for Syrian refugees.

II. FROM REFUGEES TO CITIZENS: UNIONS AS ENGINE OF CHANGE

Finding harmony between the European Union's refugee policies and a human rights perspective has been difficult. The last 10 years have seen the European Union evolve from a group of nations that jealously guarded sovereign prerogatives over refugee policy and migration to a supranational institution that is devising a regional approach to asylum (the Common European Asylum System, CEAS). Since 1999 the European Union has been working to create the CEAS and improve the current legislative framework. The reasoning of this institution relates to the necessity of establishing a hierarchy among rights – security over solidarity, borders over solidarity, and sovereignty over hospitality. In 2013 the Dublin Regulation (EU) No 604/2013 of the European Parliament and of the Council of 26 June 2013 on criteria and mechanisms for determining the Member State responsible for examining an application for international

[15] C Barnard, 'Enforcement of Employment Rights by EU-8 Migrant Workers in Employment Tribunals' (2016) 45 *Industrial Law Journal* 1.

protection,[16] and Directive 2013/32/EU of the European Parliament and of the Council of 26 June 2013 on common procedures for granting and withdrawing international protection[17] were examples of these more sophisticated measures of migration control. This ranking of rights contradicts the very foundation of the idea of human rights protection to recognise that some rights are so fundamental to human existence and human dignity that they should be enjoyed by any human being irrespective of citizenship.[18] On the other hand, cuts in public services (exacerbated in some countries by ongoing austerity programmes) put additional strain on refugees' precarious right to work.

Since the EU-Turkey Joint Action Plan was activated in November 2015, decisive action was taken by European leaders to break the cycle of uncontrolled flows of migrants creating an unsustainable humanitarian crisis.[19] In line with the EU-Turkey Statement, from 20 March 2016 all new irregular migrants and asylum seekers arriving from Turkey to the Greek islands and whose applications for asylum have been declared inadmissible should be returned to Turkey.[20]

While immigrant integration policies remain a competence of the Member States and are implemented at the regional and local level, the European Commission created a common framework for the integration of third-country nationals in 2005.[21] The Commission was supported in this effort by the Member States and their Common Basic Principles on Integration, reaffirmed by the European Council Conclusions of June 2014. Thus, the Common Basic Principles for Immigrant Integration Policy in the European Union were aimed at designing a common framework for a European approach to immigrant integration. One of the keystones of this policy was that employment is a key part of the integration process and is central to the participation of immigrants, to the contributions immigrants make to the host society, and to making such contributions visible. Nevertheless, EU directives have traditionally followed a very different path. In November 2002 the European Union adopted Directive 2002/90/EC of 28 November 2002 defining the facilitation of unauthorised entry, transit

[16] [2013] OJ L180/31.

[17] [2013] OJ L180/60.

[18] J Fudge and K Strauss, 'Migrants, Unfree Labour and the Legal Construction of Domestic Servitude. Migrant Domestic Workers in the UK' in C Costello and M Freedland (eds), *Migrants at Work. Immigration and Vulnerability in Labour Law* (Oxford, Oxford University Press, 2014) 160, 179.

[19] European Commission, 'Next Operational Steps in EU-Turkey Cooperation in the field of migration' (Communication) COM (2016)166 final, 4.

[20] European Commission, 'First Report on the progress made in the implementation of the EU-Turkey Statement' (Communication) COM (2016) 231 final, 2. The European Commission has remarked that the return of irregular migrants started on 4 April 2016. A total of 325 persons who entered irregularly have been returned from Greece to Turkey. In total, 1,292 migrants have been returned under the bilateral readmission agreement between Greece and Turkey in 2016, with most of return operations taking place in March.

[21] European Commission, 'A Common Agenda for Integration – Framework for the Integration of Third-Country Nationals in the European Union' (Communication) COM (2005) 389 final, 3.

and residence, and Framework Decision 2002/629/JHA on Strengthening the Penal Framework to prevent the Facilitation of Unauthorised Entry, Transit and Residence.[22]

Moreover, Council Directive 2003/86/EC of 22 September 2003 on the Right to Family Reunification[23] used a language of inclusion and exclusion that was a previous step towards the reality that we are now facing. Thus, article 6 states that 'the Member States may reject an application for entry and residence of family members on grounds of public policy, public security or public health'. Regarding minor children referred to in article 4,

> where a child is aged over 12 years and arrives independently from the rest of his/her family, the Member State may, before authorising entry and residence under this Directive, verify whether he or she meets a condition for integration provided for by its existing legislation on the date of implementation of this Directive.

Directive 2005/85/EC of 1 December 2005 on minimum standards on procedures in Member States for granting and withdrawing refugee status[24] provides for a number of procedural standards rather than a 'standard procedure'. The common element is the exploration of a status valid throughout the Union. The European Union must readdress its ineffective migration regulations and create a more humane response to the phenomenon of refugees' asylum. Nevertheless, with hardening attitudes at the borders, the situation is getting worse.[25]

Asylum seekers and refugees should be able to access public services without fear, without discrimination and without restrictions. Such services include emergency response, health care, education, housing, social services, access to justice, job placement and integration services.[26] According to Eurofound, 'while employers claim that refugees could help address skills shortages, unions are concerned about the consequences for the working conditions of both refugees and lower-paid segments of the existing workforce'.[27] This foundation remarks on the actions of trade unions in 15 European countries: Austria,

[22] [2002] OJ L328/17.

[23] [2003] OJ L 251/12.

[24] [2005] OJ L 326/13.

[25] According to article 6 of Council Directive 2003/86/EC, the notion of public policy may cover a conviction for committing a serious crime. In this context it has to be noted that the notion of public policy and public security also covers cases in which a third-country national belongs to an association which supports terrorism, supports such an association or has extremist aspirations.

[26] I Martin, A Arcarons and J Aumüller, *From Refugees to Workers. Mapping Labour-Market Integration Support Measures for Asylum Seekers and Refugees in EU Member States* (Florence, Migration Policy Centre, 2016) 32.

[27] Eurofound, *Approaches to the Labour Market Integration of Refugees and Asylum Seekers* (Brussels, Eurofound, 2016) www.eurofound.europa.eu/publications/report/2016/labour-market-social-policies/approaches-to-the-labour-market-integration-of-refugees-and-asylum-seekers. Conversely, the level of involvement is scarce or non-existent in Cyprus, France, Greece, Ireland, Latvia, Lithuania (trade unions only), Luxembourg, Malta, the Netherlands, Poland, Portugal, Romania, Slovakia (trade unions only) and Slovenia.

Belgium, Bulgaria, Croatia, Denmark, Estonia, Germany, Finland, Italy, Lithuania, Norway, Slovakia (employer organisations only), Spain, Sweden and the United Kingdom.

The role of transnational trade unions in defining the characterisation of refugees' protection is a crucial element of the current integration process. The actions of trade unions in relation to asylum seekers are often described as a simple way to facilitate entry into the labour market of otherwise marginalised groups. Despite the fact that in some countries no clear position has been taken, the great majority of trade unions have a proactive attitude towards integration of refugees and asylum seekers into the labour market.[28] But although trade union activism has had this positive effect, at the same time, due to the important role played by trade unions and their penetration into issues of concern to society,[29] trade unions' actions can also bring about difficulties in war-to-peace transitions.

Global trade unions are considered an engine of change by international institutions.[30] Specifically, policies developed by trade unions in areas such as gender issues, recruitment and education are crucial in the treatment of emergency issues. In this sense, the Recommendations of Global Trade Unions for the Declaration of United Nations Summit on Refugees and Migrants, signed in New York, 19 September 2016, are centred in the following proposals: (a) governments should ratify and implement, as a matter of urgency, the ILO Conventions on migration; (b) due to serious abuses by recruitment agencies, the alternative that might be considered is direct recruitment with full transparency without passing through private agencies; (c) from a gender perspective, it is especially important to increase compliance with mechanisms provided by the ILO Conventions in such areas as domestic workers (ILO Convention No. 189, 2011) or against trafficking in persons for the purposes of forced labour (ILO Convention No. 29, 1930); (d) migrants require decent work to realise their human rights; (e) it is necessary to enforce compliance with collective rights, enabling rights to form and join trade unions and engage in collective agreements.

The Recommendations of Global Trade Unions to the United Nations in 2016 remarks that the situation for migrants and refugees differs according to sectors, occupations and skills and needs to be sector sensitive.[31] The document notes that not only do problems and conditions of migrants often differ by sector, but also that global market conditions affect sector employment opportunities and practices differently. A recent European Parliament report on the labour market

[28] ibid 1.

[29] K Ewing, 'The Function of Trade Unions' (2005) 34 *Industrial Law Journal* 4.

[30] United Nations General Assembly, Draft resolution referred to the high-level plenary meeting on addressing large movements of refugees and migrants [2016] UN Doc A/71/L.1.

[31] Global Unions, *Global Trade Unions Recommendations for the Declaration of United Nations Summit on Refugees and Migrants*, 19 September 2016, www.un.org/en/development/desa/population/migration/events/ga/documents/2016/14July2016/GlobalUnions_14July2016.pdf.

integration of refugees also stresses the fundamental role of social partners in this domain, shaping collective representation in the workplace.[32] Thus, the European Parliament recalls that, to avoid a two-tiered system in the workplace, it is important that migrant workers are able to access their labour rights fully, including the right of trade union membership. To reduce social tensions, trade unions must work for the improved inclusion of refugees in the labour market and social security schemes, providing for equal treatment between national citizens and refugees. Nevertheless, the inclusion of refugees and asylum seekers in the personal scope of collective agreements is very scarce so this recommendation is far from actual implementation – as we will see in the following points.

Thus, the challenge is to find frameworks that avoid placing refugees in a position of competition and rivalry rather than solidarity. These frameworks embrace not only legal regulations, but also a collective bargaining understanding of this as a process. An example of transnational agreement is the emergency motion of the ETUC regarding the refugee crisis that was adopted at the 13th ETUC Congress on 30 September 2015. This motion highlights the role of trade unions in bringing about respect for the dignity of refugees. The ETUC calls for a proactive European asylum policy which respects internationally agreed protection standards, taking into account the UN 1951 Convention on Refugee Status and its 1967 Protocol, and encourages Member States to continue to work together in a spirit of constructive solidarity under the leadership of European institutions.[33] On a sectoral level, the European Federation of Food, Agriculture and Tourism Trade Unions (EFFAT) is another example of transnational union action. The EFFAT is focused on the effective implementation of core protective measures in the Seasonal Workers Directive 2014/36/EU[34] to prevent exploitative practices and abuses of third-country nationals and to ensure that the core content of this Directive is extended to refugees.[35] Moreover, this sectoral union is trying to ensure the offer of language courses and classes to develop refugees' knowledge of the labour market and help them learn how to apply for jobs

[32] European Parliament and the Committee on Civil Liberties, Justice and Home Affairs, *Report on the situation in the Mediterranean and the need for a holistic EU approach to migration* (2015/2095(INI), 23 March 2016).

[33] European Trade Union Confederation, *Emergency motion – refugee crisis in Europe* (Brussels, 30 September 2015) www.etuc.org/documents/emergency-motion-refugee-crisis-europe#.WTj0m-dzVCUk.

[34] Directive 2014/36/EU of the European Parliament and of the Council of 26 February 2014 on the conditions of entry and stay of third-country nationals for the purpose of employment as seasonal workers [2014] OJ L94/375.

[35] López López (n 11) 241.

III. COLLECTIVE ACTION FOR REFUGEES AND THE ERUPTION OF A COLLECTIVE CONSCIOUSNESS

Border controls, visa policies, preventing arrivals and the additional burden of suspicion of terrorism have meant that the path to safety and economic survival in Europe has been extremely arduous for refugees and asylum seekers in the last decade, exposing them to the risk of prosecution. A new way for trade unions to work at the community level is by strengthening human rights in order to fight against the criminalisation of immigrants and refugees – the phenomenon called 'crimmigration'.[36] Criminalisation[37] involves not just the bringing of criminal prosecutions or judicial processes but the treatment of whole groups of people as inherently suspect and criminal.[38]

In order to fight against this reality, national trade unions have developed a new way to work at the community level which has produced creative ways of promoting progressive messages on refugees, asylum seekers and migration. In France, the role of trade unions in mediating racism and enhancing the employment experiences of refugees has been a highlight.[39] For example, the most representative French union, CGT, analyses racism as a weapon used by employers to divide workers, so the argument is that only mobilisation can be effective. In Spain, most representative trade unions (Comisiones Obreras and Unión General de Trabajadores) have participated with other entities and non-governmental organisations in demonstrations. One of the biggest took place in Barcelona on 18 February 2017. The campaign 'Our home, your home' recalls that the Spanish government has welcomed only 516 of the more than 10,500 refugees established in the scheme of distribution by the European Commission, to be completed in two years. Organisations and unions urged the Catalan government to implement its commitment to host 4,500 people and called for action to improve the situation of immigrants in Catalonia and end 'institutional racism'.[40] In Spain, most representative unions also participate in the

[36] J Stumpf, 'The Crimmigration Crisis: Immigrants, Crime, and Sovereign Power' (2006) 56 *American University Law Review* 367.

[37] JA Brandariz García, 'Crimmigration Policies and the Great Recession: Analysis of the Spanish Case' in MJ Guia (ed), *Immigration Detention, Risk and Human Rights* (New York, Springer, 2016) 185, 197.

[38] F Webber, *Border Wars and Asylum Crimes* (London, Statewatch, 2006) 3.

[39] S Jefferys, 'Trade Unions, Migration and Racism in France' in S McKay (ed), *Refugees, Recent Migrants and Employment: Challenging Barriers and Exploring Pathways* (London, Routledge, 2009) 121, 138.

[40] Catalan News Agency, *Thousands march in Barcelona urging Spain to take in more refugees* (Barcelona, 19 February 2017) www.catalannewsagency.com/politics/item/thousands-march-along-barcelona-urging-spain-to-take-in-more-refugees. According to this report, 2016 will go down in history as one of the most death-filled years in the Mediterranean: at least 4,700 people, according to the official record, passed away trying to reach safety in Europe. The Catalan Refugee Programme is aimed at refugees who have completed the state programme without having reached sufficient

Catalan Refugee Programme, which has been developed in collaboration with civil society organisations and local authorities.[41]

This democratic movement fights against an ideology that criminalises refugees as well as immigrants.[42] The response of unions through a contra-ideology of human rights, decent work and dignity is an attempt to fight against the risks of poverty and social exclusion for refugees and asylum seekers.[43] Thus, members of this union take on the task of struggling against the wave of criminalisation and persecution of refugees and asylum seekers.

Trade unions face growing challenges of social integration, and to shoulder the task it is imperative to provide jobs for more refugees, enabling them to become part of communities. In 2016 the European Economic and Social Committee (EESC) agreed with the need to revise the current European Security Strategy (ESS) of 2003 in order to respond to the substantially altered international context.[44] In this revision, trade unions have an important role. Trade unions are on the front line of the fight for inclusion and integration of refugees in the workplace. On 15 June 2016 the ETUC, meeting in Rome, called on the EU and national governments to end all measures that endanger human dignity, rights or the physical integrity of human beings, on EU territory or at its borders. It is evidence that transnational trade unions are well aware that the segmentation of the workforce in our societies constitutes an obstacle to the realisation of collective worker consciousness on refugee policies.[45] The task

personal independence, and also refugees in situations of social exclusion. The beneficiaries must be registered in Catalonia and should have annual incomes below the Minimum Insertion Income during the previous 12 months.

[41] Another paradigmatic experience in the UK is the case of the Trades Union Congress (TUC). It is a national trade union centre, a federation of trade unions in England and Wales, representing the majority of trade unions. There are 51 affiliated unions with a total of about 5.8 million members. The TUC refers to itself as the voice of Britain at work. The TUC designed the campaign titled 'Migration Messaging Project' in which TUC General Secretary Frances O'Grady has added her voice to calls for Channel 4 to cancel its controversial documentary called 'Immigration Street'. This channel broadcast a documentary that showed racist conduct towards refugees and asylum seekers and demonised immigrants living in Derby Road, Southampton. Unfortunately, these actions are often supported by the media, which profits from domestic terrorist attacks. In the end, the issue is polarising society and the political debate is emotional with radical right-wing parties taking advantage of the dire situation of refugees. Information available at www.tuc.org.uk/about-tuc.

[42] C Barnard, 'Labour Market Integration: Lessons from the European Union' in R Craig and M Lynk (eds), *Globalization and the Future of Labour Law* (Cambridge, Cambridge University Press, 2006) 225, 241.

[43] The response of Spanish unions is described in J López López, 'Diminishing Unions' Agency: Weakening Collective Bargaining and Criminalizing Picketing in the Spanish Case' (2017) 38 *Comparative Labor Law & Policy Journal* 169, 186. According to the author, 'the unions have responded to their current challenges – including the government's efforts to diminish their role – through a set of interrelated strategies that include the following three instruments of activism: collective bargaining, judicialization, and protest'.

[44] European Economic and Social Committee, Opinion on the new EU strategy on foreign and security policy [2016] OJ C264/1.

[45] Speech delivered by Veronica Nilsson, ETUC Deputy General Secretary at the rally 'No to more walls in Europe'. She said, 'instead much richer European countries are building walls and

of the ETUC is to prevent the expression of workers' interests from being distorted by the division of the working class into various competing or rival groups.

To react against this tendency, a new form of trade union attitude is emerging, one based not on a summation of individual actions but on collectivism as an end.[46] In the fight for economic and social justice, this transformation progresses very slowly, gradually and carefully from one stage to the next. Nevertheless, those in favour of the doctrine remark that it could be the best path because as a very first goal, unionism requires an attitude oriented at partial privileges rather than at general improvement.[47] It is a complex process that goes from consultation levels to contribution to policy design, policy making and provision of services.

IV. UNIONS' LOCAL STRATEGIES: SHAPING RECOGNITION OF REFUGEES' AGENCY

Guillermo O'Donnell[48] traces the origins of the conception of the human being as an agent, emphasising its origins in the sphere of civil and social rights. The institutionalised, legally backed recognition of agency required a long process in which prior recognition of human rights and human development has been crucial. This process also entails the recognition of an agent as a 'legal person' entitled to subjective rights, who can validly claim against others and the state, including by accessing the courts. Very importantly, different national experiences show that unions decisively contribute to the existence of different spheres of decision for refugees and asylum seekers. The overall result is the formalisation of social relations concomitant with the regularisation of refugees' legal status in various nations.

The existing literature also proves that the more quickly refugees get in contact with the labour market, the sooner they integrate. As Lemaître remarks, benefits of early employment experience on later employment are much stronger than those of vocational education courses in Sweden.[49] In the trade unions' scenario of action in the field of local policies, the keystone is how to transform

closing frontiers and declaring emergencies. Now they want to pay Turkey to keep the refugees out of Europe. It is a scandal and shameful. European solidarity has been replaced by selfishness and nationalism', www.etuc.org/speeches/no-more-walls-europe-euwakeup#.WRrx9tzVCUk.

[46] AL Bogg, 'Individualism and Collectivism in Collective Labour Law' (2017) 46 *Industrial Law Journal* 91, remarks that 'a comparative perspective demonstrates how the "right to organise" might incorporate elements of "individualism" and "collectivism" in the specific design of complex rights'.

[47] R Herding, *Job Control and Union Structure* (Rotterdam, Rotterdam University Press, 1972).

[48] O'Donnell (n 12) 34.

[49] G Lemaître, 'The Integration of Immigrants into the Labour Market: The Case of Sweden' (2007) 48 *OECD Social, Employment And Migration Working Papers* 4.

refugees from spectators into participants.[50] In this complex process, unions have assumed an important role. The doctrine notes that effective representation by trade unions, especially where there is sectoral bargaining, has the capacity to promote solidarity.[51]

In the field of integration into the local labour market, an interesting initiative is contained in the German IG Metall Declaration, 'Towards a sustainable refugee policy based on solidarity', engaged by the Central Committee Meeting on 8 September 2015, and focused on improving capabilities for a better quality of life.[52] In 2016, IG Metall was providing its local units with a total of EUR 500,000. Chairs at these offices were called to use these resources to promote and initiate local activities for the benefit of refugees and encouraging the integration of refugees through patrons or mentoring programmes based on solidarity at the local level.[53] Actions go in two main directions: first, there is an initial programme of health care; second, IG Metall provides training and qualification measures. Refugees should undertake a three-month integration course, followed by a three-month internship in an enterprise. After successful completion, they can begin an apprenticeship in that company.[54] Representative bodies that are serving to implement these measures are the union's own members, works councils, trade union officers and youth training representatives, working for integration in the labour market based on solidarity.[55]

Spanish unions' good practices in this field are focused on skills recognition support and also on a function of providing assistance.[56] One interesting experience is offered by the Service for Attention to Immigrants, Emigrants and Refugees (SAIER, Servei d'Atenció Immigrants, Emigrants i Refugiats)[57]

[50] Following the expression of G Minet, 'Spectators or Participants. Immigrants and Industrial Relations in Western Europe' (1975) 117 *International Labour Review* 21, 36.

[51] Novitz (n 14) 109.

[52] A Sen, 'Development as Capability Expansion' in S Fukuda-Parr (ed), *Readings in Human Development* (Oxford, Oxford University Press, 2003) 3, 16.

[53] IG Metall, Declaration towards a sustainable refugee policy based on solidarity, Central Committee Meeting, 8 September 2015. Frankfurt, www.powerinaunion.co.uk/ig-metall-statement-on-refugees/.

[54] M Bergfeld, 'Germany's Willkommenskultur: Trade Unions, Refugees and Labour Market Integration' (2017) 8 *Global Labour Journal* 83 explains that, as a result of this strategy, in 2016 ver.di – the services union – negotiated the employment of 100 refugees as apprentices in Telekom – Germany's largest telecommunications company – on a yearly basis. Other experiences of the trade union for Mining, Chemical and Energy Industries (IGBCE) and the Food, Beverages and Catering Union (NGG) are also noted.

[55] G Mundlak, 'De-Territorializing Labor Law' (2009) 3 *Law & Ethics of Human Rights* 189, 222.

[56] See the concept of 'assistentialism' in MR Alarcón Caracuel, *La Seguridad Social en España* (Pamplona, Aranzadi, 1999).

[57] The SAIER was founded by the city council of Barcelona in 1991. It dealt with 1,041 asylum seekers in 2015, redirecting 64 to a labour-market orientation programme named AMIC, and 386 to another programme of advice for refugees on job placement called ACSAR. Over 40,000 activities were carried out in 2012, which means 4 actions per person. The main requests are for residence permits, nationality and Catalan courses. See M Fauser, *Migrants and Cities: The Accommodation of Migrant Organizations in Europe* (London, Routledge, 2012).

since 1991. This service collaborates with the most representative Spanish unions, Unión General de Trabajadores (AMIC-UGT)[58] and Comisiones Obreras (CITE-CCOO),[59] in coordination with the municipality and local administration.[60] They offer the necessary information and orientation for training and work integration. They also give advice on legal issues to refugees and asylum seekers, accompany refugees at legal processes and in regular reporting to the authorities, defend them in cases of illegal detentions and help with assisted returns[61] – see particularly the requirements of Law 12/2009 of 30 October on the regulation of asylum rights and other complementary legal instruments.[62] Recently it has begun offering Catalan courses. A similar initiative was launched in 1993 by the Association for Mutual Aid for Immigrants in Catalonia (AMIC) in coordination with the Unión General de Trabajadores. Another important service in this field is offered by the Spanish union Comisiones Obreras through the Centre of Information for Foreign Workers (CITE). Comisiones Obreras created this centre in Catalonia for the provision of legal, social and labour advice, and it has worked since 1986 for the integration of refugees, immigrants and asylum seekers.[63]

On one hand, it provides information about basic needs, such as information about reception centres for asylum seekers and refugees. Asylum claimants are frequently housed in detention, accommodation or reception centres which fail to meet basic standards of health and safety. When the Spanish Conservative Party (Partido Popular) approved, with the support of the Socialist Party, Law 4/2000 requiring immigrants to register with city councils, the main unions, Comisiones Obreras and the Unión General de Trabajadores, supported immigrants who said that such registration could in practice violate their fundamental

[58] AMIC is the Association for Mutual Aid for Immigrants in Catalonia (Associació d'Ajuda Mútua d'Immigrants a Catalunya).

[59] CITE is the Centre of Information for Foreign Workers (Centre d'Informació per Treballadors Estrangers).

[60] Other entities that collaborate with SAIER are the Barcelona Bar Association, the Red Cross, the Consortium for Linguistic Normalization and the ACSAR Foundation.

[61] Law 12/2009 of 30 October 2009 on the right to asylum, Official State Gazette (BOE) 31 October 2009, and Law 4/2000 of 11 January 2000 on rights and freedoms of immigrants and their social integration in Spain, Official State Gazette (BOE) 12 January 2000. According to the process contemplated in this regulation, after six months of the beginning of the administrative application, it is presumed as rejected (article 24.3 of the Spanish Law 12/2009).

[62] Urgency proceedings are regulated in article 25 of Law 12/2009, Official State Gazette (BOE) 31 October 2009, and the time of resolution is reduced to three months in special situations of unaccompanied minors.

[63] Its main functions are (a) advising about the creation of enterprises; self-employed activity; job intermediation; (b) social security issues: which legislation has to be applied; what are the social formalities; what are the requirements for health care assistance; (c) taxation: which fiscal system will apply; (d) legal matters: obligations concerning the Register of Commerce, VAT administration, employment contracts (models, clauses, workers' representative); (e) providing general information: living and working conditions, housing, language courses; (f) advice on legal issues, administrative processes and claims before the courts.

rights. Unions have expressed concern regarding the extensive use of detention of asylum seekers in these centres. Trade unions have also expressed indignation at 'indecent' conditions in reception centres where asylum seekers, including children, stay for up to six months or more. These protests have decisively contributed to the closure of some centres, such as the centre of Zona Franca by the city council of Barcelona. On the other hand, unions have created round tables for coordination (*taules de coordinació*) in order to mediate in some districts of the city of Barcelona where conflicts arose between refugees and settled populations.[64]

According to Eurofound, the major successes have been in countries where social partners are strongly involved in policy design for the purpose of integrating refugees. It is the so-called new perspective on 'diversity management'[65] implemented in countries such as Denmark and Sweden.[66] The Swedish trade unions have been very active in the fight for recognition of the right to organise for undocumented migrants, asylum seekers and refugees, and they have created the Swedish Trade Union Centre for Undocumented Migrant Workers, representing a new form of union activism.[67] The idea is that the line between individual and collective interests is very thin, and for this reason it is necessary to deal with these interests from a holistic perspective. In relation to Denmark, in 2016 the government, trade unions and business representatives concluded a tripartite initiative[68] with the robust participation of unions.[69] This initiative has significantly improved social integration through the intensification of fair mechanisms of job intermediation, giving effective tools for self-employment and economic activities, reducing administrative limitations for companies, and increasing the quality of collective rights – overall promoting the signing of new collective agreements, in accordance with ILO Convention

[64] Since 2005, UGT and CC.OO have coordinated networks of reception (*xarxes d'acollida*), a system for the exchange of experiences and knowledge about work integration. Activities of these networks are co-funded by the municipality of Barcelona through the Catalan Fund for the Cooperation and Development (Fons Català de Cooperació al Desenvolupament).

[65] AM Green, G Kirton and J Wrench, 'Trade Union Perspectives on Diversity Management: A Comparison of the UK and Denmark' (2005) 11 *Journal of Industrial Relations* 179, 196.

[66] Lemaître (n 49) 4.

[67] See the experience of the Swedish white-collar trade union TCO (Swedish Confederation of Professional Employees) in N Selberg, 'The Laws of Illegal Work and Dilemmas in Interest Representation on Segmented Labor Markets: A Propos Irregular Migrants in Sweden' (2014) 2 *Comparative Labour Law and Policy Journal* 263.

[68] The agreement was signed on 17 April 2016. The text is available at www.eurofound.europa.eu/observatories/eurwork/articles/working-conditions-industrial-relations/denmark-tripartite-agreement-on-integration-of-refugees.

[69] C Jørgensen, *Denmark: Tripartite Agreement on Integration of Refugees* (Brussels, Eurofound, 2016) 1.

The author remarks that this tool takes in information from the screening conducted in asylum centres, and it is used to match people with available jobs in the most convenient municipality for them.

No 98.[70] Taking this priority into account, the Danish authorities have subordinated the implementation of other tripartite agreements – in education, pensions and occupational health – to the realisation of this agreement as a necessary prerequisite.[71]

The agreement states that 'labour market inclusion is an absolute necessity for the integration of people into Danish society'. It is a joint proposal launched by social partners in the private sector – the Danish Confederation of Trade Unions (LO) and the Confederation of Danish Employers (DA) – for flexible solutions to integrate refugees with no special, or low, qualifications into the labour market as this group in particular has had difficulties in finding a job in Denmark.[72] The instrument for implementing the agreement is a so-called 'integration basic education' scheme (IGU). Companies that hire refugees under the IGU scheme can qualify for a financial bonus of up to 40,000 kroner if the refugees are employed for two years. The IGU aims to put refugees in short-term jobs at an apprentice salary level of between 50 and 120 kroner per hour (€6.72 to €16.13 in April 2016), allowing refugees a lower wage for at least a period, a so-called 'introductory pay' (*indslusningsløn*). Nevertheless, the salary was one of the most controversial matters. Some Danish unions, such as the Danish Union of Public Employees (FOA), have expressed concerns about how the IGU could affect the existing working conditions of stable workers. According to the FOA, this instrument could mean that municipalities put refugees into jobs at 49 kroner per hour, taking the risk of a 'replacement effect' or, in other words, a race to the bottom in relation to pre-existing working conditions.

The agreement aspires to the quick insertion of the refugees in the labour market, even if they do not meet language requirements. Local authorities are still obliged to offer relevant Danish language education free of charge for up to five years, irrespective of whether a refugee takes part in company-oriented initiatives or has obtained a job. Jobs under the IGU can last for up to two years and refugees will also be offered skills development or education courses of up to 20 weeks. Unions work together with local authorities, which are responsible for efficient integration programmes and seeking out the local jobs that the business sector can provide. The first stage of the integration consists of a fair transition from the asylum centre to the municipality. In this phase, refugees' skills are assessed. A new national tool is being developed to do this. It represents a new step in the maturity of trade union activity, enforcing labour rules in favour of the rights of refugees.

[70] Article 4 of the ILO Convention No 98 states that 'measures appropriate to national conditions shall be taken, where necessary, to encourage and promote the full development and utilisation of machinery for voluntary negotiation between employers or employers' organisations and workers' organisations, with a view to the regulation of terms and conditions of employment by means of collective agreements'.

[71] M Mailand, 'The European Refugee Crisis and the Reaction of Labour Market Actors: The Case of Denmark' (2017) 8 *Global Labour Journal* 91.

[72] Green, Kirton and Wrench (n 65) 179.

V. UNIONS AND REFUGEES: HETEROGENEOUS LEVELS OF PROTECTION

In the absence of specific central government responses to refugees' needs for integration and inclusion, we can observe that trade unions are currently in a process of *assistentialism* in their activities, often in collaboration with the social services of the municipalities and local authorities. This could provoke a phenomenon of 'replacement effect' where humanitarian actions are covered – or rather replaced – by trade unions instead of social services providers. The line between the union and the public administration function is very thin in the sense that it involves the implementation of public policy that the union has played a part in creating. In other words, unions could be in a process of transformation towards becoming social services providers due to the emergency activism that they are progressively undertaking in society.

Consequently, it seems that the role of trade unions could go beyond collective labour relations, taking into account that the precarious situations of refugees as individuals could justify the need for immediate attention due the provisions of the European Convention on Human Rights and ILO Conventions Nos 97 and 193. To some extent, we could be faced with the discussion of individualism as human rights or collectivism as collective rights, depending on the legal provision that serves as a frame in such Conventions,[73] taking into account the very broad material scope of such instruments, which could incorporate both perspectives.[74]

Thus, by concentrating their immediate task in the area of humanitarian aid, trade unions tackle a dilemma about what is the real focus in terms of representation of their interests and if it could be possible to combine individualist and collectivist elements in respect of these particular right holders. Following Niklas Selberg, they could take the risk of segregating themselves from adopting coordinated collective actions with positive benefits for both national workers and newcomers. In this sense, theorists of the doctrine have said that the focus of unions should be on labour market rights and collective action, not on the concrete problems of migration policy (eg regularisation issues or authorisations for residence).[75] From another point of view, Alan Bogg maintains that

[73] Two Conventions protect migrant workers and provide a framework for addressing refugees and forcibly displaced persons who enter labour markets outside their home countries: the Migration for Employment Convention (Revised), 1949 (No. 97) and the Migrant Workers (Supplementary Provisions) Convention, 1975 (No. 143). These explicitly prohibit discrimination based on nationality, and pertain to refugees and other forcibly displaced persons. In relation to the material scope, article 6 of Convention No. 97 includes the right to join and form trade unions. Both the Freedom of Association and Protection of the Right to Organise Convention, 1948 (No. 87), and Right to Organise and Collective Bargaining Convention, 1949 (No. 98), protect these rights.

[74] Bogg (n 46) 91.

[75] Selberg (n 67) 247. He remarks that the TCO (the confederation of white-collar Swedish trade unions) 'highlighted the encounter between labour law and migration law and proposed a separation between the two systems; arguing that "migrant status" and "status of employee" needed to be distinguished'. Thus, this confusion of roles opens up multiple tensions.

the distinction between individualism and collectivism is a trap, and 'we need to get beyond the tribalism of "individualism" and "collectivism" as antithetical worldviews, and recognise the multiplicity of claims that are often elided when we fall into that reductive trap'.[76] Conversely, according to Creighton, the model of collective agreement in some countries – such as Australia – is 'individualistic', in part because enterprise agreements are made between employers and employees, rather than employers and unions.[77]

Keith Ewing identifies at least the following five functions of trade unions: a service function, a representation function, a regulatory function, a government function and a public administration function. He remarks that the 'perception of trade unions as universal service providers coincides with an apparent increase in the trade union service function', such as provision of social services or legal advice or even a 'welfare function'.[78] These strategies of *assistentialism* could be characterised as a short-term process in which trade unions cover an important gap in the basic and minimum needs of refugees and asylum newcomers. In other words, trade unions, at the regional and local levels, provide the legal and first administrative information support, assisting refugees in the recertification of qualifications, which is long and arduous, in accordance with national legislation, which often imposes impossible visa requirements on nationals of all refugee-producing countries.

On the other hand, the experience in the field of local authorities is a bit different. In the 1980s many municipalities began to adapt their local structures in order to establish specific instruments for the first reception, judicial advisory and legal assistance of refugees and asylum seekers – even in their places or origin. These agreements are negotiated as a matter of social emergency. Specificities in the different sectors of activity are very important in the treatment of the emergency issues addressed by trade unions. This conception goes beyond mere measures of employment policy towards a holistic movement in which the previous situation of the refugees provokes a need for human assistance that requires an extraordinary level of action and contribution not normally vested in governmental structures.

Different models of local governance in each city lead to different approaches to the roles of trade unions and refugees' organisations, participatory channels and methods of integration. Political and administrative decentralisation improves the development of emerging models of trade unions as actors in policy implementation and decision making from a human rights perspective that coexists with the voluntaries and actions of non-governmental organisations. Nevertheless, the progress is more appreciable in the field of individual

[76] Bogg (n 46) 91.

[77] B Creighton, 'A Retreat from Individualism? The Fair Work Act 2009 and the Re-collectivisation of Australian Labour Law' (2011) 40 *Industrial Law Journal* 116.

[78] Ewing (n 29) 7.

rights and so the challenge is to improve actions in the field of collective rights and collective agreements that include special attitudes or measures of positive action towards refugees and asylum seekers.

Thus, it must be mentioned that the trade unions have evolved in refugees' and asylum seekers' issues, playing an important role in public policies from global to local strategies. From the global point of view, trade unions are trying to contribute to 'resocialisation'[79] and 'decriminalisation' due to the negative image that right-wing parties and some media have contributed to spreading. There have been efforts to increase collective consciousness in favour of refugees. From a transnational perspective, the Rome Declaration of 2016 is paradigmatic to achieving this aim. From a local point of view, unions are assisting in legal issues or administrative processes, and political actions on these matters have significantly increased. Unions are also developing important programmes for the labour-market inclusion of refugees, and put stronger emphasis on the enforcement of individual and collective rights. In sum, we can appreciate a significant eruption of collective consciousness about refugee matters among trade unions in the sense that they have included in their programmes of action substantial changes in favour of these persons, and this consciousness is being transmitted to the wider society as the different forms of integration take effect.

BIBLIOGRAPHY

Alarcón Caracuel, MR, *La Seguridad Social en España* (Pamplona, Aranzadi, 1999).

Barnard, C, 'Labour Market Integration: Lessons from the European Union' in R Craig and M Lynk (eds), *Globalization and the Future of Labour Law* (Cambridge, Cambridge University Press, 2006) 225–41.

Barnard, C, 'Enforcement of Employment Rights by EU-8 Migrant Workers in Employment Tribunals' (2016) 45 *Industrial Law Journal* 1.

Bergfeld, M, 'Germany's Willkommenskultur: Trade Unions, Refugees and Labour Market Integration' (2017) 8 *Global Labour Journal* 80.

Bogg, AL, 'Individualism and Collectivism in Collective Labour Law' (2017) 46 *Industrial Law Journal* 72.

Brandariz García, JA, 'Crimmigration Policies and the Great Recession: Analysis of the Spanish Case' in MJ Guia (ed), *Immigration Detention, Risk and Human Rights* (New York, Springer, 2016) 185–97.

Countouris, N and Freedland, M (eds), *Resocialising Europe in a Time of Crisis* (Cambridge, Cambridge University Press, 2013).

[79] N Countouris and M Freedland (eds), *Resocialising Europe in a Time of Crisis* (Cambridge, Cambridge University Press, 2013) 3.

Creighton, B, 'A Retreat from Individualism? The Fair Work Act 2009 and the Re-collectivisation of Australian Labour Law' (2011) 40 *Industrial Law Journal* 116.

Eurostat, 'Asylum in the EU Member States' (2017) 46 *News Release* 1, ec.europa.eu/eurostat/en/web/products-press-releases/-/3-16032017-BP.

—— 'Asylum decisions in the EU' (2018) 67 *News Release* 1, ec.europa.eu/eurostat/web/products-press-releases/-/3-19042018-AP.

Ewing, K, 'The Function of Trade Unions' (2005) 34 *Industrial Law Journal* 1.

Fudge, J and Strauss, K, 'Migrants, Unfree Labour and the Legal Construction of Domestic Servitude. Migrant Domestic Workers in the UK' in C Costello and M Freedland (eds), *Migrants at Work. Immigration and Vulnerability in Labour Law* (Oxford, Oxford University Press, 2014) 160–79.

Green, AM, Kirton, G and Wrench, J, 'Trade Union Perspectives on Diversity Management: A Comparison of the UK and Denmark' (2005) 11 *Journal of Industrial Relations* 179.

Herding, R, *Job Control and Union Structure* (Rotterdam, Rotterdam University Press, 1972).

Jefferys, S, 'Trade Unions, Migration and Racism in France' in S McKay (ed), *Refugees, Recent Migrants and Employment: Challenging Barriers and Exploring Pathways* (London, Routledge, 2009) 121–38.

Jørgensen, C, *Denmark: Tripartite Agreement on Integration of Refugees* (Brussels, Eurofound, 2016).

Keane, D, 'The Environmental Causes and Consequences of Migration: A Search for the Meaning of Environmental Refugees' (2004) 2 *The Georgetown International Environmental Law Review* 209.

Lemaître, G, 'The Integration of Immigrants into the Labour Market: The Case of Sweden' (2007) 48 *OECD Social, Employment And Migration Working Papers* 1.

López López, J, 'The Regulation of Temporary Immigration as Part of New Forms of the Supply Chain: Segmenting Labour Rights For Workers' in RM Owens and J How (eds), *Temporary Labour Migration in the Global Era: The Regulatory Changes* (Oxford, Hart Publishing, 2016) 241–59.

Mailand, M, 'Global Issues Refugees and Labour in Europe' (2017) 8 *Global Labour Journal* 90.

Martin, I, Arcarons, A and Aumüller, J, *From Refugees to Workers. Mapping Labour-Market Integration Support Measures for Asylum Seekers and Refugees in EU Member States* (Florence, Migration Policy Centre, 2016).

McKay, S, 'The Future of Work of Recent Migrants and Refugees' in S McKay (ed), *Refugees, Recent Migrants and Employment: Challenging Barriers and Exploring Pathways* (London, Routledge, 2009) 233–38.

Minet, G, 'Spectators or Participants. Immigrants and Industrial Relations in Western Europe' (1975) 117 *International Labour Review* 21.

Mundlak, G, 'De-Territorializing Labor Law' (2009) 3 *Law & Ethics of Human Rights* 189.

Noll, G, *Negotiating Asylum. The EU Acquis, Extraterritorial Protection and the Common Market of Deflection* (The Hague, Martinus Nijhoff Publishers, 2000).
Novitz, T, 'Collective Bargaining, Equality and Migration: The Journey to and from Brexit' (2017) 46 *Industrial Law Journal* 109.
O'Donnell, G, *Democracy, Agency, and the State: Theory with Comparative Intent* (Oxford, Oxford University Press, 2010).
Selberg, N, 'The Laws of Illegal Work and Dilemmas in Interest Representation on Segmented Labor Markets: A Propos Irregular Migrants in Sweden' (2014) 2 *Comparative Labour Law and Policy Journal* 247.
Sen, A, 'Development as Capability Expansion' in S Fukuda-Parr (ed), *Readings in Human Development* (Oxford, Oxford University Press, 2003) 3–16.
Stumpf, J, 'The Crimmigration Crisis: Immigrants, Crime, and Sovereign Power' (2006) 56 *American University Law Review* 367.
United Nations High Commissioner for Refugees, *Global Appeal 2018–2019* (Geneva, UNHCR, 2018) www.unhcr.org/publications/fundraising/5a0c05027/unhcr-global-appeal-2018-2019-full-report.html.
Webber, F, *Border Wars and Asylum Crimes* (London, Statewatch, 2006).

8

European Works Councils and the Convergence of National Collective Bargaining Processes

SERGIO CANALDA

I. THE EWCS IN THE CONTEXT OF THE EU DIRECTIVES ON INFORMING AND CONSULTING WORKERS

THE ADOPTION OF the first European Works Council (EWC) Directive was seen as the creation of the first 'transnational system of industrial relations based on European legislation'.[1] When created, it was placed among workers' recognised rights to information and consultation, which have evolved in ways that parallel the EU itself.[2] As has been pointed out, the *social acquis communautaire* has evolved as the 'social dimension' of the internal market.[3] The Treaty of Rome did not mention these rights, but it did include a Social Policy chapter where Member States agreed upon 'the need to promote improved working conditions and an improved standard of living for workers' (Article 117). In this vein, the Social Action Programme adopted in 1974 sought to increase the involvement of workers in the life of undertakings. Two Directives were adopted regarding this matter in order to approximate the laws of the Member States: Directive 75/129/EEC[4] (collective redundancies) and Directive 77/187/EEC[5] (transfers of undertakings).

[1] T Schulten, 'European Works Councils: Prospects for a New System of European Industrial Relations' (1996) 3 *European Journal of Industrial Relations* 303, 303.

[2] The European Commission stated that 'The history of the attempts to establish Community-level rules on employee information, consultation and involvement is closely linked to the history of the European Community itself'. See Commission, 'Communication from the Commission on worker information and consultation' (Communication) COM (95) 547 final, 3.

[3] I Schömann, 'EU Integration and EU Initiatives on Employee Participation and Social Dialogue' (2011) 17 *Transfer* 239, 244.

[4] Council Directive 75/129/EEC of 17 February 1975 on the approximation of the laws of the Member States relating to collective redundancies [1975] OJ L48/29.

[5] Council Directive 77/187/EEC of 14 February 1977 on the approximation of the laws of the Member States relating to the safeguarding of employees' rights in the event of transfers of undertakings, businesses or parts of businesses [1977] OJ L61/26.

The adoption of the Single European Act highlighted the social dimension of the future internal market.[6] In November 1988 the European Commission stated it was essential to have a social foundation within the Community which shows that 'the social dimension of the internal market is being completed at the same time as its economic dimension'[7] and which could be embodied in a 'European Charter of Social Rights'. This was finally adopted in 1989[8] with the name 'Community Charter of the Fundamental Social Rights of Workers'. In it, paragraph 17 states that information, consultation and participation for workers must be developed 'especially in companies or groups of companies having establishments or companies in two or more Member States of the European Community'.

This preceding background was the origin for the adoption of the first EWC Directive in 1994.[9] Indeed, the first action programme[10] to come about as part of the application of the Community Charter included a proposal for a Council Directive on the procedures for the information and consultation of employees of undertakings with complex structures, in particular transnational undertakings. Moreover, the European Parliament considered[11] the Commission's annual programme for 1990 to be insufficient for the balanced creation of a social dimension and called on the Commission to include a Directive on procedures for the information, consultation, and participation of workers, including the setting up of European consultative committees for multinational undertakings.[12]

Once the Treaty of Maastricht came into force, EU social policy, as the Commission stated,[13] was governed not only by the provisions of the EC Treaty as amended by the Treaty on the European Union, but also by the provisions introduced by the Protocol on Social Policy. With regard to the latter, the consultation and negotiation procedures with social partners provided for in the agreement were used for the first time in practice when the first Directive was

[6] Conclusions of the Presidency, European Council in Hannover, 27–28 June 1988, www.europarl.europa.eu/summits/hannover/default_en.htm.

[7] Commission of the European Communities, 'Social Dimension of the Internal Market' (Commission Working Paper) SEC (1988) 1148 final.

[8] Conclusions of the Presidency, European Council in Strasbourg, 8–9 December 1989, www.europarl.europa.eu/summits/strasbourg/default_en.htm.

[9] Council Directive 94/45/EC of 22 September 1994 on the establishment of a European Works Council or a procedure in Community-scale undertakings and Community-scale groups of undertakings for the purposes of informing and consulting employees [1994] OJ L254/64.

[10] Commission of the European Communities, 'Communication from the Commission concerning its Action Programme relating to the Implementation of the Community Charter of Basic Social Rights for Workers' (Communication) COM (89) 568 final.

[11] European Parliament, 'Resolution on the most important legislative proposals in the social field to be included in the Commission's programme for 1990' [1990] OJ C68/155.

[12] This is more developed in: European Parliament, 'Resolution on the Commission's action programme relating to the implementation of the Community Charter of fundamental social rights for workers – priorities for 1991–1992' [1990] OJ C260/167.

[13] Commission of the European Communities, 'Communication concerning the application of the agreement on social policy presented by the Commission to the Council and the European Parliament' (Communication) COM (93) 600 final.

adopted in 1994.[14] Moreover, the Commission launched a wide-ranging debate about the future direction of social policy. Because of the adoption of a Community action in the social field[15] and the EWC Directive in 1994, the Commission allowed other proposals for Council Directives concerning the information and consultation of employees to be discussed.[16]

When new Member States entered the EU, the Council embraced 'Agenda 2000',[17] which required that Member States' employment policies be coordinated. On this basis, the adaptability of employees was approached as an integral part of the employment strategy, and, concretely, it had to be 'conceived and achieved through information and consultation procedures which allow employees to face and anticipate change'.[18] That was the seed for the proposal of a Council Directive which would establish a general framework for informing and consulting employees in the European Community, which was successfully adopted in 2002.[19] Directive 2002/14 is more broadly applicable, that is to say it is applicable 'in any situation where corporate restructuring is envisaged'.[20] Two more Directives were adopted in the early 2000s regarding the involvement of employees in European companies (SE Directive)[21] and European Cooperative Societies (SCE Directive).[22]

In parallel to this, the European Council affirmed that the development of the European Union should be accompanied by the consolidation of the fundamental rights applicable at the Union level by means of a Charter to make them more evident.[23] Therefore, the European Council decided to draw up a Charter

[14] Commission of the European Communities, 'Report on the Community Charter of the Fundamental Social Rights of Workers and on the Protocol on Social Policy' (Report) COM (95) 184 Final, 42.

[15] See Commission of the European Communities, 'European Social Policy. Options for the Union' (Green Paper) COM (93) 551; Commission, 'European social policy – a way forward for the Union' (White paper) COM (94) 333 Final.

[16] Commission of the European Communities, 'Communication from the Commission on worker information and consultation' (Communication) COM (95) 547 final.

[17] Conclusions of the Presidency, European Council in Luxembourg on 12–13 December 1997, www.europarl.europa.eu/summits/lux1_en.htm.

[18] European Commission, 'Proposal for a Council Directive establishing a general framework for Informing and Consulting Employees in the European Community' (Communication) COM (1998) 612 final.

[19] Directive 2002/14/EC of the European Parliament and of the Council of 11 March 2002 establishing a general framework for informing and consulting employees in the European Community – Joint declaration of the European Parliament, the Council and the Commission on employee representation. [2002] OJ L80/29.

[20] W Njoya, 'The EU Framework of Information and Consultation: Implications for Trades Unions and Industrial Democracy' in A Bogg, C Costello and ACL Davies (eds), *Research Handbook on EU Labour Law* (Cheltenham, Edward Elgar, 2016) 367.

[21] Council Directive 2001/86/EC of 8 October 2001 supplementing the Statute for a European company with regard to the involvement of employees [2001] OJ L294/22.

[22] Council Directive 2003/72/EC of 22 July 2003 supplementing the Statute for a European Cooperative Society with regard to the involvement of employees [2003] OJ L207/25.

[23] Conclusions of the Presidency, European Council in Cologne 3–4 June 1999 www.europarl.europa.eu/summits/kol1_en.htm.

of Fundamental Rights of the EU (CFREU), which was solemnly proclaimed in Nice in 2000 and which recognised in Article 27 the right of workers to information and consultation in an undertaking. After the Treaty of Lisbon entered into force, the CFREU acquired binding force. The recast EWC Directive adopted in 2009 contains a specific reference to the CFREU in order to ensure that fundamental rights are respected and to observe the principles recognised by the CFREU.

II. THE FRAGMENTED EWC LEGAL FRAMEWORK ACROSS NATIONAL REALITIES

As stated above, the EU legislated on EWCs for the first time through Directive 94/45/EC, but Directive 2009/38/EC[24] is currently in force, recasting the former and other subsequent Directives. According to Lamers, unlike the old EWC Directive, the recast Directive stresses the European role of EWCs.[25] The EWC Directive sets out the rights of information and consultation in Community-scale companies or groups of undertakings (hereinafter, MNC) to be exercised by the EWC (or other similar procedures). However, the role of EWCs has to be analysed from a broader perspective beyond the information and the consultation of workers. As Njoya has affirmed, the EWC Directive is concerned with participation rights since it implies a permanent body within the company whose function is 'to engage with management on decisions affecting employees'.[26]

The specific competencies of EWCs are defined through a process of negotiation between central management and a negotiating committee called the Special Negotiating Body (SNB). Exercising the principle of autonomy of parties, the SNB and the management of the MNC will determine the functions and operating methods of the EWC by mutual agreement. As a key element of the role of the EWC, the Directive guarantees that it is the bearer of the right of information and consultation on transnational issues.

However, its ability to deal with transnational matters varies from one Member State to another due to the flexibility of the Directive's content. On the one hand, the Directive refers to specific provisions that must be directly regulated by national norms under the principle of subsidiarity. On the other hand, the Directive guarantees relative flexibility to Member States when transposing its content to the national level. Because of this, the EWCs' legal frameworks are

[24] Directive 2009/38/EC of the European Parliament and of the Council of 6 May 2009 on the establishment of a European Works Council or a procedure in Community-scale undertakings and Community-scale groups of undertakings for the purposes of informing and consulting employees (Recast) [2009] OJ L122/28.

[25] J Lamers, 'EWCs' Role Recast: A European Actor?' in F Dorssemont and T Blanke (eds), *The Recast of the European Works Council Directive* (Antwerp, Intersentia, 2010) 358.

[26] Njoya (n 20) 369.

not uniform but are composed of a diverse array of regulations causing EWCs' competencies and resources to differ.

A. National Circumstances Recognised Under the Subsidiarity Principle: The Definition of 'Employees' Representatives' as the Epicentre

The capacity of the EU for regulating the information and consultation of workers depends on its competence as established in the Treaties and the well-rooted basis of these rights in national traditions. In this vein, due to the fact that the issue of information, consultation and participation 'goes to the very heart of national industrial relations systems', Schömann underlines that there are different attitudes among the Member States with respect to which social policy responsibilities should be allocated to the EU.[27]

EU social policy is a shared competence between the Union and the Member States and therefore it is governed by the principles of subsidiarity and proportionality (Article 5, Treaty of the European Union, TUE). With respect to the principle of subsidiarity,[28] the EWC Directive would allow Member States to adapt the provisions of the Directive to national industrial relations and legal systems, specifically with respect to 'determining the arrangements for designating or electing employees' representatives, their protection, and determining appropriate penalties'.[29] In this sense, the idea of flexibility in designing national legal frameworks is anchored in 'the different national traditions, needs, and profiles of multinational companies'.[30] Indeed, the idea of flexibility is embraced by all information and consultation Directives.[31]

Accordingly, the Directive refers to national law and/or practice in several issues, widening the extent to which the application of the Directive may diverge. The most significant definition in the Directive is that related to 'employees' representatives'. Effectively, the term 'employees' representatives' means 'the employees' representatives provided for by national law and/or practice' (Article 2.1.d, EWC Directive). It is important to highlight that the definition was taken[32] from Directive 75/129/EEC on collective redundancies and

[27] Schömann (n 3) 245.

[28] Art 5.3 TEU states that 'the Union shall act only if and in so far as the objectives of the proposed action cannot be sufficiently achieved by the Member States, either at central level or at regional and local level, but can rather, by reason of the scale or effects of the proposed action, be better achieved at Union level'.

[29] European Commission, 'Proposal for a European Parliament and Council Directive on the establishment of a European Works Council or a procedure in Community-scale undertakings and Community-scale groups of undertakings for the purposes of informing and consulting employees (Recast)' (Communication) COM (2008) 419 final, 7.

[30] R Jagodzinski, *Variations on a Theme? The Implementation of the EWC Recast Directive* (Brussels, ETUI, 2015) 106.

[31] Njoya (n 20) 371.

[32] Commission of the European Communities, 'Proposal for a Council Directive on the establishment of European committees or procedures in Community-scale undertakings and

Directive 77/187/EEC on transfers of undertakings. The definition of 'employees' representatives' provided by Directive 75/129/EEC specified that any type of representation of workers' interests is accepted under the Directive and that they 'could function within the type of consultation/negotiation procedure'.[33]

Those implications should also be applicable to the definition found in the EWC Directive. Moreover, the Directive also specifies that the Member States shall determine the method for electing or appointing members of SNBs who are to be elected or appointed in their territories (Article 5.2, EWC Directive). As Picard affirms, SNB members could even be 'a representative from a European Industry Federation or a trade union official from a national trade union'.[34] The Directive also provides that the Member States shall provide employees who, through no fault of their own, are employed in undertakings or establishments where there are no employee representatives the right to elect or appoint members of the SNB.[35] Therefore, the EWC Directive also included this innovation, that is, the definition of 'employees' representatives' that was stipulated in the Directives on collective redundancies and transfers of undertakings.[36]

As a result, it is possible to find out a national framework's influence on the composition of an EWC, even though MNCs and workers are entitled to dictate an EWC's composition through the exercise of their autonomy (Article 6.1.b, EWC Directive). For instance, it is possible to distinguish between the German model, which establishes a joint composition of the EWC (thus including both employee and employer representatives), and the French model, which provides for employee representatives in the EWC only. Furthermore, national works councils in some countries are vested with the central role in the composition of the EWC, whereas in other countries, trade unions appoint members jointly with the works council or just play an indirect role.[37]

The EWC Directive includes other references to national frameworks. For instance, the Member States are also competent to establish the method for

Community-scale groups of undertakings for the purposes of informing and consulting employees' (Proposal for a Council Directive) COM (94) 134 final, 12.

[33] Commission of the European Communities, 'Proposal for a Council Directive on the establishment of European committees or procedures in Community-scale undertakings and Community-scale groups of undertakings for the purposes of informing and consulting employees' (Proposal for a Council Directive) COM (94) 134 final, 12.

[34] S Picard, *European Works Councils: A Trade Union Guide to Directive 2009/38/EC* (Brussels, ETUI, 2010) 73.

[35] That without prejudice to national legislation or practice laying down thresholds for the establishment of employee representation bodies (Art 5.2 of the EWC Directive).

[36] Commission of the European Communities, 'Proposal for a Council Directive on the establishment of European committees or procedures in Community-scale undertakings and Community-scale groups of undertakings for the purposes of informing and consulting employees' (Proposal for a Council Directive) COM (94) 134 final, 12.

[37] See European Commission, 'Report from the Commission to the European Parliament and the Council on the application of the Directive on the establishment of a European works council or a procedure in Community-scale undertakings and Community-scale groups of undertakings for the purposes of informing and consulting employees' (Report) COM (2000)188 final, 12.

calculating the thresholds for workforce sizes (Article 2.2, EWC Directive). Moreover, under the same rationale, 'national legislator must define the conditions under which temporary agency workers should be taken into account'.[38] Regarding the protection of employees' representatives, Article 10.3. of the EWC Directive provides that EWC members may enjoy protection and guarantees 'similar to those provided for employees' representatives by the national legislation and/or practice in force in their country of employment'.[39] Because of this, members of the same EWC may have different statutes applicable to them. Furthermore, the Directive also stipulates that Member States shall ensure information and consultation links between the EWC and national employee representation in cases where decisions likely to lead to substantial changes in labour organisation or contractual relations are envisaged and no arrangement for which is set forth in the agreement establishing the EWC (Article 12.2, EWC Directive). The links between national employee representatives and EWCs will be assessed below. Member States are also empowered to rule on confidential information (Articles 8 and 11.3, EWC Directive). Finally, it is important to highlight the statutory duty of the Member States to take appropriate measures in the event of failure to comply with the obligations laid down in the Directive (recital 35). However, this is not homogeneous, since these policies have been implemented differently in each Member State.[40]

All those references to national laws and national practices when Member States have transposed the Directive have subsequently resulted in a huge variety of national norms guaranteeing information and consultation rights at different levels of protection. Moreover, the flexibility of Member States in increasing the standards provided for by the Directive also makes the legal framework of EWCs even more complex. In the next section, the different transpositions will be assessed.

B. Divergent Information and Consultation Rights as a Result of National Transposition Laws

According to the principle of proportionality, the content and form of Union actions 'shall not exceed what is necessary to achieve the objectives of the Treaties' (Article 5.4, TEU). One of the most important factors limiting EU actions is respect for national circumstances. In doing so, Directives serve to

[38] Picard (n 34) 59.

[39] However, as recital 34 EWC Directive states, 'They must not be subject to any discrimination as a result of the lawful exercise of their activities and must enjoy adequate protection as regards dismissal and other sanctions'.

[40] R Jagodzinski, *Implementation of Enforcement Provisions of the European Works Councils Recast Directive: Are Sanctions Really 'Effective, Proportionate and Dissuasive'?* ETUI Policy Brief 7/2014, www.etui.org/content/download/16943/133161/file/Policy+Brief+2014-07.pdf.

set minimum standards in the EU, which may be eclipsed by a Member State's transposed legislation. Indeed, the weight of national transposing legislation is highlighted in all information and consultation Directives since the Directives may be less effective 'in the absence of a supportive domestic legal framework'.[41]

As for the practical functioning of EWCs, this is influenced not only by the home country's industrial relations, but also by 'company-specific industrial relations considerations, including structures and forms of employee representation and participation'.[42] Workforce size was also indicated as an attribute of an MNC which might affect compliance with the EWC Directive.[43] Concretely, as De Spiegelaere argues, employees, unions and management are more likely to take an interest in organising and making resources available to an EWC in countries with strong information and consultation rights.[44]

If we compare national frameworks for informing and consulting workers, we find that strong differences exist between countries. For example, there is a higher percentage of establishments with structures for employee representation in Denmark (80 per cent) or Finland (70 per cent) than in the UK, Hungary, Malta, Greece, the Czech Republic, Latvia and Portugal (less than 20 per cent).[45] Furthermore, there are also striking differences in terms of information rights. In more than 80 per cent of establishments in Austria, the Czech Republic, Denmark, Germany and the Netherlands, employee representatives receive information about the employment and financial situation, whereas these percentages drop to 52 per cent and 38 per cent in Cyprus and Portugal, respectively.[46] Taking industrial relations regimes into account, it is possible to detect similar trends:[47] employee representation in countries with 'organised corporatism'[48] is based in unions and has a high level of coverage. Under a 'social partnership'[49] regime, employee representation is based in a dual system but also has a high level of coverage. Conversely, employee representation in countries whose systems are based in 'liberal pluralism'[50] or the 'fragmented,

[41] Njoya (n 20) 371.

[42] Eurofound, *European Works Councils in Practice: Key Research Findings* (Luxembourg, Office for Official Publications of the European Communities, 2008) 17.

[43] Eurofound, *European Works Council Developments Before, During and After the Crisis* (Luxembourg, Publications Office of the European Union, 2015) 10.

[44] S De Spiegelaere, *Too Little, Too Late? Evaluating the European Works Councils Recast Directive.* (Brussels, ETUI, 2016) 30.

[45] Eurofound, *Third European Company Survey – Overview Report: Workplace Practices – Patterns, Performance and Well-being* (Luxembourg, Publications Office of the European Union, 2015) 99.

[46] ibid 103.

[47] Eurofound, *Mapping Key Dimensions of Industrial Relations* (Luxembourg, Publications Office of the European Union, 2016) 40.

[48] Denmark, Finland, Sweden.

[49] Austria, Belgium, Germany, Luxembourg, the Netherlands, Slovenia.

[50] Cyprus, Ireland, Malta, United Kingdom.

state-centred' regime[51] are both union based and show limited coverage in terms of the percentage of the workforce covered.

This plurality of national frameworks influences the definitions of information and consultation when they are transposed from the EWC Directive into the national legal framework. Therefore it becomes crucial to assess the parameters contained in the EWC Directive, which Member States must respect when they adopt definitions of 'information', 'consultation', and 'transnational', as well as the links between national and supranational levels of information and consultation. The extent to which Member States eclipse the minimum standards of the EWC Directive will explain the divergences in workers' information and consultation rights among EWCs' national legal frameworks.

First of all, the recast EWC Directive involved two new developments which serve as parameters to regulate the EWCs' competencies in informing and consulting employees. On one hand, it introduced a definition of 'information' – which did not exist in the previous Directive – and revised the old definition of 'consultation' in light of the other definitions included in Directives 2002/14, 2001/86 and 2003/72. Accordingly, the definitions contained in the current EWC Directive could be approached in the context of the effects of the Directives on information and consultation from the 2000s, so they have to be interpreted in an interrelated way with the other information and consultation Directives. On the other hand, the revised Directive introduced the general principle of effectiveness via Article 1.2 (EWC Directive), so the arrangements for informing and consulting employees shall be defined and implemented in such a way that their effectiveness is increased and so as 'to enable the undertaking or group of undertakings to take decisions effectively'.

The definitions of both 'information' and 'consultation' and the idea of effectiveness behind the procedures serve to delimit the minimum standards which should be respected by Member States when transposing workers' rights of information and consultation into national legal frameworks. However, some countries define 'consultation' more broadly.[52] In this vein, Jagodzinski pointed out that only five countries (Germany, Estonia, the Czech Republic, Lithuania and Slovakia) have implemented a broader definition of consultation, covering the right of an EWC to obtain a detailed response. For instance, whereas the UK legislation defines 'consultation' in similar terms to those of the EWC Directive, the German law provides employee representatives with the right to express an opinion and to meet with central management to obtain a reasoned response to any opinion they have expressed. Moreover, the same author argues that not all countries include references to the requirement of ensuring effectiveness either in information and consultation procedures or in the decision-making process.

[51] Bulgaria, Croatia, Czech Republic, Estonia, Hungary, Latvia, Lithuania, Poland, Romania, Slovakia.

[52] Jagodzinski (n 30) 65.

For example, social partners in Belgium specified in the transposed collective agreement that the arrangements for informing and consulting employees need to be defined and implemented in such a way that their effectiveness with regard to the provisions of the agreement is guaranteed.

One of the main issues where Member States may diverge is in the transposition of the definition of transnationality. The concept of 'transnational' becomes the material frontier of EWCs' competencies for being informed and consulted.[53] This is why Picard argues that clarity should be given to the notion of transnationality so as to prevent management from challenging EWCs' powers and capabilities.[54] In this vein, two aspects should determine the transnational scope of the EWCs' competencies regarding information and consultation: the scope of an issue's potential effects and the level of management and representation involved in it (recital 16, EWC Directive).[55] However, Jagodzinski concludes[56] that there are few countries that include references to recital 15 in their national laws or even broader definitions of 'transnational' than in recital 16. For instance, Spain included a specific reference to recital 16 in the Preamble of its transposed law whereas Hungary included its content in the operative part of its transposed law.

Finally, the EWC Directive states that EWCs' information and consultation procedures and those of national bodies of employee representation shall be linked with due regard to the competencies and areas of action of each (Article 12, EWC Directive). When an EWC's establishing agreement does not include arrangements for linking EWCs and national employee representation bodies and management takes a decision likely to significantly affect labour organisation, or contractual relations are envisaged, the Member States shall ensure that the procedures for informing and consulting employees are conducted both through the EWC and national employee representation bodies (Article 12.3, EWC Directive). Once more, countries have transposed the provisions of the EWC Directive in non-harmonious ways since some of them do not provide any statutory solution if the agreement does not include any arrangement for linking the procedures at the national and the European levels. Furthermore, of those countries that have transposed Article 12.3 from the EWC Directive, only a few add more precision regarding how both levels have to be linked.[57] Moreover, it has been stated that the way Member States and social partners

[53] According to the Directive, the competence of the EWC shall be limited to transnational issues (Art 1.3 EWC Directive).

[54] Picard (n 34) 24.

[55] The Directive illustrates the idea of the 'potential effects' of the matter subjected to the competence of the EWC as those 'regardless of the number of Member States involved, [which] are of importance for the European workforce in terms of the scope of their potential effects or which involve transfers of activities between Member States' (recital 16, EWC Directive).

[56] Jagodzinski (n 30) 65.

[57] Jagodzinski (n 30) 66.

at each level perceive the issue of linking may be influenced by 'the existence of co-determination rights, injunction rights, or more or less dissuasive sanctions to enforce local-level information and consultation rights'.[58]

In conclusion, divergences in the laws governing the competencies and functioning of EWCs are a consequence of references contained in the EWC Directive to national law or practices and, consequently, the distinct forms in which countries have transposed the Directive's minimum requirements. In spite of that, the principle of autonomy of parties rules the capacity of employee representatives and management to determine the scope of EWCs' competencies. Therefore, the principle of autonomy implies that new possibilities for convergence lie among the distinct national traditions.

III. THE EWC AS A SOURCE OF CONVERGENCE FOR NATIONAL COLLECTIVE BARGAINING PROCESSES: THE POTENTIAL OF THE AGENCY OF LABOUR

Despite the fragmentation characterising EWCs' legal frameworks, they are likely to undergo a lengthy process of change by which an increasing number of EWCs are enlarging their competencies even to include collective bargaining power. The myriad of factors influencing the negotiation process establishing an EWC and its functioning may range from the managerial structure of a company[59] to transnational variables such as the sector.[60] Even when the EWC is already in operation, divergences arising among an EWC's members can also be attributed to 'representation cultures, trade union policies, and [the] labour market situation' in the countries of their constituencies.[61] Moreover, actors' strategies may be decisive in the functioning of EWCs.[62]

The concept of agency may be useful to explain why the process of empowering the EWC's role is taking place. Though the concept of agency has been used in distinct scientific fields,[63] the approach given by labour geography literature will prove insightful. Labour geographers have brought the role of labour

[58] Eurofound, *Linking Information and Consultation Procedures at Local and European Level* (Luxembourg, Publications Office of the European Union, 2015) 1.

[59] C Gilson and A Weiler, 'Transnational Company Industrial Relations: The Role of European Works Councils and the Implications for International Human Resource Management' (2008) 50 *Journal of Industrial Relations* 697.

[60] P Marginson, 'The Eurocompany and the Euro Industrial Relations' (2000) 6 *European Journal of Industrial Relations* 9, 30.

[61] H Bicknell and H Knudsen, 'Comparing German and Danish Employee Representatives on European Works Councils: Do Differences in National Background Matter?' (2006) 48 *Journal of Industrial Relations* 435, 449.

[62] V Mählmeyer, L Rampeltshammer and M Hertwig, 'European Works Councils During the Financial and Economic Crisis: Activation, Stagnation or Disintegration?' (2017) *European Journal of Industrial Relations* 225.

[63] SP Shapiro, 'Agency Theory' (2005) 31 *Annual Review of Sociology* 263.

to the forefront in the study of the global economy and, more concretely, in the development of transnational production systems.[64] From their perspective, the potential for worker action is embedded in 'the formation of capital, the state, the community, and the labour market'.[65] In this vein, they use the geographical concept of 'political scale' to explain that workers have employed scalar strategies through which labour has managed to 'reconfigure political landscapes and renegotiate social hierarchies in ways which are more beneficial to the interests of workers'.[66] The evolution of the role of EWCs shows this trend.

Since their emergence, EWCs have, effectively, been seen as formal structures making a European labour movement possible.[67] Workers have, thus, shown great interest in the new representative body in that they could use EWCs to defend their interests at the transnational level. Furthermore, they have been approached as a primary European institution that offers 'a basis for international cooperation between the various unions represented at both [the] group- and workplace-levels within transnational companies'.[68] For those reasons, the expansion of the competencies of new EWCs may denote a strategy on behalf of workers to expand the role of these transnational representative bodies towards the adoption of new competencies, provoking a process of convergence of the different national traditions.

Although the idea of convergence may be elusive in the field of industrial relations,[69] the idea is to approach EWCs as bodies where national divergences converge through new competencies that are distinct from those prescribed by both the EWC Directive and national regulations. It deals with the idea of the 'vertical Europeanisation' of labour relations by means of the establishment and functioning of EWCs.[70] 'Vertical Europeanisation' refers to the establishment of a distinctive trans- and supranational sphere of communication and cooperation used as a level of problem solving beyond the nation state.[71]

[64] A Cumbers, C Nativel and P Routledge, 'Labour Agency and Union Positionalities in Global Production Networks' (2008) 8 *Journal of Economic Geography* 369.

[65] NM Coe and DC Jordhus-Lier, 'Constrained Agency? Re-evaluating the Geographies of Labour' (2010) 35 *Progress in Human Geography* 211, 214.

[66] ibid 219.

[67] L Turner, 'The Europeanization of Labour: Structure Before Action' (1998) 2 *Europen Journal of Industrial Relations* 325, 328.

[68] WE Lecher, 'European Works Councils. Experiences and Perspective' in WE Lecher and HW Platzer (ed), *European Union – European Industrial Relations? Global Challenges, National Developments and Transnational Dynamics* (London and New York, Routledge, 2002) 249.

[69] L Turner and J Windmuller, 'Convergence and Diversity in Industrial Relations' in MF Neufeld and JT McKelvey (eds), *Industrial Relations at the Dawn of the New Millennium* (Ithaca, NY, Cornell University Press, 1998) 195.

[70] H Katz and N Wailes, 'Convergence and Divergence in Employment Relations' in A Wilkinson, G Wood and R Deeg (eds), *The Oxford Handbook of Employment Relations: Comparative Employment Systems* (Oxford, OUP, 2014) 55.

[71] HW Platzer, 'Approaching and Theorising European Works Councils: Comments on the Emergence of a European Multi-level-structure of Employee Involvement and Participation' in M Hertwig, L Pries and L Rampeltshammer (eds), *European Works Councils in Complementary Perspectives* (Brussels, ETUI, 2009) 56.

Complementing it, 'horizontal Europeanisation' refers to the horizontal, cross-national interactions that form 'an integral part of the whole EWC-communication structure' and play 'an important role in the shaping of the actor-profile of the EWC'.[72] Notwithstanding the convergence that will be discussed below, it is interesting to highlight the existence of a previous convergence of European industrial relations systems 'on a pattern of representative consultation – or participation – at the workplace' in Western countries up to the 1980s.[73]

A. The Articulation of the Multi-level System of Worker Participation as a Starting Point for Convergence

It has been argued that EWCs should be analysed as multi-level, multi-dimensional organisations due to the fact that driving forces, fields of power, and interests have been inserted into EWCs' structures, their internal dynamics and their external impacts – from 'the local plant level, through the level of national companies and unions, up to the European level'.[74] This complexity is institutionalised when, as part of the autonomy of the parties, an EWC's functioning is established. The EWC Directive includes provisions reinforcing the effective functioning of EWCs, including some which trigger the convergence of national practices.

The most relevant provision is the need to coordinate EWC information and consultation procedures and those of national employee representation bodies. Furthermore, it is likely for national and transnational information and consultation procedures to take place simultaneously since the issue at stake is relevant at both levels. Therefore, it becomes necessary to anticipate the articulation of these procedures, taking into account that they may happen simultaneously, or even that informing and consulting the EWC may come first.[75] Indeed, the articulation of both levels is already considered in several agreements. For example, the ING's EWC agreement establishes that, where 'there are transnational issues that also call for information and consultation at the national or local level, … parties shall endeavour to ensure that the information and

[72] ibid 55.

[73] W Streeck, 'Works Councils in Western Europe: From Consultation to Participation' in J Rogers and W Streeck (eds), *Works Councils: Consultation, Representation, and Cooperation in Industrial Relations* (Chicago, IL, University of Chicago Press, 1995) 347.

[74] M Hertwig, L Pries and L Rampeltshammer, 'European Works Councils as International Non-profit-organisations' in *European Works Councils in Complementary Perspectives* (Brussels, ETUI, 2009) 28.

[75] Recital 37 stipulates that national legislation and/or practice 'may have to be adapted to ensure that the European Works Council can, where applicable, receive information earlier or at the same time as the national employee representation bodies but must not reduce the general level of protection of employees'.

consultation process at the European level and national level shall begin in a coordinated manner'.[76] In a similar way, the SE-Banken EWC agreement states that information 'shall, if possible, be given to the EWC at the same time as to the local employee representative body concerned'. The level of priority the EWC is given is also included in some agreements such as the Novartis EWC agreement, whose Article 6.2 stipulates that EWC employee members should be informed and consulted 'prior to national works councils to allow them to provide their timely input to the national works councils'.

The Directive also makes it mandatory for members of the EWC to inform employee representatives or, when there are no representatives, the workforce as a whole of the content of the information and consultation procedure carried out as well as its outcome (Article 10.2, EWC Directive). This duty to report through a top-down process guarantees that the information from the management is distributed and ensures the fully representative role of the EWC (Recital 33, EWC Directive).[77] Jagodzinski has pointed out that the duty to report back was hoped to 'improve articulation and facilitate a factual exchange of information between national and transnational fora'.[78] However, these processes may transform into a bottom-up process inasmuch as some agreements make it possible for local representatives or appropriate constituents to give feedback to EWC members. For example, GlaxoSmithKline's EWC agreement states that the EWC employee representatives will afford reasonable time 'to communicate with their constituents and give them the opportunity to express their views and opinions'.

Thirdly, the Directive opens the door to negotiating the establishment of a select committee set up within the EWC whose 'composition, appointment procedure, functions, and procedural rules' shall be also provided for in the agreement (Article 6.2.e, EWC Directive). The idea behind the select committee is to promote coordination and greater effectiveness of the EWCs' regular activities and to make information and consultation procedures available at the earliest opportunity when exceptional circumstances arise (Recital 30, EWC Directive). Whereas the operative part of the Directive does not include any more references to the select committee, the subsidiary requirements contained in Annex 1 establish that the EWC 'shall elect a select committee from among its members, comprising at most five members, which must benefit from conditions enabling it to exercise its activities on a regular basis'.[79] It is relevant to highlight that the same rights ascribed to the EWC shall apply to the select committee's members.[80]

[76] It also says that where 'possible and required, all levels will be informed at an early stage, allowing for enough time for consultation to have a meaningful effect'.

[77] Without prejudice to the provisions on confidential information in Art 8 EWC Directive.

[78] Jagodzinski (n 30) 101.

[79] Indeed, recital 44 also foresees that the select committee should be able to consult regularly.

[80] The select committee is provided with the same rights and duties as the EWC, according to points four (to meet without the management concerned being present), five (to be assisted by

The ability of the Select Committee to impel the convergence of collective bargaining processes is based upon the development of its role. For instance, in the case of BNP Paribas, the select committee (called the Bureau) 'represents the countries which are part of the European Economic Area but do not have their own representative on the European Works Council'. Another example would be the Select Committee of the Donnelley EWC being able to participate in resolving disputes (presumably also at the national level). The convergence process is even more strongly apparent when exceptional circumstances occur and the select committee acts on behalf of the EWC.[81] For example, General Dynamics' EWC agreement provides for a procedure whose provisions are more similar to those contained in a national information procedure than those in the EWC itself.

B. Building a New Transnational Participation Structure: The Convergence of Collective Bargaining Processes Beyond National Industrial Relations

EWCs are becoming a powerful structure where different traditions of worker participation converge. Indeed, social partners have highlighted the capacity of EWCs to become a mechanism for reconciling different national cultures regarding industrial relations.[82] This is also the role of European Industry Federations (EIFs) when they give support to SNBs. For example, the trade union UNI Europa may appoint SNB coordinators whose task is to make SNB members aware of the differences in national legislation and industrial relations and to promote 'the position that the interests of employees from all countries should be fairly represented'.[83]

The EWCs' competencies have evolved from information and consultation to other forms of participation. For example, some EWCs are entitled to give recommendations and to receive a reasoned response (eg, the EWCs established with MNCs Ecolab & Nalco,[84] Rolls-Royce,[85] and David S. Smith[86]). Other EWCs

experts of its choice), and six (cost of organising meetings and arranging for interpretation facilities and accommodation and travel expenses) of the subsidiary requirements.

[81] The subsidiary requirements state that 'there are exceptional circumstances or decisions affecting the employees' interests to a considerable extent, particularly in the event of relocations, the closure of establishments or undertakings, or collective redundancies' (point three of the subsidiary requirements).

[82] CEEP, ETUC, UEAPME, UNICE, 'Lessons learned on European Works Councils'.

[83] UNI Global Union, 'UNI Europa Guidelines on European Works Councils', www.uniglobalunion.org/publications/uni-europa-guidelines-european-works-councils-full-version.

[84] The 2015 agreement states in Art 8.3 that 'Central Management shall take the EWC's opinion and recommendation into account in its decision-making process and shall give a reply to the EWC with a reasoned response within fifteen (15) days'.

[85] The 2011 agreement defines 'consultation' as including the right to 'obtain a response and the reasons for that response, to any opinion the MNC might express'.

[86] According to the agreement of 2013, the EWC is able to submit suggestions that will also be considered by the management.

are even able to adopt resolutions, as in the case of ThyssenKrupp.[87] This phenomenon lies in the potential of agreements established while setting up the EWC to fulfil and develop the different procedures used to inform and consult workers. Some factors may influence the negotiations establishing the EWCs' functions. For instance, the subsidiary requirements might influence the parties negotiating the agreement establishing the EWC, though they are not applicable.[88] Moreover, the European Union's *social acquis* may also be an influential factor. For example, references to consultation aimed at reaching an agreement contained in some Directives 'blur the distinction between consultation and bargaining'.[89]

Analytically, 'information' and 'consultation' have been seen 'as initial stages within an overall employee participation process, preceding, but differing from, employee participation and co-decision making'.[90] In the same vein, Njoya has stated that information and consultation rights 'offer a valuable support for other avenues of worker voice and participation'.[91] However, the lines between all of these are hard to define. Blurred frontiers between consultation and negotiation would also be transferred from national practices to the EWCs' functions. As has been argued, the consultation process tends to blur into negotiation 'or into the other, stronger forms of co-determination-type employee involvement that exist in some countries, such as Austria, Finland, Germany, the Netherlands, Slovenia, and Sweden'.[92] The same report maintains that the relationship between collective bargaining and consultation within dual-channel systems may blur, such as in the cases of Italy, Spain and Sweden.

The blurred boundaries between consultation and negotiation, which have been transposed to the competencies of EWCs in their establishing agreements, may be explained by the so-called headquarters' homeland effect. This refers to the 'clear influence of the national political and especially the industrial relations regime of the home country of the European company'.[93] The German case may be a good example as Germany has transposed the definition of information and consultation given by the EWC Directive with a broader scope, thereby enriching the procedures of EWCs linked to German companies. According to the headquarters' homeland effect, it is likely that the broader competencies of EWCs established in a German MNC, and thus influenced by the co-determination basis of the German model, may be transferred to the functions exercised by the EWC's members, regardless of the national tradition of their home country.

[87] Agreement of establishment of ThyssenKrupp's EWC adopted in 2009.
[88] Picard (n 34) 85.
[89] C Barnard, *EU Employment Law* (Oxford, OUP, 2012) 639.
[90] E Ribarova, 'Information and Consultation Arrangements: Results from a Transnational Study' (2011) 17 *Transfer* 231.
[91] Njoya (n 20) 229, 365.
[92] Eurofound, *National Practices of Information and Consultation in Europe* (Luxembourg, Publications Office of the European Union, 2013) 57.
[93] Hertwig et al (n 74) 24.

If we look at the data provided by the European Works Councils Data Base (EWCdb),[94] EWCs may carry out five activities other than those of information and consultation: EWCs can give opinion/comments; make recommendations; initiate projects; negotiate; and, finally, reach consensuses. Focusing on EWCs that were established in 2009 onwards and are still in force, it is possible to see the following results: first, 72 per cent of EWCs established at companies headquartered in Germany have been endowed with the capacity to give opinions or comments, whereas only 38 per cent of EWCs established at French companies have the same right. Secondly, the percentage of EWCs established at French companies whose competencies include initiating projects or reaching consensuses with management is significantly lower (3 per cent and 2 per cent, respectively) than the percentage of EWCs endowed with those competencies at German MNCs (23 per cent and 27 per cent, respectively). In general, it is often the case that EWCs are entitled to expanded procedures when MNCs are headquartered in or expand their operations throughout continental Europe. For example, none of the EWCs established at MNCs headquartered in the UK have been given the capacity to negotiate, while 36 EWCs established at MNCs with a subsidiary in the UK but headquartered elsewhere have been empowered to negotiate; most of these are headquartered in Germany (17), France (7) and the Netherlands (3).

The headquarters' homeland effect should be less relevant than the agency of labour when the EWCs' competencies come close to collective bargaining and the capacity to conclude Transnational Company Agreements (TCAs). Given that neither the EWC Directive nor any national transposed laws give EWCs negotiating power, it is likely that worker action would trigger the signature of a TCA. Despite other factors, such as the willingness of management and others[95] to facilitate the development of EWCs as negotiating actors, expanding the competencies of EWCs, including incorporating negotiating powers, runs in direct contradiction with the effects management try to avoid when signing TCAs: 'the transfer of social and economic standards from their countries of origin to other countries' and 'paving the way for international trade union organisations to become real negotiating partners for working conditions on a much greater scale'.[96] Therefore, whether or not the convergence of national collective bargaining processes will entail transcending national differences in industrial relations and reinforcing the role of EWCs at the transnational arena, it should be concluded that labour will act as a catalyst for the empowerment of EWCs.

[94] ETUI, 'European Works Councils Data Base' (European Works Councils and SE Works Councils Data Base of the ETUI), www.ewcdb.eu.

[95] Hertwig et al (n 74) 37.

[96] Eurofound, *The Impact of Codes of Conduct and International Framework Agreements on Social Regulation at Company Level* (Luxembourg, Office for Official Publications of the European Communities, 2008) 46.

Regarding the capacity of EWCs to negotiate with management, although it would seem that they are limited to an EWC's instalment agreement, the number of TCAs concluded by EWCs is significant and some of them have been published as annexes to the establishment agreements for some EWCs.[97] In this vein, Lamers has argued that all agreements directly related to the EWC's functions and the execution of its rights should be legally covered by the provisions related to renegotiations of the EWC agreement.[98] From this perspective, most of these kinds of agreements would be legally binding. For instance, MNC Air France-KLM signed the 'Framework agreement regarding the Outstations in Europe' in 2013, which settled the role and information and consultation procedures of the company's EWC as well as those of local councils. MNC Diageo and its EWC signed the framework agreement entitled 'Best practice guidelines on redeployment, redundancy, and outplacement' as an appendix to their 2007 EWC agreement. Yet another example includes MNC Daimler Chrysler, which agreed to the 'Framework Regulation with the EWC on the Realignment of the Sales Organization in the EU' in 2007. Finally, the EWC of France Telecom negotiated with the management the establishment of the 'France Telecom World Works Council' in 2010.

IV. THE DISRUPTIVE ROLE OF EWCS THROUGHOUT THE CONVERGENCE OF COLLECTIVE BARGAINING PROCESSES

European Works Councils are representative bodies where the rights of workers to information and consultation may evolve into other procedures that reinforce the role of workers' voices in the workplace. As has been said, the competencies of some EWCs have transformed into other capabilities, including the capacity to negotiate with management on transnational matters. As was also discussed above, expanding the reach of EWCs involves converging national traditions in the new procedures and going above and beyond the simple methods of information and consultation provided for by the EWC Directive and national laws. On the other hand, those far-reaching procedures may be influenced by national industrial relations traditions regarding worker participation. This may happen at the enterprise level, but it also may happen by way of the workforce encouraging the EWCs' roles to be developed.

As a consequence, EWCs may be the source of an authentic, new level of participation for workers. In this sense, Njoya has argued that information and consultation rights, operating in conjunction with other mechanisms that allow workers' voices to be heard, should be understood as promoting the ideals of

[97] European Commission, 'The Role of Transnational Company Agreements in the Context of Increasing International Integration' (Staff Working Document) SEC (2008) 2155, 6.

[98] Lamers (n 25) 394.

industrial democracy.[99] This should be the principal reason behind discussing the need to empower EWCs with new competencies, always with respect for each party's autonomy when the agreement is signed. Moreover, if they are to play a role in the construction of industrial relations at the European level, Lamers affirms that 'an effective dialogue will evoke more EWCs to conclude transnational texts at the European level'.[100] In doing so, co-determination models referring to the competencies conferred to EWCs cannot be a taboo subject for the European Commission,[101] which should also be said of their capacity as negotiators at the transnational level.[102]

BIBLIOGRAPHY

Barnard, C, *EU Employment Law* (Oxford, OUP, 2012).

Bicknell, H and Knudsen, H, 'Comparing German and Danish Employee Representatives on European Works Councils: Do Differences in National Background Matter?' (2006) 48 *Journal of Industrial Relations*, 435–51.

Coe, NM and Jordhus-Lier, DC, 'Constrained Agency? Re-evaluating the Geographies of Labour' (2010) 35 *Progress in Human Geography* 211–33.

Cumbers, A, Nativel, C and Routledge, P, 'Labour Agency and Union Positionalities in Global Production Networks' (2008) 8 *Journal of Economic Geography* 369–87.

De Spiegelaere, S, *Too Little, Too Late? Evaluating the European Works Councils Recast Directive* (Brussels, ETUI, 2016).

Eurofound, *European Works Councils in Practice: Key Research Findings* (Luxembourg, Office for Official Publications of the European Communities, 2008).

——, *The Impact of Codes of Conduct and International Framework Agreements on Social Regulation at Company Level* (Luxembourg, Office for Official Publications of the European Communities, 2008).

——, *National Practices of Information and Consultation in Europe* (Luxembourg, Publications Office of the European Union, 2013).

——, *Third European Company Survey – Overview Report: Workplace Practices – Patterns, Performance and Well-being* (Luxembourg, Publications Office of the European Union, 2015).

[99] Njoya (n 20) 365.

[100] Lamers (n 25) 394.

[101] In 1997, the European Parliament affirmed the need to clarify 'what role the EWC can play in an overall concept of codetermination and whether, after a few years' consolidation, it can participate in negotiations on the codetermination model of the European company'. See European Parliament, 'Resolution on the communication from the Commission on worker information and consultation' [1997] OJ 33/130.

[102] European Commission, 'The role of transnational company agreements in the context of increasing international integration' (Communication) COM (2008) 419 final.

——, *European Works Council Developments Before, During and After the Crisis* (Luxembourg, Publications Office of the European Union, 2015).
——, *Linking Information and Consultation Procedures at Local and European Level* (Luxembourg, Publications Office of the European Union, 2015).
——, *Mapping Key Dimensions of Industrial Relations* (Luxembourg, Publications Office of the European Union, 2016).
Gilson, C and Weiler, A, 'Transnational Company Industrial Relations: The Role of European Works Councils and the Implications for International Human Resource Management' (2008) 50 *Journal of Industrial Relations*, 697–717.
Hertwig, M, Pries, L and Rampeltshammer, L, 'European Works Councils as International Non-profit-organisations' in *European Works Councils in Complementary Perspectives* (Brussels, ETUI, 2009) 13–46.
Jagodzinski, R, *Variations on a Theme? The Implementation of the EWC Recast Directive* (Brussels, ETUI, 2015).
Katz, H and Wailes, N, 'Convergence and Divergence in Employment Relations' in A Wilkinson, G Wood and R Deeg (eds), *The Oxford Handbook of Employment Relations: Comparative Employment Systems* (Oxford, OUP, 2014) 42–61.
Lamers, J, 'EWCs' Role Recast: A European Actor?' in F Dorssemont and T Blanke (ed), *The Recast of the European Works Council Directive* (Antwerp, Intersentia, 2010) 357–97.
Lecher, WE, 'European Works Councils. Experiences and Perspective' in WE Lecher and HW Platzer (eds), *European Union – European Industrial Relations? Global Challenges, National Developments and Transnational Dynamics* (London and New York, Routledge, 2002) 234–53.
Marginson, P, 'The Eurocompany and the Euro Industrial Relations' (2000) 6 *European Journal of Industrial Relations* 9–34.
Mählmeyer, V, Rampeltshammer, L and Hertwig, M, 'European Works Councils During the Financial and economic Crisis: Activation, Stagnation or Disintegration?' (2017) *European Journal of Industrial Relations* 225–42.
Njoya, W, 'The EU Framework of Information and Consultation: Implications for Trades Unions and Industrial Democracy' in A Bogg, C Costello and ACL Davies (eds), *Research Handbook on EU Labour Law* (Cheltenham, Edward Elgar, 2016) 363–88.
Picard, S, *European Works Councils: A Trade Union Guide to Directive 2009/38/EC* (Brussels, ETUI, 2010).
Platzer, HW, 'Approaching and Theorising European Works Councils: Comments on the Emergence of a European Multi-level-structure of Employee Involvement and Participation' in M Hertwig, L Pries and L Rampeltshammer (eds), *European Works Councils in Complementary Perspectives* (Brussels, ETUI, 2009) 47–69.
Ribarova, E, 'Information and Consultation Arrangements: Results from a Transnational Study' (2011) 17 *Transfer* 229–37.

Schömann, I, 'EU Integration and EU Initiatives on Employee Participation and Social Dialogue' (2011) 17 *Transfer* 239–49.

Schulten, T, 'European Works Council: Prospects for a New System of European Industrial Relations' (1996) 3 *European Journal of Industrial Relations* 303–24.

Shapiro, SP, 'Agency Theory' (2005) 31 *Annual Review of Sociology* 263–84.

Streeck, W, 'Works Councils in Western Europe: From Consultation to Participation' in J Rogers and W Streeck (eds), *Works Councils: Consultation, Representation, and Cooperation in Industrial Relations* (Chicago, IL, University of Chicago Press, 1995) 313–48.

Turner, L, 'The Europeanization of Labour: Structure Before Action' (1998) 2 *European Journal of Industrial Relations* 325–44.

Turner, L and Windmuller, J, 'Convergence and Diversity in Industrial Relations' in MF Neufeld and JT McKelvey (eds), *Industrial Relations at the Dawn of the New Millennium* (Ithaca, NY, Cornell University Press, 1998) 192–208.

Part III

Collective Action and Inclusive Governance

9

Autonomous Collective Bargaining in Sweden under Pressure

MIA RÖNNMAR

I. INTRODUCTION

THE SWEDISH LABOUR law and industrial relations system is based to a large extent on self-regulation through autonomous collective bargaining. Wages and employment conditions are generally set by collective agreements. There is no minimum-wage legislation or system for extension of collective agreements. In practice, the coverage of collective bargaining is almost complete. The relationship between trade unions and employers' organisations has traditionally been characterised by cooperation and social partnership.

It is generally recognised that a number of trends currently influence and challenge national collective bargaining systems and industrial relations in Europe and worldwide.[1] Collective bargaining in Sweden is thus framed within a European and international context, and is under pressure.

The aim of this chapter is to analyse the functions and legal regulation of collective bargaining in the Swedish system of labour law and industrial relations in light of EU law and current pressing developments. Two examples are in specific focus: European integration and posting of workers and the need to promote labour market inclusion of specific groups of workers, respectively.[2]

A global trend towards individualisation and decentralisation weakens trade unions and collective bargaining, and results in a decrease in trade union organisation rates and collective bargaining coverage rates. In Sweden, the trade union organisation rate is still high at about 70 per cent (even though there has been

[1] Cf eg S Hayter (guest ed), 'What Future for Industrial Relations? Special Issue' (2015) 154(1) *International Labour Review*; OECD, *OECD Employment Outlook 2016* (OECD 2016); and European Commission, *Industrial Relations in Europe 2014* (European Commission 2015).

[2] See also M Rönnmar, 'Aktuella utmaningar för det svenska kollektivavtalssystemet' in K Ahlberg, P Herzfeld Olsson and J Malmberg (eds), *Niklas Bruun i Sverige. En vänbok* (Uppsala, Iustus, 2017) for a similar analysis.

a significant drop in the last 10 years) and the employers' organisation rate is about 90 per cent. There are, however, important differences between sectors and groups of employees. Thus, in the hospitality and retail sectors the trade unionisation rates are significantly lower, and the same applies for younger workers. The collective bargaining coverage is about 90 per cent.[3] Since the 1990s, there has been a clear tendency towards individualisation and 'organised' decentralisation of industrial relations and wage negotiations in Sweden.[4]

Globalisation and European integration trends also shape the conditions for collective bargaining systems. EU industrial relations are simultaneously acting above, beside and within national industrial relations.[5] Attempts at transnational collective bargaining are made through international framework agreements and agreements with European works councils. Increased global competition, global supply chains and relocation of businesses run in parallel with an EU emphasis on freedom of establishment, free movement of services and posting of work. In the EU context, the rulings by the Court of Justice of the European Union (CJEU) in *Viking* and *Laval*[6] (as well as in the wider *Laval Quartet*[7]) have restricted fundamental trade unions rights linked to collective bargaining and collective action, and challenged national systems for collective bargaining, wage setting and industrial relations, especially systems based on collective autonomy and self-regulation. Thus, trade unions have limited possibilities to address worker issues through collective bargaining and collective action in an integrated, cross-border European market.[8,9]

Paradoxically, fundamental rights are not only challenged, but also increasingly highlighted and protected through a 'constitutionalisation' trend in the International Labour Organization (ILO), the Council of Europe and the EU,

[3] See Medlingsinstitutet, *Avtalsrörelsen och lönebildningen 2017. Medlingsinstitutets årsrapport* (Stockholm, Medlingsinstitutet, 2018) 224ff.

[4] Cf eg F Traxler, 'Farewell to Labour Market Associations? Organized versus Disorganized Decentralization as a map for Industrial Relations' in C Crouch and F Traxler (eds), *Organized Industrial Relations in Europe: What Future?* (Aldershot, Ashgate, 1995).

[5] See further M Rönnmar (ed), *EU Industrial Relations v National Industrial Relations. Comparative and Interdisciplinary Perspectives* (Alphen aan den Rijn, Kluwer Law International, 2008) for an analysis along these lines.

[6] See Case C-341/05 *Laval un Partneri Ltd v Svenska Byggnadsarbetareförbundet*, EU:C:2007:809 and Case C-438/05 *International Transport Workers' Federation v Viking Line ABP*, EU:C:2007:772.

[7] See also Case C-346/06 *Rüffert* [2008] ECR I-1989 and Case C-319/06 *Kommissionen mot Luxemburg* [2008] ECR I-4323.

[8] See M Rönnmar, 'Labour Law in the Courts' in U Neergard, R Nielsen and L Roseberry (eds), *The Role of Courts in Developing a European Social Model. Theoretical and Methodological Perspectives* (Copenhagen, DJØF Publishing, 2010) and S Deakin and R Rogowski, 'Reflexive Labour Law, Capabilities and the Future of Social Europe' in R Rogowski, R Salais and N Whiteside (eds), *Transforming European Employment Policy. Labour Market Transitions and the Promotion of Capability* (Cheltenham, Edward Elgar Publishing, 2011).

[9] See A Iossa, *Collective Autonomy in the European Union. Theoretical, Comparative and Cross-border perspectives on the Legal Regulation of Collective Bargaining* (Lund, Lund University, 2017) for an interesting, multifaceted and thorough analysis of collective autonomy and collective bargaining in the EU.

reflected, for example, by the adoption and legal effects of the EU Charter of Fundamental Rights. However, fundamental rights need to be balanced against each other, and the EU Charter of Fundamental Rights protects not only the rights to collective action and collective bargaining, but also the freedom to conduct a business.[10]

The economic crisis led both to financial and governance reforms at EU level and to far-reaching austerity measures in many Member States. These measures targeted basic tenets of national labour law and industrial relations: collective bargaining, wage setting, and employment protection, and were harshly criticised by international human rights bodies, trade unions and labour law scholars. These reforms have also been legally challenged at several levels – in national constitutional courts, in the CJEU and before international human rights bodies, such as the ILO and the Council of Europe.[11]

Demographical and societal trends are also influential. The rapidly ageing population within the EU implies challenges not only to social inclusion, pension systems, health care systems and solidarity between the generations, but also to labour markets, labour law and industrial relations. There is a need to advance the inclusion of both older and younger workers in the labour market, to promote active ageing and longer working lives, and to combat youth unemployment.[12] Furthermore, the refugee situation emphasises the need to advance the inclusion of newly arrived immigrants in the labour market.

In addition, the stability of the Swedish collective bargaining system has been brought into question in recent years, and a trend towards increased tension and diversity characterises the collective bargaining system and its different sectors and levels. Failed attempts at renegotiation of key cross-sectoral collective agreements, such as the Saltsjöbaden Agreement on industrial peace and the SN-PTK Omställningsavtal on redundancy transition, may also indicate a weakening of the tradition of cooperation and social partnership.

[10] See Case C-426/11 *Alemo-Herron*, EU:C:2013:82, relating to the (2001/23/EC) Transfers of Undertakings Directive, the application of collective agreements and the freedom to conduct a business. See further J Prassl, 'Freedom of Contracts as a General Principle of EU Law? Transfers of Undertakings and the Protection of Employer Rights in EU Labour Law. Case C-426/11 Alemo-Herron and others v Parkwood Leisure Ltd' (2013) 42(4) *Industrial Law Journal*. Cf, however, also the ruling in the subsequent Case C-201/15 *AGET Iraklis*, EU:C:2016:972 on the (1998/59/EC) Collective Redundancies Directive, the freedom of establishment and the freedom to conduct a business, representing a partly different approach.

[11] See eg S Deakin and A Koukiadaki, 'The Sovereign Debt Crisis and the Evolution of Labour Law in Europe' in N Countouris and M Freedland (eds), *Resocialising Europe in a Time of Crisis* (Cambridge, Cambridge University Press, 2013) and C Kilpatrick, 'On the Rule of Law and Economic Emergency: The Degradation of Basic Legal Values in Europe's Bailouts' (2015) 35(2) *Oxford Journal of Legal Studies* 325.

[12] See, for example, A Numhauser-Henning and M Rönnmar (eds), *Age Discrimination and Labour Law. Comparative and Conceptual Perspectives in the EU and Beyond* (Alphen aan den Rijn, Kluwer Law International, 2015) and A Numhauser-Henning (ed), *Elder Law. Evolving European Perspectives* (Cheltenham, Edward Elgar Publishing, 2017).

The outline of the chapter is as follows. Section II provides a discussion of the Swedish labour law and industrial relations system and functions and regulation of collective bargaining. Sections III and IV discuss implications for Swedish collective bargaining of European integration and posting of workers and the need to promote labour market inclusion of specific groups of workers (older workers, younger workers and newly arrived immigrants), respectively. Finally, Section V provides some concluding remarks.

II. THE SWEDISH LABOUR LAW AND INDUSTRIAL RELATIONS SYSTEM AND FUNCTIONS AND REGULATION OF COLLECTIVE BARGAINING

Important traditional functions of collective bargaining in the Swedish labour law and industrial relations system are, for example, to create a peace obligation and social truce; regulate wages and employment conditions; adapt the statutory regulation to sectoral or company circumstances; complement the statutory social security system;[13] protect individual employees; regulate and facilitate negotiations and other collaboration between the social partners; and supervise and enforce employment conditions. More recently, the promotion of the labour market inclusion of specific groups, such as older workers, younger workers and newly arrived immigrants, has surfaced as a function of collective bargaining.[14] Thus, in the Swedish labour law and industrial relations system collective agreements constitute an important legal source, and the majority of an employee's terms and conditions of employment are regulated by collective agreements.

The main legal regulation of collective bargaining in Swedish law is to be found in the (1976:580) Co-determination Act (MBL), which in turn is set within an international, European and constitutional framework (including ILO Conventions, the European Convention on Human Rights, The European Social Charter, the EU Charter of Fundamental Rights and the Swedish Instrument of Government). A collective agreement is statutorily defined as 'an agreement in writing between an organisation of employers or an employer and an organisation of employees about conditions of employment or otherwise about the relationship between employers and employees' (section 23 MBL). Within its area of application, a collective agreement is legally binding, not only for the contracting parties to the agreement but also for their members (section 26 MBL). In addition, an employer bound by a collective agreement is obliged to

[13] For example, through additional regulation of occupational pensions, unemployment benefits and parental leave benefits.

[14] Cf, eg, A Adlercreutz, *Kollektivavtalet. Studier över dess tillkomsthistoria* (Lund, CWK Gleerup, 1954) and F Schmidt, R Eklund, H Göransson, K Källström and T Sigeman, *Facklig arbetsrätt* (Stockholm, Norstedts juridik, 1997).

apply it to all employees, regardless of trade union membership. A collective agreement has both a normative and mandatory effect (section 27 MBL). Unless otherwise provided for by the collective agreement, employers and employees being bound by the agreement may not deviate from it by way of an individual employment contract. Such a contract is null and void, and breaches of the collective agreement are sanctioned by the payment of economic and punitive damages. In most cases collective agreements set minimum standards only, allowing employers, trade unions and employees to agree on better terms and conditions of employment by way of a local collective agreement concluded at workplace level, or an individual employment contract.[15]

There is no minimum-wage legislation or system for extension of collective agreements. However, in practice, the coverage of collective bargaining is almost complete and a de facto *erga omnes* effect is achieved. The collective bargaining coverage rate is about 90 per cent.[16] In line with the autonomous collective bargaining system, it is the role of the social partners to safeguard a general level of pay and employment conditions.[17] Supervision and enforcement of terms and conditions of employment are carried out to a large extent by the trade unions or the social partners in cooperation. Effective enforcement depends to a large degree on the workplace being covered by a collective agreement.[18]

Collective bargaining is closely linked to the freedom of association and the right to take collective action, both protected by constitutional law and regulated in the Instrument of Government. Furthermore, the (1976:580) Co-determination Act also contains an elaborate regulation not only of collective bargaining, but also of freedom of association, collective action and information, consultation and co-determination, all complemented by collective agreements.

The positive side of the freedom of association is protected by the Instrument of Government and the (1976:580) Co-determination Act.[19] Freedom of association is defined as a right of the employer and the employee to belong to an employers' organisation or a trade union, to exercise the rights of membership, and to participate in such an organisation and the establishment thereof (section 7 MBL). A violation of the freedom of association is deemed to have

[15] See J Malmberg, *Anställningsavtalet. Om anställningsförhållandets individuella reglering* (Uppsala, Iustus, 1997) 144ff. and M Hansson, *Kollektivavtalsrätten. En rättsvetenskaplig berättelse* (Uppsala, Iustus, 2010).

[16] See Medlingsinstitutet, *Avtalsrörelsen och lönebildningen 2017*.

[17] The trade unions do this by trying to force employers who are not members of an employers' organisation (and thereby not automatically bound by collective agreements) to conclude 'application agreements' (*hängavtal*). If agreement cannot be reached by way of negotiations, the trade unions have the right to take collective action.

[18] Cf N Bruun and J Malmberg, '*Lex Laval* – Collective Actions and Posted Work in Sweden' in R Blanpain and F Hendrickx (eds), *Labour Law between Change and Tradition. Liber Amicorum Antoine Jacobs* (Alphen aan den Rijn, Kluwer Law International, 2011).

[19] The negative side of the freedom of association is protected by Article 11 of the European Convention on Human Rights, and the Convention was incorporated into Swedish law in 1995. See also *Gustafsson v Sweden*, judgment of the European Court of Human Rights of 25 April 1996.

occurred where an employer or employee, or the representative of either, engages in such conduct detrimental to the other party as a consequence of such party's exercise of his or her freedom of association, or where an employer or employee, or the representative of either, engages in conduct towards the other party for the purpose of inducing that party not to exercise his or her right to freedom of association (section 8 MBL). The violation of the freedom of association of an individual member also constitutes a violation of the activities of the employers' organisation or the trade union.[20]

There is a wide scope for collective action. The mutual right to take collective action is protected by the Instrument of Government, and more specifically regulated in sections 41 to 44 MBL. The right to take collective action can be further specified or limited by way of legislation or collective agreement. A peace obligation, and social truce, follows from the collective agreement and is strictly upheld by the Swedish Labour Court; during the period of validity of a specific collective agreement, collective action must not be taken. Furthermore, collective action may not contravene peace obligation provisions in collective agreements. Basic agreements on collective action and social truce cover large parts of the Swedish labour market. Sympathy action is allowed, and the right to take sympathy action is vast and applies even during the peace obligation as long as the primary collective action is permitted. There is no general principle of proportionality in Swedish law on collective action. If no peace obligation prevails, collective action is permitted.[21]

An important characteristic of the (1976:580) Co-determination Act – and Swedish labour law legislation in general – is its so-called 'semi-compelling' nature, which allows for deviations by way of collective agreement, both to the advantage and detriment of individual employees. Thus, collective agreements can be used to adapt the legislation to the circumstances of a certain sector or company. Swedish labour law is thus characterised by an important interplay between legislation and collective bargaining.

Worker participation is channelled through trade unions and their representatives, at local and central levels, in a single-channel system. Trade unions both negotiate and conclude collective agreements on wages and other working conditions, and take part in information and consultation at workplace level. The regulation of information, consultation and co-determination in the (1976:580) Co-determination Act is elaborate and complemented by collective bargaining regulation. So-called established trade unions, ie trade unions which

[20] See further P Herzfeld Olsson, *Facklig föreningsfrihet som mänsklig rättighet* (Uppsala, Iustus, 2003) and Schmidt et al (n 14) 108ff.

[21] See Schmidt et al (n 14) 97ff and Labour Court judgment AD 1998:17. A measure of collective action, however, must always be decided by the relevant organisation in due order. The (1976:580) Co-determination Act and basic agreements provide for rules on notice, mediation, postponement of collective action and other measures to favour a responsible bargaining process. The National Mediation Office plays a central role here. In addition, the Labour Court can make interim decisions on the lawfulness of collective actions.

are currently or customarily bound by a collective agreement with the employer (or the employers' organisation), are privileged in this context. They enjoy more far-reaching rights of primary negotiation and co-determination, for example, when it comes to management decisions regarding important alterations in the working conditions of employees or in the employer's activities and business (section 11 MBL).[22]

The Swedish Labour Court was established in 1928, originally aiming at resolving disputes relating to the collective bargaining system and promoting industrial peace. Nowadays the jurisdiction of the Labour Court encompasses all kinds of labour disputes. The Labour Court is a tripartite body comprised of judges with judicial backgrounds and of members from both sides of the labour market.[23]

Collective agreements in Sweden are entered into at different levels. Nationwide collective agreements are concluded at sectoral level and supplemented by local collective agreements concluded at workplace level. In addition, some master agreements are concluded at national top level. In line with the trend towards individualisation and 'organised' decentralisation, wages are today set mostly through individual and local bargaining within a – sometimes very general – framework of national sectoral bargaining. The Swedish labour market is covered by about 670 national sectoral collective agreements.

The legal regulation of collective bargaining in EU law is related to the European tradition of involving the social partners in the legislative processes. The Maastricht Treaty resulted in a similar process at EU level – the European social dialogue. Article 28 of the EU Charter of Fundamental Rights, now legally binding, recognises the right to collective bargaining and collective action.

In the Swedish context, an important difference has developed between collective bargaining in domestic and cross-border situations. While the legal regulation of collective bargaining in the (1976:580) Co-determination Act and main collective agreements has been relatively stable in domestic situations, EU law, the (1996/71/EC) Posted Workers Directive, and *Viking* and *Laval* have brought about important regulatory changes in cross-border situations (Section III).

III. SWEDISH COLLECTIVE BARGAINING, EUROPEAN INTEGRATION AND POSTING OF WORKERS

European integration has important implications for the Swedish collective bargaining system. *Viking* and *Laval* – and the resultant multifaceted and

[22] Furthermore, representatives of established trade unions are given paid time off for their assignment, and enjoy a far-reaching protection against dismissal, deteriorated terms and conditions of employment, and harassment from the employer according to the (1974:358) Act on Trade Union Representatives.

[23] See further the (1974:371) Labour Disputes (Judicial Procedure) Act.

complex developments at national, European and international level – challenge the Swedish collective bargaining system in different ways.[24] It relates to the EU internal market, free movement and posting of work, but also to fundamental trade union rights, collective action and collective bargaining and the scope for national sovereignty and social partner autonomy.

The (1996/71/EC) Posted Workers Directive was implemented in Sweden through the (1999:678) Act on Posting of Workers. Section 5 of the Act refers to Swedish legislation relating to terms and conditions of employment in Article 3 of the (1996/71/EC) Posted Workers Directive, such as working time, annual holiday, health and safety, and non-discrimination, which are to be applied to posted workers in Sweden. The Act makes no mention of the minimum rate of pay although this is one of the mandatory terms listed in Article 3. In Sweden the Directive was implemented in line with the autonomous collective bargaining system through the right of trade unions to negotiate and ultimately to take collective action in order to force foreign service providers to conclude collective agreements.[25]

In *Viking* and *Laval* the CJEU declared that collective action falls within the scope of the Treaty and that Articles 56 and 49 TFEU can be invoked against trade unions. The CJEU, with reference to Article 28 of the EU Charter of Fundamental Rights, also recognised the right to take collective action as a fundamental right, which forms an integral part of the general principles of Union law. However, the exercise of the right to collective action may be restricted. The Court concluded in *Laval* that the collective action constituted a restriction on the free movement of service. The right to take collective action for the protection of the workers of the host state against social dumping may constitute an overriding reason of public interest. However, the specific obligations linked to the signature of the collective agreement in the building sector in *Laval* (also going beyond the nucleus of mandatory rules for minimum protection in Article 3(1) of the Directive) could not be justified as necessary to attain such an objective. Similarly, in *Viking*, the CJEU found that the collective action constituted a restriction on the freedom of establishment. When it came to justification the Court left the assessment to the national court.[26]

The *Laval Quartet* also clarified that the (1996/71/EC) Posted Workers Directive establishes only a minimum protection of a nucleus of mandatory rules, and does not provide for equal treatment of domestic and foreign employers. Thus,

[24] See, for a more developed analysis, Rönnmar (n 8) and M Rönnmar, 'The Impact of *Viking* and *Laval* in Swedish Labour Law and Industrial Relations' in M Freedland and J Prassl (eds), *EU Law in the Member States. Viking and Laval and Beyond* (Oxford, Hart Publishing, 2015).

[25] See Government Bill Prop. 1998/99:90.

[26] The final judgment of the Swedish Labour Court in the *Laval* case, AD 2009:89, concerned the question of trade union liability in relation to the collective action, found to be in breach of EU law. The Swedish Labour Court, controversially, ordered the trade unions to pay punitive damages of approximately 55,000 Euro.

the Directive establishes a 'ceiling' for the terms and conditions of employment that a trade union or a state may require foreign service providers to apply to employees. The *Laval Quartet* creates specific challenges for Member States – such as Sweden (and its Nordic neighbour Denmark) – with industrial relations systems built on collective autonomy and self-regulation. For example, the strong emphasis of the CJEU on transparency of terms and conditions of employment runs counter to the decentralised and flexible character of the Swedish collective bargaining system (where, inter alia, collective agreements can be 'numberless' and not specify yearly wage increases, or lack specific minimum wages).

The controversial so-called *Lex Laval*, aimed at implementing *Viking* and *Laval* into Swedish law, became effective law in 2010 and entailed changes to the (1976:580) Co-determination Act and the (1999:678) Act on Posting of Workers.[27] The changes related to the regulation of collective action and collective bargaining, and measures aimed at transparency and simplification.

According to a new section 5a of the (1999:678) Act on Posting of Workers, collective action against an employer for the purpose of regulating conditions for posted workers through a collective agreement may be taken only if the conditions demanded (1) correspond to the conditions contained in a collective agreement concluded by a trade union and an employer's organisation at central level, and which are applied throughout Sweden to corresponding workers within the sector in question, (2) do not refer to anything other than a minimum rate of pay or other minimum conditions in the areas covered by section 5 of the Act (specifying the statutory rules employers must apply to posted workers according to Article 3(1) of the Posted Workers Directive), and (3) are more favourable for the worker than those prescribed by the statutory rules referred to in section 5 of the Act.

In addition, and importantly, such collective action must not be taken if the employer can show when it comes to pay or the areas covered by section 5 of the Act that the posted workers have essentially at least such conditions as follow from the minimum conditions of such a central collective agreement. This applies regardless of whether the conditions are established in a collective agreement, a personal employment contract or merely as a result of managerial prerogative. This rule is often referred to as the 'evidential' rule.

Collective action in contravention of section 5a of this Act is unlawful according to the (1976:580) Co-determination Act, section 41c, and regular sanctions for unlawful collective action apply.

Furthermore, *Lex Britannia*, the trade union's right to take collective action in order to set aside or amend an existing foreign collective agreement, is not to be applied when it comes to collective action against an employer who posts workers to Sweden according to the (1999:678) Act on Posting of Workers.

[27] See Government Inquiry Report SOU 2008:123 and Government Bill prop. 2009/10:48.

The implications for Swedish labour law and industrial relations of the *Laval Quartet* and *Lex Laval* have been far reaching. The rights to collective action and collective bargaining have been restricted, arguably in contravention of international law; the autonomous collective bargaining system has been weakened and the means for fighting social dumping has changed. Swedish trade unions submitted a report to the ILO Committee of Experts on Swedish developments post *Laval*. The Committee reviewed the Swedish developments in relation to ILO Conventions Nos 87 and 98 and expressed serious concern.[28] Swedish trade unions also made a collective complaint to the European Committee of Social Rights concerning the right to collective bargaining and the right to take collective action and legislative developments in Sweden following *Laval*. The Committee concluded that there was a violation of Articles 6§2, the right to bargain collectively, and 6§4, the right to collective action, of the European Social Charter.[29] In general, *Viking* and *Laval* have led to an intensified debate on fundamental rights in working life in Sweden, and increased attention is being paid not only to the EU Charter of Fundamental Rights and the European Convention on Human Rights, but also to the European Social Charter and ILO Conventions.

Post *Viking* and *Laval* there has been a decrease both in the number of disputes with foreign employers and in the number of concluded collective agreements with foreign companies in the construction sector (the sector where posted work in Sweden is most common). According to statistics from the Swedish Work Environment Authority (the Swedish liaison office according to the (1996/71/EC) Posted Workers Directive) since 1 July 2013 approximately 86,800 postings to Sweden have been reported, corresponding to 203,200 posted employees in total. More than 23,100 postings were reported in 2017, and that is approximately 1,000 more compared with 2016.[30] In 2014 there were 1.9 million postings in the EU, which represents 0.7 per cent of the total EU labour force. Between 2010 and 2014 there was a 44.4 per cent increase in the number of postings.[31]

There are no clear signs of a 'spillover effect' from the cross-border situation to the domestic situation, as regards collective bargaining or the right to collective action, demands for justification and proportionality, or damage liability. However, although the introduction of minimum-wage legislation or a system

[28] See Comments by Swedish Trade Union Confederation (LO) and Swedish Confederation of Professional Employees (TCO) to the CEACR on Sweden's application of C. 87 and 98 and the 2013 General Report on the Application on Conventions and Recommendations.

[29] See *Swedish Trade Union Confederation (LO) and Swedish Confederation of Professional Employees (TCO) v Sweden*, Complaint No. 85/2012.

[30] Cf the National Mediation Office's Yearbooks from 2007–2012 and Arbetsmiljöverket, *Helårsrapport 2017 – Register för företag som utstationerar arbetstagare i Sverige*, Rapport 2018:3 (Stockholm, Arbetsmiljöverket, 2018).

[31] See European Commission, Proposal for a Directive of the European Parliament and of the Council amending Directive 96/71/EC of the European Parliament and of the Council of 16 December 1996 concerning the posting of workers in the framework of the provision of services, COM (2016) 128 final, 2.

for extension of collective agreements was rejected in Sweden when *Viking* and *Laval* were first implemented, arguments in favour of extending collective agreements have later been raised in the domestic debate, for example by social partners in the transport sector. Furthermore, there seems to be a growing influence of government authorities in aspects linked to wage setting and collective bargaining, for example when it comes to posting of work, public procurement and labour migration. This burgeoning influence appears alien to the Swedish autonomous collective bargaining system.[32]

A parliamentary Government Inquiry on posted work, aimed at an evaluation of *Lex Laval*, was appointed in 2012 and delivered its report in 2015.[33] In February 2017 the government presented a Government Bill containing legislative proposals aimed at reforming *Lex Laval* and strengthening the Swedish collective bargaining system and the protection of posted workers. The Government Bill was approved by Parliament in April and became effective law from June 2017.[34] The possibilities to conclude collective agreements in posting situations with the support of collective action are increased, which will, for example, enable trade unions to more effectively control and enforce terms and conditions of employment.

The 'evidential' rule has been abolished. Section 5a of the (1999:678) Act on Posting of Workers now states that collective action against an employer for the purpose of regulating conditions for posted workers through a collective agreement may be taken only if the conditions demanded (1) comply with the terms and conditions contained in a collective agreement concluded at central level that are generally applied throughout Sweden to corresponding workers in the sector in question; (2) relate only to a minimum rate of pay or other minimum terms and conditions within the areas referred to in section 5 without prejudice to the application of terms and conditions that are more favourable to workers; and (3) are more favourable to the workers than those prescribed by section 5.

However, these collective agreements will have specific and limited legal effects in comparison with regular Swedish collective agreements. The trade unions that conclude these collective agreements will, for example, not be awarded the status of established trade unions in relation to the employer, and be afforded with specific rights of information, consultation and co-determination according to the (1976:580) Co-determination Act) (section 5b of the (1999:678) Act on Posting of Workers). At the same time, 'outside' posted workers (ie workers that are unorganised or members of trade unions, other than the trade union that concluded or is bound by the collective agreement in question)

[32] Compare in this context also K Ahlberg and N Bruun, 'Har det bästa blivit det godas fiende? Om försvaret av den svenska modellen' in M Rönnmar and J Julén Votinius (eds), *Festskrift till Ann Numhauser-Henning* (Lund, Juristförlaget i Lund, 2017).

[33] See Kommittédirektiv Dir. 2012:92 and Government Inquiry Report SOU 2015:83.

[34] See Government Bill prop. 2016/17:107.

are provided with an individual right to some collectively bargained conditions (section 5c of the (1999:678) Act on Posting of Workers) in ways that 'outside employees' (*utanförstående arbetstagare*) normally are not according to Swedish law. Thus, also in this context there is a difference between the domestic and the cross-border situation. Consequently, in the debate following the presentation of the Bill, some have argued that these rules run contrary to the Swedish labour law and industrial relations system.[35]

Post *Viking* and *Laval* a number of different measures to increase transparency, simplification and effective enforcement have been introduced. A foreign service provider posting workers to Sweden is required to register at the Swedish Work Environment Authority and to appoint a contact person in Sweden (sections 10–20 of the (1999:678) Act on Posting of Workers). The latest reform of *Lex Laval* introduced an obligation for the foreign service provider, if requested to do so by a Swedish trade union, to appoint a representative who is authorised to negotiate and conclude collective agreements on behalf of the employer (section 21 of the (1999:678) Act on Posting of Workers). Furthermore, Swedish trade unions are obliged to give in collective agreements potentially applicable to posted workers so-called 'posting work collective agreements' (*utstationeringsavtal*) to the Swedish Work Environment Authority (section 9a of the (1999:678) Act on Posting of Workers).[36]

At EU level, post-*Viking* and *Laval*, proposals were put forward for the need to revise the (1996/71/EC) Posted Workers Directive or to revise the Treaty. The Commission initially concentrated on issues of transparency and enforcement. In 2014 the (2014/67/EU) Enforcement Directive was adopted, and established a common framework of provisions, measures and control mechanisms necessary for better and more uniform implementation and enforcement of the (1996/71/EC) Posted Workers Directive.

In March 2016 the European Commission presented a proposal for a targeted revision of the (1996/71/EC) Posted Workers Directive, aimed at facilitating the provision of services across borders within a climate of fair competition and respect for the rights of posted workers.[37] The proposal was challenged by 14 chambers of national parliaments on grounds of subsidiarity according to Protocol No 2. However, in July 2016 the Commission concluded that the proposal complied with the principle of subsidiarity and that the proposal was maintained.[38]

In June 2018, following a long period of negotiation, Directive 2018/957/EU of the European Parliament and of the Council of 28 June 2018 amending

[35] Cf, for example, Government Bill prop. 2016/17:107.

[36] These collective agreements together with contact details of Swedish trade unions and employers' organisations are available online at the website of the Work Environment Agency, see www.av.se/arbetsmiljoarbete-och-inspektioner/utlandsk-arbetskraft-i-sverige/utstationering---utlandsk-arbetskraft-i-sverige/kollektivavtal/.

[37] See COM (2016) 128 final.

[38] See COM (2016) 505 final.

Directive 96/71/EC concerning the posting of workers in the framework of the provision of services was adopted. The new Directive addresses, for example, the rate of pay a posted worker is entitled to, long-term posting[39] and temporary work agencies. The subject matter and scope of the (1996/71/EC) Posted Workers Directive is clarified, and Article 1(1) now states that the Directive 'shall ensure the protection of posted workers during their posting in relation to the freedom to provide services, by laying down mandatory provisions regarding working conditions and the protection of workers' health and safety that must be respected'. The relationship between the Posted Workers Directive and fundamental rights, including trade union rights, is addressed in a new Article 1(1a), which states that the Directive

> shall not in any way affect the exercise of fundamental rights as recognised in the Member States and at Union level, including the right or freedom to strike or to take other action covered by the specific industrial relations systems in Member States, in accordance with national law and/or practice. Nor does it affect the right to negotiate, to conclude and enforce collective agreements, or to take collective action in accordance with national law and/or practice.

In relation to pay, the Directive implies an important shift from minimum rates of pay to a broader notion of remuneration and equality of treatment between posted workers and workers in the host country (Article 3(1)).[40]

In 2017 and 2018 there has been a development related to collective action and collective bargaining in the domestic Swedish context arising out of a local industrial conflict, with specific characteristics, at the docks in the city of Gothenburg. This development relates inter alia to issues regarding industrial peace, the aim of collective action, and trade union pluralism and competition. In comparative terms, the Swedish industrial relations system is characterised by industrial peace, and relatively few working days are lost each year due to collective action. In the collective bargaining round of 2017, 497 national sectoral

[39] A new provision, Article 3(1a) is inserted, which states that 'Where the effective duration of a posting exceeds 12 months, Member States shall ensure, irrespective of which law applied to the employment relationship, that undertakings as referred to in Article 1(1) guarantee, on the basis of equality of treatment, workers who are posted to their territory, in addition to the terms and conditions of employment referred to in paragraph 1 of this Article, all the applicable terms and conditions of employment which are laid down in the Member State where the work is carried out …'.

[40] Posted workers are entitled to remuneration, including overtime rates (c), as well as conditions of workers' accommodation (h) and allowances or reimbursement of expenditure to cover travel, board and lodging expenses for worker away from home for professional reasons (i). Article 3 also specifies that for the purposes of the (1996/71/EC) Posted Workers Directive 'the concept of remuneration shall be determined by national law and/or practice of the Member State to whose territory the worker is posted and means all the constituent elements of remuneration rendered mandatory by national law, regulation or administrative provision, or by collective agreements or arbitration awards which, in that Member State, have been declared universally applicable or otherwise apply in accordance with paragraph 8'. Cf also Case C-396/13 *Sähköalojen ammattiliitto ry v Elektrobudowa spółka Akcyjna*, EU:C:2015:86.

collective agreements were renegotiated without a single working day being lost due to strike or lock-out. Despite this, in 2017, in total 2,570 working days were lost in Sweden due to collective action, more or less all related to the local industrial conflict in Gothenburg.[41]

The Swedish trade union movement is centralised, with three central trade union confederations: the Swedish Confederation of Trade Unions (LO), organising blue-collar workers; the Swedish Confederation for Professional Employees (TCO), organising white-collar workers; and the Swedish Confederation of Professional Associations (SACO), organising university graduates and academics. All trade unions in Sweden enjoy the same basic rights regarding freedom of association, general negotiation, collective bargaining, and collective action. In practice, owing to the principles of labour market organisation, the dominance of nationwide industrial unions, and the policies and practices of the central trade union confederations and the Confederation of Swedish Enterprise, there are only a few so-called minority trade unions – with the Swedish Dockworkers Union being one exception, and a nationwide syndicalist trade union movement being another.[42] Employers and trade unions alike are free to refrain from signing collective agreements. An employer is therefore under no obligation to sign a collective agreement with a minority or competing trade union – such as the Swedish Dockworkers Union – even if the agreement is identical to collective agreements already signed. Employers are often reluctant to conclude such collective agreements. However, trade unions may make use of collective action in order to persuade the employer to sign such a collective agreement.[43] If the employer chooses to conclude a competing collective agreement, the trade union will gain the status of so-called established trade union, but according to the legal principles related to competing collective agreements the employer is, in principle, obliged to apply the terms and conditions of employment regulated in the first collective agreement concluded.

[41] See Medlingsinstitutet, *Avtalsrörelsen och lönebildningen* 2017. The dispute concerns the following. The local branch of the Swedish Dockworkers Union, a trade union *not* affiliated to the Trade Union Confederation (LO), has for a longer period of time organised the majority of the employees at the docks in Gothenburg, but is not bound by collective agreement with the employer. Instead the employer, APM Terminals Gothenburg AB, is, through its membership in the employers' organisation Ports of Sweden (affiliated to the Confederation of Swedish Enterprise), bound by a collective agreement in relation to the Swedish Transport Workers Union, affiliated to the Trade Union Confederation. The Swedish Dockworkers Union wants to conclude a collective agreement with the employer, and has used strike and other forms of collective action to achieve this aim. The employer has made use of lock-out. Negotiation and mediation have proved unsuccessful (the Swedish Dockworkers Union has, for example, denied the offer to conclude a so-called application agreement, linked to the existing collective agreement at the workplace).

[42] See further A Christensen, 'Den etablerade fackföreningen och minoritetsorganisationen' in R Fahlbeck and CM Roos (eds), *Perspektiv på arbetsrätten. Vänbok till Axel Adlercreutz* (Lund, Juridiska föreningen i Lund, 1983).

[43] However, according to the so-called *Britannia principle* there is a general ban in Swedish law on collective action with the aim of setting aside or amending an existing collective agreement (section 42 MBL).

Despite these general industrial relations practices, well-established legal rules on collective action and competition between trade unions and collective agreements, a tradition of autonomous collective bargaining and the specific and local character of the industrial conflict at the docks in Gothenburg, the government in 2017 appointed a Government Inquiry in order to 'safeguard' the Swedish labour law and industrial relations system and consider amendments and possible restrictions on the right to collective action. Before the Government Inquiry presented its proposals in the spring of 2018 a number of key social partners presented a proposal of their own, asking the government to turn their proposal into legislation (ie revisions to the (1976:580) Co-determination Act).[44] The Minister of Employment declared that she would proceed, not with the proposal of the Government Inquiry, but with the proposal of the social partners. The proposal contains inter alia a general ban on collective action in disputes of rights, and restrictions on the right to collective action in cases where the employer is already bound by a collective agreement.

IV. SWEDISH COLLECTIVE BARGAINING AND LABOUR MARKET INCLUSION OF SPECIFIC GROUPS OF WORKERS

An increasing number of precarious and vulnerable workers, such as older workers, younger workers and refugees and newly arrived immigrants, is presenting new challenges that have to be handled within the collective bargaining context. This development is partly provoked by structural conditions such as the flexibilisation of work and demographic changes stemming from an ageing population as well as from the economic crisis with its resultant high levels of unemployment, most specifically among the young population, and the refugee situation and great numbers of newly arrived immigrants.

Inclusion of these workers is fundamental not only to increase employment and growth, but also to achieve and maintain overall stability and legitimacy, in society in general and for the collective bargaining system. New demands have to be accommodated by the trade union movement, where the recognition of gender inequality and the need for diversity perspectives at times have been marked by ambiguity and reluctance.[45]

In general, Swedish labour law and collective bargaining are characterised by a uniform and extensive personal scope, and a traditionally high degree of equal treatment of different categories of employees, such as blue- and white-collar employees and private- and public-sector employees.

[44] See Government Inquiry Report SOU 2018:40.

[45] See eg Y Hirdman, *Med kluven tunga. LO och genusordningen* (Stockholm, Atlas, 1998) and R Mahon, 'Sweden's LO Learning to Embrace the Differences Within?' in F Colgan and S Ledwith (eds), *Gender, Diversity and Trade Unions. International Perspectives* (London, Routledge, 2002).

In promoting labour market inclusion, equal treatment is an important legal technique, although non-discrimination law (and its protected grounds) also limit the extent to which collective bargaining can protect specific groups of workers or promote their labour market inclusion.[46] EU non-discrimination law is extensive and regulated in a rather complex way by the Treaties, the EU Charter of Fundamental Rights, secondary law, case law of the CJEU, and soft law and policy.

The ban on age discrimination is regulated both by EU law (the (2000/78/EC) Employment Equality Directive and the EU Charter of Fundamental Rights) and by Swedish law (the (2008:567) Non-Discrimination Act). The protection against age discrimination covers all ages, and both older and younger workers are protected.[47] In principle, EU age discrimination law – through a large scope for justification of age-related differential treatment, specific exemptions and a broad margin of appreciation for Member States and social partners – enables direct and indirect age-related regulation as well as collective bargaining on age-related measures for older and younger workers and intergenerational bargaining. In its case law the CJEU has emphasised that collective agreements differ from measures adopted unilaterally by Member States as they are the result of negotiations between social partners engaged in exercising their fundamental right to bargain collectively.[48] A comparative analysis of a number of EU Member States reveals that there are still a large number of directly and indirectly age-related labour law rules and practices in the areas of recruitment, working conditions, flexible employment, employment protection and compulsory retirement. This is related to the traditional role given to age in the organisation of the labour market and the design of labour law.[49]

The Swedish labour market is generally characterised by high employment rates. In comparative European terms, the labour market situation of older workers in Sweden is good. The employment rate among older workers is high – about 73 per cent in the age group 55–64 – and the average retirement age is about 65 years. Still, in some sectors, such as industry and health care, it is difficult for employees (especially blue-collar employees) to stay in working life until 'normal' retirement age. Thus, there is a need to adjust work, work organisation and working environment – and to prolong working life for older workers beyond 'normal' retirement age in order to cover the increased costs of pensions,

[46] See J Julén Votinius, 'On the Gendered Norm of Standard Employment in a Changing Labour Market' in J Fudge and R Owens (eds), *Precarious Work, Women and the New Economy: the Challenge to Legal Norms* (Oxford, Hart Publishing, 2006).

[47] See further Numhauser-Henning and Rönnmar (eds) (n 12).

[48] Cf Joined Cases C-297/10 and C-298/10 *Hennigs and Mai* [2011] ECR-07965 and Case C-152/11 *Johann Odar v Baxter Deutschland GmbH*, EU:C:2012:772.

[49] See M Rönnmar, 'Age Discrimination and Labour Law: A Comparative Analysis' in A Numhauser-Henning and M Rönnmar (eds), *Age Discrimination and Labour Law. Comparative and Conceptual Perspectives in the EU and Beyond* (Alphen aan den Rijn, Kluwer Law International, 2015).

health care and elder care linked to an ageing population. Youth unemployment and younger workers' difficulties in entering and establishing themselves on the labour market are fundamental problems, from both an individual and a societal perspective. In Sweden the debates on ways to combat youth unemployment and promote labour market inclusion of younger workers revolve around such factors as lower entry wages for younger workers, the scope for flexible employment contracts, the strength of employment protection, and implications of seniority rules.[50]

The labour market situation of older and younger workers differs and there is an increased risk of intergenerational conflict, especially when it comes to the perceived competition for jobs, at both micro and macro level. Such intergenerational conflict relates, for example, to the entry into the labour market and access to permanent, instead of flexible or precarious, employment, and to the access and strength of employment protection in restructuring and redundancy situations. Employment protection and seniority rules can both be seen as affording necessary protection for older workers and as barriers to the entry of younger workers into the labour market.

The *iNGenBar* research project aimed at a comparative and interdisciplinary analysis of intergenerational bargaining in EU law and a number of EU Member States, including Sweden.[51] Intergenerational bargaining referred here to the integration of policies and strategies for older and younger workers through collective bargaining and social dialogue.

Swedish labour law, industrial relations and collective bargaining lack a clear intergenerational dimension, as well as an articulated debate on intergenerational solidarity or conflict. The interests of younger and older workers, and the labour market inclusion of these groups, are to a large degree dealt with separately and in parallel. The strategies to combat youth unemployment and to promote active ageing and a prolonged working life for older workers, respectively, are in principle seen as separate, equally important and non-conflicting strategies. Given the lack of direct intergenerational bargaining in the Swedish context, it was not possible to select only the case studies that displayed a direct and central intergenerational element. Thus, the Swedish study focused on three case studies on *introduction agreements* for younger workers

[50] See further M Rönnmar, *Intergenerational Bargaining in Sweden*, Report for the project iNGenBar, Intergenerational Bargaining: towards integrated bargaining for younger and older workers in EU countries (2014) and M Rönnmar, 'Does Age Matter? Sweden, Younger and Older Workers and the Intergenerational Dimension of Contingent Work' in E Ales, O Deinert and J Kenner (eds), *Core and Contingent Work in the European Union. A Comparative Analysis* (Oxford, Hart Publishing, 2017) for a more developed analysis of older workers, younger workers and collective bargaining in Sweden. See also in relation to younger workers J Julén Votinius, 'Young Employees – Securities, Risk Distribution and Fundamental Social Rights' (2014) 5(3–4) *European Labour Law Journal* 387.

[51] The *iNGenBar* research project was coordinated by AIAS at Amsterdam University and funded by the European Commission, see intergenerationalbarganing.eu. On the Swedish study, see further Rönnmar, *Intergenerational Bargaining in Sweden* (n 50).

(*yrkesintroduktionsavtal*), collective agreements on *partial retirement* for older workers, and *transition agreements* (*omställningsavtal*), linked to labour market restructuring, employment protection and redundancy, where the interests and inclusion or exclusion of younger and older workers may be competing.[52]

Youth unemployment and labour market inclusion of younger workers form a background for the *introduction agreements* for younger workers.[53] They regulate employment for younger workers, combining work with education, training and supervision. The first agreement was concluded in 2010, and in 2012 the government started negotiations with the social partners on a tripartite job pact, aimed at tackling youth unemployment. In 2014 a government regulation entered into force for a government scheme to support and subsidise introduction employment for younger workers.[54,55]

Several collective agreements, for both blue-collar and white-collar employees, offer possibilities for employees to apply for *partial retirement* from the age of 60 or 62.[56] The aim of the provisions of partial retirement is to provide an opportunity for a longer working life and to create fruitful conditions for generational renewal. In line with the strategy on active ageing, this right to partial retirement is not about early retirement or about making room for younger workers. Instead it is a question of prolonging working life from the individual (older) employee's perspective. A crucial question for the realisation of the right to partial retirement is of course the level of economic compensation. Here, a long-term perspective must be applied in relation to the build-up of adequate funds for partial retirement pension benefits.

Transition agreements cover all sectors (private and public, blue-collar, white-collar and professional employees) and large parts of the labour market. They constitute a key feature of Swedish labour law and collective bargaining, and comprise an important complement to the statutory employment protection

[52] Within each type of collective agreement, one or a few collective agreements were studied more closely. The collective agreements covered both the private and public sector of the labour market and blue-collar and white-collar/professional employees. Analysis of specific collective agreements was complemented by interviews with leading representatives of social partners to gain further insights into the context, goals, content and implementation of collective agreements, as well as the views and strategies of the social partners.

[53] In 2010 Teknikföretagen and IF Metall concluded a 'pioneer' introduction agreement in the industry sector, and introduction agreements have since been concluded, for example in municipal/regional healthcare and care, the retail sector, and the wood and graphical sector.

[54] The government scheme has been authorised by the European Commission under EU state aid rules, see decision C (2013) 4053 final. See also Government Inquiry Report Ds 2013:20 and Förordning (2013:1157) om stöd för yrkesintroduktionsanställningar.

[55] The scope of the introduction agreements was subsequently extended, see below in relation to the discussion on newly arrived immigrants.

[56] See National Mediation Office, *Avtalsrörelsen och lönebildningen 2013. Medlingsinstitutets årsrapport* (Stockholm, National Mediation Office, 2014) 137. See, for example, provisions on partial retirement for older workers in the collective agreements in the industry sector – so-called *Teknikavtalen* – between Teknikarbetsgivarna and the blue-collar trade union IF Metall and the white-collar and professional employees' trade unions Unionen/Sveriges Ingenjörer, respectively.

regulation on redundancy dismissals – but also to active labour market policies and unemployment insurance.[57] The transition agreements provide employees facing dismissal owing to reasons of redundancy with different rights to severance pay and economic compensation and active transition support measures, by way of coaching, job-searching services, training and re-education etc.[58] The agreements also provide support for employers in reorganisations and redundancy situations. The transition agreements are administered by transition foundations, set up by the social partners and collective bargaining, and the severance pay and transition support are financed by the employers, often through an insurance and premium-based scheme.

This study reflects the fact that autonomous collective bargaining – in this case, introduction agreements for younger workers, collective agreements on partial retirement for older workers and transition agreements on restructuring and redundancy – can serve to protect older and younger workers and promote their labour market inclusion. Although Swedish collective bargaining developments display a lack of direct and explicit intergenerational bargaining, several indirect and implicit intergenerational elements can be found in the collective agreements studied. These indirect intergenerational elements relate, for example, to generational renewal in terms of future skills provision, competence development and transfer of knowledge and experience between older and younger workers, and older workers' participation in education and supervision of younger workers, as a way of adapting the working environment to enable a longer working life.

The refugee situation in recent years has created an urgent societal need to advance the inclusion of newly arrived immigrants in the labour market. This is clearly the case in Sweden, where many persons have sought and received refuge. In 2015, for example, 160,000 persons sought refuge in Sweden, and among them were 70,000 children (half of whom were unaccompanied). The Swedish labour market is marked by an increasing segmentation and difference between, on the one hand, the majority of workers, and, on the other hand, groups of workers that have a particular difficulty in establishing themselves in the labour market, such as refugees and newly arrived immigrants, early school leavers and older unemployed persons. In January 2018 the unemployment rate

[57] See Sebardt for a historical account of the early agreements and the developments in this area, G Sebardt, *Redundancy and the Swedish Model. Swedish Collective Agreements on Employment Security in a National and International Context* (Uppsala, Iustus förlag, 2005).

[58] See, for example, the leading transition agreement, *Omställningsavtalet*, covering private-sector and white-collar and professional employees and concluded by Svenskt Näringsliv (Confederation of Swedish Enterprise) and PTK (the Council for Negotiation and Cooperation, a joint negotiation organisation of trade unions representing private-sector white-collar and professional employees). In recent years Svenskt Näringsliv and PTK have been in the process of renegotiating their transition agreement. The renegotiations have focused on seniority rules, an extended coverage of the agreement and rights to education and competence development. However, these renegotiations failed in September 2015.

for persons born outside of Sweden was 21 per cent, in comparison to 4 per cent for persons born in Sweden. Thus, the labour market situation for refugees and newly arrived immigrants is very challenging, and, in general, it takes a long time for these persons to establish themselves in the Swedish labour market.[59] In order to address this situation and to promote the labour market inclusion of newly arrived immigrants, Sweden – as well as other EU Member States – has put in place a number of policy measures such as early skills assessment, the recognition of qualifications, language courses, vocational training, job training and general education for low-educated learners. In most of the key destination countries, social partners play an active role, and focus, for example, on topics such as education and apprenticeships, accelerating labour market access and recruitment of refugees.[60]

In Sweden the social partners have contributed to the creation of so-called 'fast tracks' into the labour market for newly arrived immigrants. There are now 14 different 'fast tracks' and since 1 January 2016 more than 5,000 persons have entered a 'fast track'. The 'fast tracks' aim at securing the skills provision in professions and sectors marked by skills and labour shortage, and at reducing the time newly arrived immigrants spend in unemployment. The 'fast tracks' are developed and run in collaboration between the social partners, the Public Employment Office and other authorities and actors. They cover a range of different measures such as validation and recognition of qualifications, vocational training, job training and language course of different kinds.[61] Furthermore, the scope of existing introduction agreements has been extended to include also newly arrived immigrants. This is, for example, the case with the introduction agreement concluded between Teknikföretagen and IF Metall in the industry sector.[62]

The debate has also revolved around the creation of so-called 'simple jobs' and the use of lower wages for newly arrived immigrants and other groups of workers. In this context, the political opposition (the four centre-right political parties in the so-called *Alliansen*) in August 2017 presented a proposal for a new form of statutorily regulated form of employment, so-called entry employment

[59] See further S Eriksson, L Hensvik and O Nordström Skans, *Den svenska arbetsmarknaden och dess utmaningar*, IFAU Rapport 2017:5 (Uppsala, IFAU, 2017) and Arbetsförmedlingen, *Ungdomsarbetslösheten och ungdomsgarantin – en översikt* (Stockholm, Arbetsförmedlingen, 2017).

[60] See further F Tanay and J Peschner, *Labour Market Integration of Refugees in the EU* (Thematic Analysis Unit and EMPL Refugee Task Force, European Commission, 2017) and Eurofound, *Approaches to the Labour Market Integration of Refugees and Asylum Seekers* (Luxembourg, Publications Office of the European Union, 2016).

[61] See Arbetsförmedlingen, *Arbetsförmedlingens nulägesbedömning av arbetet med snabbspår. December 2017* (Stockholm, Arbetsförmedlingen, 2017).

[62] Likewise the regulation governing the government scheme to support and subsidise introduction employment, Förordning (2013:1157) om stöd för yrkesintroduktionsanställningar, has been revised to cover also newly arrived immigrants and long-term unemployed. Cf also Government Bill prop. 2016/17:100.

(*inträdesjobb*), for newly arrived immigrants and some categories of younger workers. Controversially – and at odds with the autonomous collective bargaining system – this proposal builds on statutorily regulated wages of no more than 70 per cent of the collectively bargained starting wage in the relevant sector.[63]

In November 2017 – partly as a reaction to the proposal regarding entry employment – a number of key social partners, ie the Swedish Trade Union Confederation (LO), Unionen[64] and the Confederation of Swedish Enterprise, agreed, in principle, on concluding collective agreements on a new form of employment, so-called establishment employment (*etableringsanställning*). In developing this agreement they built, and sought to improve upon, the introduction agreements. The aim of the agreements and establishment employment is to help newly arrived immigrants and long-term unemployed to become established in the labour market and to facilitate future skills provision for employers. In March 2018 the government and these social partners signed a declaration of intent whereby the government agrees to financially and otherwise support this initiative. The intention is to ensure that newly arrived immigrants and long-term unemployed people have opportunities to acquire knowledge and experience that are sought after in the labour market. Establishment employment will be open for newly arrived immigrants who have been granted residence permits in Sweden in the past 36 months, and for persons with more than 12 months of unemployment (or six months of unemployment for those below 25 years of age). An employment contract under the scheme should generally be able to lead to a permanent, full-time employment contract with the employer. The employee will be given the opportunity to take part in the language course Swedish for Immigrants and other short training courses as agreed on by the employer and the employee.[65,66]

[63] Up to a maximum of around SEK 21,000 per month. During the period of employment, which could last for a maximum of three years, the employer would not have to pay pay-roll tax for the employed person. See further Alliansen, *Inträdesjobb för fler i arbete* (Stockholm, 2017).

[64] Sweden's largest white-collar trade union on the private labour market.

[65] See further Declaration of Intent of 5 March 2018 between the government, the Swedish Trade Union Confederation (LO), Unionen and the Confederation of Swedish Enterprise, www.government.se/49381d/contentassets/ae057fea761949e6950ad9a56dc81350/declaration-of-intent-between-the-government-the-swedish-trade-union-confederatio-lo-unionen-and-the-confederation-of-swedish-enterprise.pdf. Cf also the previous proposal along similar lines presented by the Swedish Trade Union Confederation, LO, *LOs förslag om utbildningsjobb för stärkt etablering* (Stockholm, LO, 2017).

[66] In 2019 an employer's total payroll expenses for an employment of this kind will amount to SEK 8,400 per month. In addition, the employee will receive a tax-free, individual state benefit amounting to at most SEK 9,870 per month in 2019. The government and the social partners agree that the salary and the individual benefit will follow wage developments. The individual state benefit can be claimed for no more than two years. The basic premise is that the size of the individual benefit should mean that there is an incentive for the individual to obtain regular employment. Before the establishment employment can be introduced, the government must file a state aid notification to the European Commission.

V. CONCLUDING REMARKS

This chapter has aimed at an analysis of the functions and legal regulation of collective bargaining in the Swedish system of labour law and industrial relations against the background of current challenging trends, and with a specific focus on the examples of European integration and posted work and labour market inclusion of specific groups of workers, respectively.

Autonomous collective bargaining is central to the Swedish labour law and industrial relations system, where it fulfils a number of important – and diverse – functions. Thus, in Sweden, collective bargaining is set at the intersection of labour law, social security law, and welfare state and labour market policy. Furthermore, collective bargaining forms part of a wider multi-level system of regulation composed of international and human rights law; European and EU law; and national constitutional and statutory law. In addition, collective bargaining and labour law interplay, and potentially conflict, with other areas of law, such as free movement law, economic law and non-discrimination law.

In a comparative context – and in light of the global trends towards individualisation and decentralisation – Sweden (and the Nordic countries) in many ways stands out with their system of autonomous and strong collective bargaining, high rates of trade unionisation and employers' organisation, and extensive collective bargaining coverage. Wages and terms and conditions of employment are set within a system of national sectoral collective bargaining, characterised by 'organised' decentralisation and an emphasis on individual and local bargaining.

However, there are also signs of increased tension and diversity within the collective bargaining system. This relates, for example, to differences in trade unionisation rates between sectors and groups of employees, to differences in the legal regulation and industrial relations practices of collective bargaining and collective action in domestic and cross-border situations, and to a growing influence of government authorities in aspects linked to wage setting and collective bargaining. So far, despite pressures linked to European integration, posted work and the *Laval Quartet*, the introduction of a statutory minimum wage or a system of extension of collective agreements has been rejected. The functioning, strength and effective enforcement of autonomous collective bargaining – and thus of terms and conditions of employment and labour law regulation more generally – in Sweden is linked to high rates of trade union and employers' organisation. Given the overall decrease in trade unionisation in recent years, and the particular decrease in some sectors and among some groups of employees, the high rate of employers' organisation plays – together with the legal regulation and legal effects of collective agreements – a particularly important role when it comes to maintaining an extensive collective bargaining coverage.

European integration, posted work and legal developments post *Laval Quartet* have had important implications for Swedish collective bargaining, labour law and industrial relations. The rights to collective action and collective bargaining have been restricted and the autonomous collective bargaining system has been weakened, at least in the cross-border situation. At the same time, there is now a greater debate and awareness of the international and European regulation of fundamental rights in working life. Although the number of postings and posted workers to Sweden has increased in recent years, it still accounts for only a small portion of the total labour force, as is also the case in the EU as a whole.

It is still too early to assess the full implications of the revisions of *Lex Laval* and the Swedish regulation of collective action and collective bargaining and the (1996/71/EC) Posted Workers Directive, respectively. The revision of *Lex Laval* strengthens the rights to collective action and collective bargaining in the cross-border situation, and the mechanisms for supervision and enforcement of collectively bargained conditions. At the same time, some of the rules introduced regarding the legal effects of collective agreements in cross-border situations depart from traditional rules in Swedish labour law applicable in domestic situations. This can be seen both as a necessary legal adaptation and as an introduction of 'alien' and disruptive legal elements in the Swedish autonomous collective bargaining system. The revision of the (1996/71/EC) Posted Workers Directive strengthens the protection of posted workers in different ways and introduces an important shift from minimum rates of pay to a broader notion of remuneration and equality of treatment. The revision also clarifies that the (1996/71/EC) Posted Workers Directive shall not in any way affect the exercise of fundamental rights, including the right or freedom to strike and the rights to collective action and collective bargaining. However, it is unclear how this provision in an act of EU secondary law will impact on case law principles related to the Treaty freedom of establishment and freedom to provide services developed by the CJEU in *Viking* and *Laval*. And what will in this context be the role of other fundamental rights, such as the freedom to conduct a business, protected by Article 16 of the EU Charter of Fundamental Rights?

The recent domestic Swedish development linked to a local industrial conflict at the docks in Gothenburg, and the social partner agreement and proposal to restrict the right to collective action in certain ways in order to 'safeguard' the Swedish labour law and industrial relations system, reflect both a strengthening and a weakening of collective autonomy.

One function of collective bargaining in the Swedish labour law and industrial relations system is to promote the labour market inclusion of specific groups of workers, such as older workers, younger workers and refugees and newly arrived immigrants. These groups of workers have different, and possibly conflicting, needs, as is clear from the debate on intergenerational tension. In this area collective bargaining interplays in important ways with welfare state and active labour market policy. The different initiatives and collective agreements in this area display the dynamic societal responsibility and pragmatism of the Swedish social partners and the autonomous collective bargaining system.

Here, the urgent need to secure the future skills provision, and to address labour market segmentation and existing labour and skills shortage in some sectors of the Swedish labour market also plays an important role. As always, there is a potentially conflicting relationship between collective bargaining and non-discrimination law when it comes to the protection of specific groups of workers and the promotion of their labour market inclusion. At the same time, EU non-discrimination law and CJEU case law affords a broad margin of appreciation for the social partners and collective agreements.

10

Collective Bargaining on Social Protection in the Context of Welfare State Retrenchment: The Case of Unemployment Insurance

ALEXANDRE DE LE COURT*

I. UNEMPLOYMENT INSURANCE AND RECENT TRENDS IN COLLECTIVE BARGAINING ON SOCIAL PROTECTION

RECENT RESEARCH INCREASINGLY shows that collective bargaining plays a role in social protection schemes and that it should be taken into account when analysing the evolution of the programmes and structures of European welfare states.[1] Trampusch, for example, on the basis of a study of collectively bargained benefits in occupational pensions, early retirement and further training, argues that there is a growing tendency towards the integration of welfare issues in collective agreements. This contradicts the general view that the role of social partners in the management of welfare is decreasing, and suggests that welfare state retrenchment does not necessarily need to be analysed in terms of privatisation or individualisation of social risks.[2]

* The research for this work was carried out during a stay at the Max-Planck-Institute of Social Law and Social Policy in Munich. The author would like to thank Pr Dr Ulrich Becker and the staff of the Institute for their support and valuable aid.

[1] C Trampusch, 'Industrial Relations as a Source of Solidarity in Times of Welfare State Retrenchment' (2007) 2 *Journal of Social Policy* 197; A Johnston, A Kornelakis and C Rodriguez d'Acri 'Social Partners and the Welfare State: Recalibration, Privatization or Collectivization of Social Risks?' (2011) 4 *European Journal of Industrial Relations* 349; M Yerkes and K Tijdens 'Corporatism and the Mediation of Social Risks. The Interaction between Social Security and Collective Labour Agreements' in R van der Veen, M Yerkes and P Achterberg (eds), *The Transformation of Solidarity. Changing Risks and the Future of the Welfare State* (Amsterdam, Amsterdam University Press, 2012) 115–68.

[2] C Trampusch, 'Industrial Relations as a Source of Solidarity in Times of Welfare State Retrenchment' (2007) 2 *Journal of Social Policy* 197.

Johnston, Kornelakis and d'Acri have provided additional evidence that unions and employers have filled gaps in welfare provisions or regulation through collective bargaining.[3] In addition to compensation through collective agreements for disability benefit cuts in the Netherlands, their study also describes the successful creation, without state intervention, of a training fund by the Greek social partners, who decided on their own initiative to extend the fund to the unemployed as an answer to the a lack of any effective state policy in that field. This move occurred without the social partners having any strong involvement in the design and management of unemployment protection policies.

The case of unemployment insurance benefits has so far received little study, perhaps because it is not intuitively associated with collective bargaining. In general, the role of social partners seems to be limited to weaker forms of involvement in the design of unemployment protection systems.

A comprehensive report published in 2013 by the European Observatory of Working Life, 'Social partners' involvement in unemployment benefit regimes in Europe', shows that the involvement of social partners varies from systematic, institutionalised, tripartite and/or bipartite participation in most EU Member States, to informal or occasional consultation in countries like Italy, Sweden, Norway and the United Kingdom and an absence of involvement (except through lobbying) in the Republic of Ireland and Malta.[4] However, even in a country like Spain, which the report classifies as demonstrating an institutionalised participation of social partners in tripartite bodies, consultation has in reality been limited, including because of a consolidated tendency to regulate the system through urgent legislative governmental decrees.[5] Moreover, in Spain, against a background of negative press coverage, the role of unions and employers in the design and management of training policies for employed and unemployed workers has been limited in favour of the state-driven market of private providers, with whom social partners must compete. This does not mean that unions have no recourse to other strategies to reinforce unemployment protection. In Spain over the past few years this has occurred through consultations with government regarding the consolidation of a (still very partial and insufficient) system of unemployment subsidies, or via participation in the promotion of a popular legislative initiative on a universal social assistance benefit system in the Catalan Parliament. Although the latter initiative

[3] A Johnston, A Kornelakis and C Rodriguez d'Acri, 'Social Partners and the Welfare State: Recalibration, Privatization or Collectivization of Social Risks?' (2011) 4 *European Journal of Industrial Relations* 349.

[4] I Regalia and S Gasparri, 'Social Partners' Involvement in Unemployment Benefit Regimes in Europe' (Dublin, European Foundation for the Improvement of Living and Working Conditions, 2013) 32–34.

[5] A de le Court, *Protección por desempleo y derechos fundamentales. El caso español en contexto* (Valencia, Tirant lo Blanch, 2014); A de le Court, 'Decommodifying Social Rights: Welfare State Policies in a Comparative Perspective', PhD thesis (Universitat Pompeu Fabra, 2013), www.tdx.cat/handle/10803/283752.

is apparently not directly connected to protection against unemployment, it should be noted that in Spain, protection of unemployed workers who have exhausted their insurance benefits is fragmentary and insufficient, as seems to be confirmed by the European Commission's 2017 proposal of the Country-Specific Recommendations for that country.[6]

Social partners do not play a specific role in the management and administration of unemployment benefit programmes in most Member States (with the exception of those where a Ghent system exists) even if they have a certain institutional presence in the organs administering the schemes.[7] In this context, it does not seem straightforward that aspects of unemployment protection would be determined through collective bargaining agreements.

It is against this background that this chapter seeks to identify and conduct a legal analysis of cases where involvement of social partners in the governance of unemployment protection has taken the form of collective bargaining. In addition to the French case, which demonstrates a system of unemployment insurance benefits that, since 1958, has been created, designed and reformed through inter-professional collective agreements, the following sections also analyse collective agreements related to supplementary benefits in Sweden as well as the recent evolution in insurance benefits in the Netherlands. A section is also devoted to the role of the Italian 'bilateral bodies' in matters of unemployment protection.

II. THE FRENCH CASE AS A SYSTEM OF COLLECTIVELY BARGAINED UNEMPLOYMENT INSURANCE

The French system of unemployment insurance governance can be viewed as an exception within the EU. Since 1958, contributions, benefits and access conditions have been the object of an inter-professional collective agreement that is renegotiated between employers' associations and representative trade unions every two or three years. This agreement is commonly referred to as the Unedic agreement in reference to the bipartite institution managing the system. The relevant law (*Code du travail*) limits itself to the establishment of a right to unemployment insurance, enforceable against the (contractual) system,[8] by defining basic conditions (definition of the notion of unemployed worker; the minimum duration to be fixed by governmental decree; the obligation of the

[6] European Commission, 'Recommendation for a Council Recommendation on the 2017 National Reform Programme of Spain and delivering a Council opinion on the 2017 Stability Programme of Spain', COM (2017) 508 final.

[7] I Regalia and S Gasparri, 'Social Partners' Involvement in Unemployment Benefit Regimes in Europe' (Dublin, European Foundation for the Improvement of Living and Working Conditions, 2013) 38.

[8] A Supiot, 'Un faux dilemme: la loi ou le contrat ?' (2003) 1 *Droit Social* 58, 64.

Unedic agreement to take into account 'unused' benefit periods; reference to previous remuneration for the calculation of benefits; the contributory character of the system and the possibility of adapting contribution levels in function of different contractual circumstances). Article L5422-20 of the *Code du travail* explicitly reserves the execution of legal provisions to inter-professional agreements. Such agreements must, however, be authorised by the government and this authorisation, like decisions regarding the extension of collective agreements, renders the agreement generally applicable. Conditions for authorisation relate to how representative those negotiating the agreement are and also stipulate an absence of contradictions with legal provisions, in particular those related to the control of unemployed workers and to the organisation of their placement, orientation and retraining.

Consideration of the reference to the placement, orientation and retraining of unemployed workers should take into account the fact that, until 2008, Active Labour Market Policies (ALMPs) for unemployed workers in receipt of insurance benefits were also managed by Unedic under the Unedic agreements. Unedic shared these responsibilities with the Agence Nationale pour l'Emploi (ANPE), a state-run institution that was responsible for activation policies for all unemployed workers, whether or not they were in receipt of insurance or assistance benefits. In 2005 legislation was passed requiring the negotiation and conclusion of a tripartite convention between the state, ANPE and Unedic to establish rules for coordinating the activities of the various institutions and to ensure communication flow between them. In 2008 most of Unedic's services (ALMPs and the recognition and payment of benefits) and ANPE itself were taken over by the new state-run body Pôle Emploi, a tripartite institution that centralised all aspects of unemployment protection regulations and ALMPs.[9] It seems that, even though social partners are for the most part present on the board of Pôle Emploi, in reality they have not been left a great deal of room within the framework of the decisions already taken by the government and introduced in the laws on the state budget. This is perhaps because the competence of this new body to take strategic decisions is more formal than real.[10] Ten per cent of Unedic's budget (which comes from the contribution agreed upon in the inter-professional agreement) goes towards the financing of Pôle Emploi.

Further, even if the procedure for authorising and extending the cross-branch Unedic agreement is to be construed as a matter of routine, on critical occasions it has threatened the autonomy of the social partners. In 2000, for example, the government refused to authorise the agreement (which had not been signed

[9] J-P Alduy, 'Rapport d'information No. 713 (2010–2011) fait au nom de la Mission commune d'information relative à Pôle emploi, déposé le 5 juillet 2011' (Paris, Sénat, 2011).

[10] D Jamme, Pôle emploi et la réforme du service public de l'emploi: bilan et recommandations (Paris, Conseil économique, social et environnemental, 2011) 15.

by all the representative unions) on several grounds. These included the fact that the agreement did not guarantee the sustainability of the system; that it attempted to introduce definitions of the employment that benefit holders must accept that were stricter than the legal definitions; that it introduced a compulsory reintegration plan; and that it introduced a new sanctions regime for the insurance scheme that differed from the legal sanctions regime. The agreement was authorised following further negotiations (formally bipartite, but in reality tripartite) in which government and unions shared common objectives, and which recognised the role of the state (and the *Code du travail*) in defining and applying infractions and sanctions.[11] Prior to this, in 1982, the government had intervened in the financial crisis of the unemployment protection system by issuing a decree setting out the need for previous contribution periods for access to insurance benefits, as well as a social assistance track for unemployed workers whose contribution periods were insufficient.[12] These principles were confirmed in the subsequent inter-professional agreement of 1984, thus establishing the improper bipartite character of the system.[13] Further, following its move to preserve its competences on activation strategies for unemployed workers during the 2000 crisis, the state gradually brought the design and implementation of ALMPs and activation strategies under its control via the tripartite institution with state dominance which Pôle Emploi is.

This context is also important when considering the reforms proposed by the recently elected French President, tending towards universalisation and the suppression of financing through social contributions, which should result in the 'statalisation' of the system, admittedly by the implementation of tripartism in its design and management.

III. THE SWEDISH CASE: COLLECTIVE AGREEMENTS AS ONE OF DIFFERENT ASPECTS OF COLLECTIVISATION

While not directly involved in establishing the conditions, level and regulation of benefits and contributions, Swedish social partners have a long tradition of supplementing unemployment benefits,[14] in both amount and duration, not

[11] A Supiot, 'Un faux dilemme: la loi ou le contrat ?' (2003) 1 *Droit Social* 58, 64–66; J Freyssinet, 'La réforme de l'indemnisation du chômage en France' (2002) 38 *Revue de l'IRES* 1; C Tuchszirer, 'La nouvelle convention d'assurance-chômage: le PARE qui cache la forêt' (2001) 14 *Mouvements* 2, 15.

[12] Actually, the law provides for the competence of the government to 'execute' its provisions in matters of unemployment insurance in case of the absence of collective agreement.

[13] C Daniel and D Tuchszirer, L'État face aux chômeurs, l'indemnisation du chômage de 1884 à nos jours (Paris, Flammarion, 1999).

[14] The system is composed of a basic, relatively low, universal tax-financed benefit, and an alternative income-related benefit for members of unemployment insurance funds (closely linked with unions as an expression of the 'Ghent' character of the system. On the Ghent system and its connection with union membership, see J Lind, 'The End of the Ghent System as Trade Union Recruitment Machinery?' (2009) 40 *Industrial Relations Journal* 510.

only through collective bargaining, but also via collective and individual insurance provided by unions.

While complementary insurance does not generally extend to industries with high unemployment risks, around 80 per cent of workers are covered by Job Security Agreements (now also known as Transition Agreements).[15] These are collective agreements that institute Job Security Councils, which are responsible for providing support to unemployed workers in their transition between jobs. From that point of view, these agreements could be said to embody a vision of unemployment protection that goes beyond guaranteeing income security to focus on labour market reintegration. The first of these agreements was created in the 1970s in the context of mass unemployment amongst white-collar workers, who were considered to be insufficiently supported by public employment services.[16] After a pause during the 1990s, new Job Security Agreements were created in 2004 (for blue-collar workers)[17] and were strongly linked to the reintegration of workers in restructuration processes (collective redundancies) as compensation for the fact that public employment services) focused on the reintegration of those already unemployed, and above all on the long-term unemployed.[18] From that perspective, Job Security Agreements can also be seen as instruments of a preventive ALMP as their provisions begin to apply even before redundancies are effective.

In reality, these agreements are not directly connected with supplementing unemployment protection as part of social security or social protection, but were negotiated within the framework of employment protection legislation.[19] However, in addition to a series of services related to placement and outplacement provided through the Job Security Councils, the Job Security Agreements also provide supplementary benefits on top of basic or insurance benefits,[20] and even include salary complements for a certain duration in cases where workers accept a new job with a lower salary than their previous salary.[21] For example, in 2014, the Job Security Agreement for government employees provided for top-up payments to unemployment benefits up to 80 per cent (70 per cent after 200 days) of their salary for permanent workers included in collective redundancies, as well as for fixed-term workers who had been working for at

[15] OECD, Back to Work: Sweden: Improving the Re-employment Prospects of Displaced Workers (Paris, OECD Publishing, 2009) 103.

[16] O Bergström and A Diedrich, 'The Swedish Model of Restructuring' in b Cazier and F Bruggeman (eds), *Restructuring Work and Employment in Europe. Managing Change in an Era of Globalisation* (Cheltenham, Edward Elgar Publishing, 2008) 160.

[17] ibid.

[18] A Diedrich and O Bergström, *The Job Security Councils in Sweden* (IMIT, 2006) 8.

[19] The 1974 Employment Protection Act (*Lagen om anställningsskydd, LAS*); A Diedrich and O Bergström, *The Job Security Councils in Sweden* (IMIT, 2006) 9.

[20] OECD, Back to Work: Sweden: Improving the Re-employment Prospects of Displaced Workers (Paris, OECD Publishing, 2009) 103–04.

[21] A Diedrich and O Bergström, *The Job Security Councils in Sweden* (IMIT, 2006) 12.

least three of the last four years and whose contracts had not been renewed. The Job Security Agreement for local authority workers provides the same benefits plus an additional lump sum payment when the benefit period expires. The oldest agreement, for white-collar workers, instituting the *Trygghetsrådet*, only applies to redundant workers over the age of 40, and provides top-ups to basic unemployment benefits up to a level of 70 per cent of salary (dropping to 50 per cent after six months), as well as unemployment benefit extensions for older workers. For private sector blue-collar workers, the Job Security Agreement provides redundant workers over the age of 40 with a one-time lump sum depending on their age.[22]

The financing of Job Councils and benefits are the responsibility of the employer. This is linked to the fact that Job Security Agreements are formally conceived as complementary protection in the event of redundancy. These agreements apply not only to trade union members, but to all workers within their scope.[23] As the Swedish legal system does not have a mechanism of extension of collective agreements,[24] the comprehensive applicability of the Job Security Agreements is set out in the agreements themselves.

One could thus argue that in Sweden an element of unemployment protection has been developed through collective bargaining, even if the scope of protection by collective agreement is limited to restructuring processes. This limitation is also connected to a trend of provision by the unions of supplementary unemployment protection through individual, and above all collective, insurance. This development can be explained by the fact that, since the 1990, the generosity of the income-related unemployment insurance system has been gradually reduced. Replacement rates decreased (with some reversal) from 90 per cent to 80 or 70 per cent (depending on duration of unemployment), as did the maximum level of benefits. This, in addition to the scrapping of an automatic benefit indexation system, has meant that protection has moved away from income-related insurance towards a system of basic benefits,[25] or a 'basic security model'.[26]

[22] OECD, Back to Work: Sweden: Improving the Re-employment Prospects of Displaced Workers (Paris, OECD Publishing, 2009).

[23] GS Lindquist and E Wadensjo 'Social and Occupational Security and Labour Market Flexibility in Sweden: The Case of Unemployment Compensation' (2006) IZA Discussion Paper 2943, 10 https://ssrn.com/abstract=1006195.

[24] P Kerckhofs, 'Extension of Collective Bargaining Agreement in the EU' (2011) EUROFOUND background paper, EF/11/54/EN, www.eurofound.europa.eu/sites/default/files/ef_publication/field_ef_document/ef1154en.pdf.

[25] P Rasmussen, 'Privatizing Unemployment Protection – The Rise of Private Unemployment Insurance in Denmark and Sweden' (2014) Centre for Comparative Welfare Studies Working Paper 2014/38, 34–38; the research shows that, while at the beginning of the 1990s, 'net replacement rate of average earners more or less corresponded to the maximum replacement rate of 90% stipulated in the insurance … by 2009 it had dropped to below 60% of former wage'.

[26] W Korpi and J Palme, 'New Politics and Class Politics in the Context of Austerity and Globalization: Welfare State Regress in 18 Countries, 1975–95' (2013) 97 *American Political Science Review* 425.

In this context, union strategies (increasing or maintaining members), combined with favourable taxation of private insurance, has led to the growth of collective (and individual) insurance to top up the dwindling maximum benefits and restore the income-related character of unemployment protection.[27]

In conclusion, it should be said that the regulation of certain aspects of unemployment protection through collective agreements in Sweden does not constitute welfare state retrenchment as such. Rather, it is more a collective response to the new needs of workers within the context of a changing and more volatile labour market. Retrenchment in unemployment protection has been answered autonomously by unions, without negotiations with employers, through the reinforcement of supplementary, collective private insurance for their members.

IV. 'REPAIRING' RETRENCHMENT IN UNEMPLOYMENT INSURANCE IN THE NETHERLANDS

In the Netherlands, the participation of social partners in the development of social legislation has been well established since the end of the twentieth century. This occurred mainly through bipartite and tripartite institutions like the *Stichting voor de Arbeid* (Foundation for Work) and the *Sociaal Economische Raad* (Social and Economic Council).

Moreover, until the 1990s, these social partners participated in the administration and execution of social insurance programmes, including unemployment benefits. Through the *Bedrijfsverenigingen* – the bipartite, sectoral organisations that administered the various schemes – social partners also assessed individual cases directly.[28] In 1993 a parliamentary investigation was conducted in response to a report by the Public Audit Office (*Rekenkamer*) regarding failing control over the execution of social security programmes. The investigation concluded that priority to rapid and fair recognition of benefits was being granted to the detriment of control over the total volume of benefits. Further, it seemed that unemployed workers were also being funnelled into the more generous disability benefit system as a way to defend workers' interests and prevent conflict through creative solutions to workforce management problems.[29]

[27] P Rasmussen, 'Privatizing Unemployment Protection – The Rise of Private Unemployment Insurance in Denmark and Sweden' (2014) Centre for Comparative Welfare Studies Working Paper 2014/38, 63–64.

[28] While the social insurance funds themselves were tripartite institutions; H Bekke and N van Gestel, *Publiek Verzekerd, Voorgeschiedenis en start van het Uitvoeringsinstituut Werknemersverzekeringen (UWV 1993–2003)* (Antwerp, Garant, 2004) 23.

[29] KP Goudswaard, 'Gedonder in de Polder: een beknopte geschiedenis van de veranderingen in de uitvoeringsstructuur sociale zekerheid' in DA Albergste, AL Bovenberg and LGM Stevens (eds), *Er zal geheven worden!: Opstellen, op 19 oktober 2001, aangeboden aan prof. dr. S. Cnossen ter gelegenheid van zijn afscheid als hoogleraar aan de Erasmus Universiteit Rotterdam* (Deventer, Kluwer, 2001).

As a result, between 1995 and 2002, the *Bedrijfsverenigingen* were forced to merge into fewer structures and cooperate with private insurers, before they were finally abolished altogether. Their role in public local job placement services was terminated and those services centralised and nationalised. Since that time, the involvement of social partners in unemployment protection seems to have been limited to the policy development level, through formulating recommendations to the government as well as involvement in tripartite consultation and agreements which led to the reforms of 1998[30] and 2006.[31,32] This trend, which expressed the traditional dynamics of the Dutch *Poldermodel*, was continued with the reforms embodied in the 2013 *Wet werk en zekerheid*, which were based on a bipartite agreement agreed in the *Stichting voor Arbeid* in April of the same year and which were, in reality, negotiated with the government.

Continuing with the Dutch comprehensive 'flexicure' approach to labour market reform that had begun in the 1990,[33] the law provided for a number of changes in the Law on Unemployment (*Werkloosheidswet*). The obligation of unemployed workers to seek suitable employment was made more strict and the law also introduced a compensation system for cases where an unemployed worker accepted employment at a lower salary than her previous salary. Above all, the law stipulated a gradual reduction, starting from 2016, in the maximum duration of benefits from 38 to 24 months, which mostly affected workers with long employment tenure. As a 'compensation' (concession to the unions during the negotiation of the agreement), the law, in line with the agreement, expressly provides that collective bargaining can 'repair' the reduction of the duration of benefits via private insurance coverage.

Negotiation between social partners regarding the design of the scheme following the 2013 social agreement and reform law remained inconclusive, even if undertakings to implement the principle of 'repairing' duration reduction were included in collective agreements in the construction, agricultural, local government and youth/child protection sectors. In 2017 the government seemed to have resolved the situation by providing proposals for the basic principles of the 'repair' scheme (which consisted of general collective agreements, applicable to entire economic sectors, that would create ad hoc funds as well as financing by workers) and by reaffirming its 2013 promise that such collective agreements would be declared generally applicable.[34] After another refusal in April 2017,

[30] Law on Flexibility and Security, with only limited impact on protection against unemployment.

[31] Law on revision of the Unemployment Law, which shortened maximum duration to 3 years and 2 months, and modified unemployment benefits system for those with short qualifying periods.

[32] EurWORK, 'The Netherlands: Social Partners' Involvement in Unemployment Benefit Regimes' (2012) Report, www.eurofound.europa.eu/fr/observatories/eurwork/comparative-information/national-contributions/netherlands/the-netherlands-social-partners-involvement-in-unemployment-benefit-regimes.

[33] A de le Court, 'Decommodifying Social Rights: Welfare State Policies in a Comparative Perspective' (PhD thesis, Pompeu Fabra University, 2014) 253–54, www.tdx.cat/handle/10803/283752.

[34] In principle, Dutch collective agreements only bind those workers and employers affiliated to the organisations which concluded them, but the government can make them generally binding in their scope of application by Decree.

employers finally agreed to the scheme, with certain conditions: that the scheme would not serve as a precedent for future 'repair' of social security retrenchments; that administrative costs for the scheme's management would be kept to a minimum; and a guarantee that worker contributions would not lead to claims for compensatory salary increases in further collective bargaining.

It is important to note that this evolution did not come out of the blue. There was already a certain trend of recourse to collective agreement to complement the existing unemployment benefit regime. In 2012, for example, 38 per cent of the most important (branch-level) collective agreements contained provisions for complementary protection to 'public' unemployment benefits in the form of complementary benefits,[35] which covered around 2.6 million workers at a cost of €170 million (in 2011), or 3.7 per cent of legal benefits.[36] The sectors in which complementary benefits seem to be most present are industry (11.4 per cent of legal benefits), health care (10.1 per cent), the public sector (8 per cent) and education (6 per cent).[37]

The clauses of the agreements regulate the level of the supplementary benefits (generally guaranteeing from 75 to 100 per cent of the previous salary); their duration (coinciding with the duration of legal benefits, or a certain duration depending on the age of the unemployed person);[38] or conditions (generally, minimum employment period in the company).[39] The systems are administered by private pension fund administrators for a whole sector,[40] but also by companies themselves or their salary administration contractors.[41] Also, it seems that financing generally occurs at the expense of the employer, or is shared between employer and worker. Financing by the worker only does not seem to be significant.[42]

[35] *Bovenwettelijke aanvulling* WW, or complementary addition to legal benefits; also 61% of the agreements contained provisions for supplementary disability benefits (*Wet Werk en Inkomen naar Arbeidsvermogen*).

[36] B Cuelenaere, WS Zwinkels and AA Oostveen, 'Praktijk en effecten van bovenwettelijke CAO-aanvullingen ZW, loondoorbetalingbijziekte, WIA en WW' (2014) Report for the Ministry of Social Affairs and Employment, 11 and 54, http://onderzoekwerkeninkomen.nl/rapporten/6vya47nr/praktijk-en-effecten-van-bovenwettelijke-cao-aanvullingen-zw-loondoorbetaling-bij-ziekte-wia-en-ww.pdf.

[37] B Cuelenaere, WS Zwinkels and AA Oostveen, 'Praktijk en effecten van bovenwettelijke CAO-aanvullingen ZW, loondoorbetalingbijziekte, WIA en WW' (2014) Report for the Ministry of Social Affairs and Employment, 56, http://onderzoekwerkeninkomen.nl/rapporten/6vya47nr/praktijk-en-effecten-van-bovenwettelijke-cao-aanvullingen-zw-loondoorbetaling-bij-ziekte-wia-en-ww.pdf.

[38] It seems that half of the studied collective agreements contain a right to complementary unemployment benefits until pension age for workers of a certain age, with the condition of having been employed by the company for a certain time.

[39] AM Wilms, PW Feenstra, A Houtkoop and A Machiels-van Es, 'Bovenwettelijke Aanvullingen Bij Ziekte, Arbeidsongeschiktheid En Werkloosheid. Een onderzoek naar cao-afspraken over bovenwettelijke aanvullingen bij ziekte, arbeidsongeschiktheid en werkloosheid' (2013) Report for the Ministry of Social Affairs and Employment, http://cao.minszw.nl/pdf/174/2013/174_2013_13_10797.pdf.

[40] ibid; it seems that only the collective agreement for the construction sector provides for equal participation of employers and workers in the financing of the system. The benefit is, however, only a one-off lump sum of €450 (suppressed since 2015).

[41] ibid.

[42] ibid.

The inclusion of supplementary unemployment benefits in collective agreements should also be viewed from the perspective of the greater tradition of complementary protection by collective agreement in other branches of social security, in particular temporary and permanent disability, as a response to the trend of privatisation in these areas.[43] The example of disability insurance reform is of particular interest in this context, not only because alleged misuse by social partners was the basis for their expulsion from the management the benefits, just as in the case of unemployment, as detailed above. Following the 'unilateral' imposition of a disability insurance system reform, which basically narrowed access criteria and reduced benefit levels (and which social partners strongly opposed), unions managed to 'repair' some of the cuts through worker and employer contributions to funds negotiated in several sectoral collective agreements. However, this provoked a conflict with the government, which tried to impose limitations on the rules on extending collective agreements.[44] When the government conducted reforms to the system for a second time in 2002 and then again in 2004 – which resulted in a reduction of the level of benefits – those were again 'repaired', as two years later, 71 per cent of collective agreements contained supplementary benefits.[45]

The new development, however, demonstrates considerable differences with other cases of collectively bargained supplementary benefits, in that, as decided from the outset of the negotiations between social partners following the 2013 bilateral agreement, the 'private' extension of unemployment benefits would be financed exclusively by workers' contributions. Despite this early agreement by the unions to exempt employers from financing the system, employers' associations blocked a final agreement and then delayed its implementation until May 2017, likely in part because they perceived the 'repair' of welfare state retrenchment through collective bargaining as a consolidating trend in the evolution of Dutch social protection.

It was government intervention that finally persuaded employers to agree to collaborate to 'repair' retrenchment. In contrast to the 'repair' of the first disability insurance reforms, here the state had a supporting role. Moreover, state involvement in the negotiations from the outset, as well as the power conferred

[43] A Rommelse, 'De arbeidsongeschiktheidsverzekering: tussen publiek en privaat. Een beschrijving, analyse en waardering van de belangrijkste wijzigingen in het Nederlandse arbeidsongeschiktheidsstelsel tussen 1980 en 2010' (PhD thesis, Leiden University, 2014) https://openaccess.leidenuniv.nl/handle/1887/23081, or Trampusch, C, 'Sozialpolitik durch Tarifvertrag in den Niederlanden. Die Rolle der industriellen Beziehungen in der Liberalisierung des Wohlfahrtsstaates' (2004) MPIfG Discussion Paper 04/12, http://hdl.handle.net/10419/19914.

[44] A Johnston, A Kornelakis and C Rodriguez d'Acri, 'Social Partners and the Welfare State: Recalibration, Privatization or Collectivization of Social Risks?' (2011) 17 *European Journal of Industrial Relations* 349.

[45] M Yerkes and K Tijdens, 'Corporatism and the Mediation of Social Risks. The Interaction between Social Security and Collective Labour Agreements' in R van der Veen, M Yerkes and P Achterberg (eds), *The Transformation of Solidarity. Changing Risks and the Future of the Welfare State* (Amsterdam, Amsterdam University Press, 2012) 125–26.

on the state by its role in the extension mechanism required to make the repairs comprehensive, nuanced the bipartite character of the collective bargaining. It is also interesting to note the inclusion in the law of a reference, or rather an authorisation, to 'repair' the reduction in the duration of benefits. Given that some collective agreements already extended benefit periods for certain categories of workers (mainly older workers) without express legal authorisation[46] it is not clear that this reference was necessary. On the other hand, the reference is a clear indication of the role of the state in this particular process of privatisation (and collectivisation) of unemployment insurance.

V. FRAGMENTED CONTRACTUAL WELFARE AND SUPPLEMENTING ACTIVE LABOUR MARKET POLICIES: THE ITALIAN CASE

In Italy, the collectivisation of welfare through collective bargaining is often cited in the context of the development of social protection for atypical workers, in particular temporary agency workers.[47] Central to what is referred to by some authors as contractual welfare,[48] which for the purpose of this chapter can be included in the idea of collectivisation, are the *Enti Bilaterali*, the bilateral bodies instituted by sectoral or inter-professional agreements. Their development can be associated with the general evolution of the system of industrial relations from a lack of a formalised framework for collective interest negotiations towards a system of collaborative corporatism.[49] Since the 1990s, bilateral bodies have emerged whose aim is to mutualise the provision of benefits related to employment contracts (eg severance pay, illness) in economic sectors whose characteristics (such as an important presence of small and medium enterprises) do not favour such advantages. Even if the inclusion of unemployment-related benefits in those systems has been marginal,[50] these bilateral

[46] For example, the WOPO, collectively bargained regulation of supplementary unemployment benefits in the sector of basic education.

[47] A Johnston, A Kornelakis and C Rodriguez d'Acri, 'Social Partners and the Welfare State: Recalibration, Privatization or Collectivization of Social Risks?' (2011) 4 *European Journal of Industrial Relations* 349.

[48] M Tiraboschi, 'Bilateralism and Bilateral Bodies: The New Frontier of Industrial Relations in Italy' (2013) 1 *E-Journal of International and Comparative Labour Studies*.

[49] A Johnston, A Kornelakis and C Rodriguez d'Acri, 'Social Partners and the Welfare State: Recalibration, Privatization or Collectivization of Social Risks?' (2011) 4 *European Journal of Industrial Relations* 349, 355.

[50] Examples can be found, among others, in the bilateral body in the sector of temporary agency work (EBITEMP), which in 2009 provided, in case of cessation of work which did not give right to unemployment benefits (because of lack of minimum working days) for a lump sum of €700, as well as a lump sum of €1,300, paid by the INPS (national social security institute) but partially financed by the bilateral body; see P Sandulli, M Faioli, P Bozzao, M Bianchi and G Croce, *Indagine sulla Bilateralità in Italia e in Francia, Germania, Spagnia, Svezia*, Quaderni Fundazione G. Brodoloni. Studi e Ricerche (Rome, Fondazione Giacomo Brodolini, 2015) 94; According to the current agreement and EBITEMP's website, those benefits are not paid anymore, which could be linked to an improvement of the public unemployment benefit system with the latest reforms.

bodies are worth mentioning because they have started to take on key functions related to the active support of unemployed workers – including services related to professional and lifelong training – that would normally be carried out by public employment services. This has also been promoted by the law via the creation of special funds financed in part by unemployment protection contributions.[51]

This response to the lack of services offered by public institutions has further been promoted by the law through a legal integration of the role of the bilateral bodies. Law 276/2003 seems to be a turning point in that it explicitly recognises these bilateral bodies as privileged for the regulation of the labour market, not only in terms of health and safety or income security, but also in promoting 'standard employment of quality' through various services to employers and workers. These include services of job placement for unemployed workers, aimed at promoting matching between job offers and the supply of work. In so doing, the bilateral bodies have above all begun to collaborate with public employment services by exchanging information, via signing agreements with the various regional or local public actors involved.[52] It is also important to note that the bilateral bodies have created funds for sectors and workers not covered by Wage Guarantee Funds, which provide financial support in case of redundancies and short-time work schemes.[53]

VI. COLLECTIVISATION OF UNEMPLOYMENT PROTECTION: COLLECTIVE BARGAINING BETWEEN TRIPARTISM AND VERTICAL DEMUTUALISATION

With the exception of a few cases, protection against unemployment (or at least unemployment benefits) has not been the object of collective bargaining to any great extent. Nevertheless, this chapter has identified both existing and new cases where welfare benefits have been provided through collective bargaining, contributing to the existing literature on the subject. However, with the exception of the French system, which for historical reasons rests in great part on periodically renegotiated inter-professional collective agreements, collective bargaining seems to be limited to supplementing existing systems of unemployment insurance.

Even in a Ghent country like Sweden, which has a strong tradition of union involvement in the management of unemployment insurance, collective

[51] M Tiraboschi, 'Bilateralism and Bilateral Bodies: The New Frontier of Industrial Relations in Italy' (2013) 1 *E-Journal of International and Comparative Labour Studies*.

[52] M D'Onghia, 'Bilateralità e politiche attive' in D Gottardi, and T Bazzani (eds), *Il workfare territoriale. Collana del Dipartimento di Scienze Giuridiche dell'Università di Verona* (Naples, Edizioni Scientifiche Italiane, 2013) 201.

[53] ibid.

agreements that also imply employer financing of benefits have only been concluded within the framework of support for workers made redundant during restructuring. Even if such collective agreements are related more to the employer's (social) responsibility regarding redundancies than to protection against unemployment, they are still the product of the reaction of social partners to gaps in state-provided social protection, and in this particular case to the emergence of new needs, or new social risks.[54]

On the other hand, the Swedish case demonstrates that collective bargaining is not the only instrument of collectivisation of unemployment protection through benefits in the context of welfare state retrenchment. In Sweden, cutbacks in the generosity of the system have been addressed through the establishment of collective insurance for union members. This can be partly explained by the fact that the Swedish unemployment protection system is considered a Ghent system, and that also (and partly linked to this) Sweden has a high union density. On the other hand, despite taking the form of collective agreements, the Dutch 'reparation', which addresses the decrease in duration of unemployment insurance benefits, does not involve sharing responsibility for the risk of long-term unemployment between workers and employers since financing of the scheme will come exclusively from workers' contributions.

From this perspective, these developments could be characterised as a one-sided collectivisation of a social risk (as opposed to a collectivisation where employers also contribute), or also, to use the approach of Freedland and Kountouris, a 'vertical demutualisation'[55] of that risk, since in the past, mutualisation of the risk via state intervention rested on a system that had been financed through employer contributions as well as those of workers.

Another aspect, characteristic of the Dutch evolution and the French system that emerges from this analysis, is that, despite taking the bipartite form of collective bargaining, the role of the state in the negotiation and further development of agreements is important, even if sometimes informal. This brings us to a certain contradiction, in that while there is a reduction of state responsibility that occurs through retrenchment of unemployment benefit programmes (at least in the Dutch system), any subsequent collectivisation of risk is almost impossible without the involvement of the self-same state. As the Dutch case shows, (one-sided) collectivisation seems not to have been possible without

[54] On the notion of new social risks, see, among others, P Taylor-Gooby, *New Risks, New Welfare: The Transformation of the European Welfare State* (Oxford, OUP, 2004) or R van der Veen, M Yerkes and P Achterberg (eds), *The Transformation of Solidarity. Changing Risk and the Future of the Welfare State* (Amsterdam, Amsterdam University Press, 2012).

[55] M Freedland and N Kountouris, *The Legal Construction of Personal Work Relations* (Oxford, OUP, 2011); M Freedland, 'Regulating for Decent Work and the Legal Construction of Personal Work Relations' in D McCann, S Lee, P Belser, C Fenwick, J Howe and M Luebker (eds), *Creative Labour Regulation. Indeterminacy and Protection in an Uncertain World* (Basingstoke, Palgrave Macmillan, 2014) 63–83.

state participation, technically through the promised extension of the relevant collective agreements, and – more politically – through its role in persuading employers. Common to both cases also is the legal integration of collective bargaining through the recognition by law (necessary or not) of the importance of collective bargaining in the field. The Italian case also shows an important degree of legal (and financial) integration in the functions of bilateral bodies, not only in unemployment protection but also in terms of training and other work-related benefits. A certain interplay between social dialogue, law and collective bargaining can also be observed in the Dutch and French cases, given the legal recognition of the 'repair' system in the Netherlands, or through legal integration and posterior legal reforms to permit the legality of the agreements in France.[56]

Further, some divergence between France and other states should be noted. In France, the state has removed the competence of collective bargaining in terms of activation and management of benefits, as the Netherlands did in the early 1990s, by expelling social partners from the design and implementation of unemployment protection. However, the Netherlands does not seem to have challenged the social partners' control of supplementary and 'repair' benefits in unemployment protection, and does not seem to intend to do so in the case of the generalised extension of the reduced duration of benefits (which might echo the shift of responsibility onto employers for the reintegration of workers receiving disability benefits). Moreover, current French proposals around the universalisation of unemployment insurance threaten the model, and an even weaker involvement of social partners in the system is to be expected. On the other hand, the importance of these changes could be put into perspective when considering the de facto quasi-tripartite character of the governance of unemployment insurance benefits. This argument confirms previous research, which has indicated the important role played by the state in industrial relations when determining the extent of social solidarity that can be provided by collective agreements.[57]

This aspect, however, is not as relevant in the case of Sweden. From a technical point of view, this might be related to the fact that Sweden lacks the system of extending collective agreements through state intervention that is a defining element of the French and the Dutch systems. However, from a more systemic point of view, and taking the strategies of social partners into account, other factors come to mind. One is the importance of the autonomy of social partners in Sweden. Another is the fear of decreasing union membership in cases where such membership is not required for a worker to be covered by complementary

[56] See, for the French case, A Supiot, 'Un faux dilemme: la loi ou le contrat ?' (2003) 1 *Droit Social* 58, 66.

[57] C Trampusch, 'Industrial Relations as a Source of Solidarity in Times of Welfare State Retrenchment' (2007) 36 *Journal of Social Policy* 197, 210.

collective solidarity. With regard to this, it could be said that there is tension between the extension of collectivised solidarity and the use of such solidarity as a power resource by unions. This tension is also visible in the Dutch case, where unions seem to have constrained themselves to accept extended unemployment protection as a bargaining tool, without employers having to participate in its financing – a move that in principle should weaken the bargaining position of the unions.

Finally, to be complete, a study of the regulation of unemployment protection should take into account activation and ALMPs (including training). From this point of view it seems that, in terms of further training of workers and of unemployed, there are some cases where collective bargaining has played a role. These include Greece, as shown above, but also France, Sweden, the Netherlands and, though not studied here, Denmark.[58] A survey of employers in Denmark found that collective bargaining coverage was a positive factor in the systematic participation of employers in ALMP schemes.[59] In France, as noted above, there is an apparent tendency towards increased state control over these matters. On the other hand, in Italy, the evolution of the *Enti Bilaterali* towards assuming tasks that public employment services do not effectively fulfil reveals the emergence of a different trend, which, though it echoes the emergence of Job Security Agreements in Sweden, is different in that its evolution seems to be promoted by the state. Due to the conceptual shift in the notion of unemployment protection to include worker activation and non-monetary benefits to support workers in labour market reintegration (or, depending on the perspective, to support a more rapid reintegration),[60] more research on the role of collective bargaining in these areas is needed in order to gain a more complete picture of how it interacts with gaps and retrenchment in unemployment protection policies.

BIBLIOGRAPHY

Alduy, J-P, 'Rapport d'information No. 713 (2010–2011) fait au nom de la Mission commune d'information relative à Pôle emploi, déposé le 5 juillet 2011' (Paris, Sénat, 2011)

Bekke, H and van Gestel, N, *Publiek Verzekerd, Voorgeschiedenis en start van het Uitvoeringsinstituut Werknemersverzekeringen (UWV 1993–2003)* (Antwerp, Garant, 2004)

58 ibid 197.

59 J Ingold, and D Valizade, 'Employer Engagement in Active Labour Market Policies in the UK and Denmark: A Survey of Employers' (2015) Centre for Employment Relations, Innovation and Change Policy Report 6, https://lubswww.leeds.ac.uk/fileadmin/webfiles/ceric/Documents/CERIC_Policy_Report_6.pdf.

60 A de le Court, *Protección por desempleo y derechos fundamentales. El caso español en contexto* (Valencia, Tirant lo Blanch, 2016); A de le Court, 'Decommodifying Social Rights: Welfare State Policies in a Comparative Perspective' (PhD thesis, Pompeu Fabra University, 2014) 253–54, www.tdx.cat/handle/10803/283752.

Bergström, O and Diedrich, A, 'The Swedish Model of Restructuring' in B Cazier and F Bruggeman (eds), *Restructuring Work and Employment in Europe. Managing Change in an Era of Globalisation* (Cheltenham, Edward Elgar Publishing, 2008)

Cuelenaere, B, Zwinkels, WS and Oostveen, AA, 'Praktijk en effecten van bovenwettelijke CAO- aanvullingen ZW, loondoorbetalingbijziekte, WIA en WW', Report for the Ministry of Social Affairs and Employment, 2014

Daniel, C and Tuchszirer, D, *L'État face aux chômeurs, l'indemnisation du chômage de 1884 à nos jours* (Paris, Flammarion, 1999)

de le Court, A, 'Decommodifying Social Rights: Welfare State Policies in a Comparative Perspective' (PhD thesis, Pompeu Fabra University, 2014)

——, *Protección por desempleo y derechos fundamentales. El caso español en contexto* (Valencia, Tirant lo Blanch, 2016)

Diedrich, A and Bergström, O, *The Job Security Councils in Sweden* (IMIT, 2006)

D'Onghia, M, 'Bilateralità e politiche attive' in D Gottardi and T Bazzani, *Il workfare territoriale. Collana del Dipartimento di Scienze Giuridiche dell'Università di Verona* (Naples: Edizioni Scientifiche Italiane, 2013)

EurWORK, 'The Netherlands: Social Partners' Involvement in Unemployment Benefit Regimes', Report, 2012

Freedland, M, 'Regulating for Decent Work and the Legal Construction of Personal Work Relations' in D McCann, S Lee, P Belser, C Fenwick, J Howe and M Luebker (eds), *Creative Labour Regulation. Indeterminacy and Protection in an Uncertain World* (Basingstoke, Palgrave Macmillan, 2014)

—— and Kountouris, N, *The Legal Construction of Personal Work Relations* (Oxford, OUP, 2011)

Freyssinet, J, 'La réforme de l'indemnisation du chômage en France' (2002) 38 *Revue de l'IRES* 1

Goudswaard, KP, 'Gedonder in de Polder: een beknopte geschiedenis van de veranderingen in de uitvoeringsstructuur sociale zekerheid' in DA Albergste, AL Bovenberg and LGM Stevens (eds), *Er zal geheven worden!: Opstellen, op 19 oktober 2001, aangeboden aan prof. dr. S. Cnossen ter gelegenheid van zijn afscheid als hoogleraar aan de Erasmus Universiteit Rotterdam* (Deventer, Kluwer, 2001)

Ingold, J and Valizade, D, 'Employer Engagement in Active Labour Market Policies in the UK and Denmark: A Survey of Employers' (2015) Centre for Employment Relations, Innovation and Change Policy Report 6

Jamme, D, 'Pôle emploi et la réforme du service public de l'emploi: bilan et recommandations' (Paris, Conseil économique, social et environnemental, 2011)

Johnston, A, Kornelakis, A and Rodriguez d'Acri, C, 'Social Partners and the Welfare State: Recalibration, Privatization or Collectivization of Social Risks?' (2011) 4 *European Journal of Industrial Relations* 349

Kerckhofs, P, 'Extension of Collective Bargaining Agreement in the EU' (2011) EUROFOUND background paper, EF/11/54/EN

Korpi, W and Palme, J, 'New Politics and Class Politics in the Context of Austerity and Globalization: Welfare State Regress in 18 Countries, 1975–95' (2013) 97 *American Political Science Review* 425

Lind, J, 'The End of the Ghent System as Trade Union Recruitment Machinery?' (2009) 40 *Industrial Relations Journal* 510

Lindquist, GS and Wadensjo, E, 'Social and Occupational Security and Labour Market Flexibility in Sweden: The Case of Unemployment Compensation' (2006) IZA Discussion Paper 2943

OECD, *Back to Work: Sweden: Improving the Re-employment Prospects of Displaced Workers* (Paris, OECD Publishing, 2009)

Rasmussen, P, 'Privatizing Unemployment Protection – The Rise of Private Unemployment Insurance in Denmark and Sweden' (2014) Centre for Comparative Welfare Studies Working Paper 2014/38

Regalia, I and Gasparri, S, 'Social Partners' Involvement in Unemployment Benefit Regimes in Europe' (Dublin, European Foundation for the Improvement of Living and Working Conditions, 2013)

Rommelse, A, 'De arbeidsongeschiktheidsverzekering: tussen publiek en privaat. Een beschrijving, analyse en waardering van de belangrijkste wijzigingen in het Nederlandse arbeidsongeschiktheidsstelsel tussen 1980 en 2010' (PhD Thesis, Leiden University, 2014)

Sandulli, P, Faioli, M, Bozzao, P, Bianchi, M and Croce, G, *Indagine sulla Bilateralità in Italia e in Francia, Germania, Spagnia, Svezia*, Quaderni Fundazione G. Brodoloni. Studi e Ricerche (Rome, Fondazione Giacomo Brodolini, 2015)

Supiot, A, 'Un faux dilemme: la loi ou le contrat ?' (2003) 1 *Droit Social* 58, 64

Taylor-Gooby, P, *New Risks, New Welfare: The Transformation of the European Welfare State* (Oxford, OUP, 2004)

Tiraboschi, M, 'Bilateralism and Bilateral Bodies: The New Frontier of Industrial Relations in Italy' (2013) 1 *E-Journal of International and Comparative Labour Studies*

Trampusch, C, 'Sozialpolitik durch Tarifvertrag in den Niederlanden. Die Rolle der industriellen Beziehungen in der Liberalisierung des Wohlfahrtsstaates' (2004) MPIfG Discussion Paper 04/12

——, 'Industrial Relations as a Source of Solidarity in Times of Welfare State Retrenchment' (2007) 2 *Journal of Social Policy* 197

Tuchszirer, C, 'La nouvelle convention d'assurance-chômage: le PARE qui cache la forêt' (2001) 14 *Mouvements* 2

van der Veen, R, Yerkes, M and Achterberg, P (eds), *The Transformation of Solidarity. Changing Risk and the Future of the Welfare State* (Amsterdam, Amsterdam University Press, 2012)

Wilms, AM, Feenstra, PW, Houtkoop, A and Machiels-van Es, A, 'Bovenwettelijke Aanvullingen Bij Ziekte, Arbeidsongeschiktheid En Werkloosheid.

Een onderzoek naar cao-afspraken over bovenwettelijke aanvullingen bij ziekte, arbeidsongeschiktheid en werkloosheid' (2013) Report for the Ministry of Social Affairs and Employment

Yerkes, M and Tijdens, K, 'Corporatism and the Mediation of Social Risks. The Interaction between Social Security and Collective Labour Agreements' in R van der Veen, M Yerkes and P Achterberg (eds), *The Transformation of Solidarity. Changing Risks and the Future of the Welfare State* (Amsterdam, Amsterdam University Press, 2012) 115

Index

Note: Alphabetical arrangement is word-by-word, where a group of letters followed by a space is filed before the same group of letters followed by a letter, eg 'legal status' will appear before 'legality'. In determining alphabetical arrangement, initial articles and prepositions are ignored.

www.ingramcontent.com/pod-product-compliance
Ingram Content Group UK Ltd.
Pitfield, Milton Keynes, MK11 3LW, UK
UKHW020905190926
475560UK00010B/279

9 781509 923168